THE MOVEMENT OF THE *CANTERBURY TALES*
CHAUCER'S LITERARY PILGRIMAGE

By

David R. Pichaske

NORWOOD EDITIONS / 1977

for Ernesto, Enrichetta, and Inez

the remembrance
With which the happy spirit contemplates
Its well-spent pilgrimage on earth,
Shall never pass away.

—*Shelley*

His image, wandering, he met. I mine.

—*Joyce*

CONTENTS

Preface
I. Preliminary Considerations 1
notes 17
II. Fragments I and II: Dialectic 19
Knight's Tale 27
Miller's Tale 36
Reeve's Tale 41
Cook's Tale 46
Man of Law's Tale 47
notes 57
III. Fragments III Through V: the Matter of Order 64
Wife of Bath's Tale 64
Friar's and Summoner's Tales 70
Clerk's Tale 78
Merchant's Tale 86
Squire's Tale 94
Franklin's Tale 100
notes 111
IV. Fragments VI and VII: the Matter of Art 120
Physician's Tale 120
Pardoner's Tale 125
Shipman's Tale 133
Prioress's Tale 137
Thopas and Melibee 141
Monk's Tale 146
Nun's Priest's Tale 149
notes 156
V. Fragments VIII Through X:
the Pilgrimage Completed 163
Second Nun's Tale 163
Canon's Yeoman's Tale 167
Manciple's Tale 173
Parson's Tale 178
Retraction 181
notes 185
Index 188

PREFACE

The view of the *Canterbury Tales* taken in this study represents an extension of one direction Chaucerian scholarship has been taking for well over a decade now. It is a respectable, although far from universally held view (many would doubt the *Tales* have the kind of thematic and structural integrity) I suggest, especially to the degree I suggest they have it. Others, having settled irrevocably on orders of the tales other than the Ellesmere, may find a priori reasons for dismissing the arguments of the following pages. Still others, reluctant to see things like the Miller's and Friar's, even the Wife's and Knight's tales rejected at pilgrimage's end, may reject the notion of movement from one position to another, settling for two views (or several) of equal validity held concurrently by the poet.

With these I sympathize. I too am reluctant to lose the *Miller's Tale* and the style of art and view of human experience it represents. I prefer the Ellesmere order as most probably that intended by Chaucer, although I can see reasonable arguments against it. Most of all, I am aware that the kind of thematic and structural unity I see in the *Tales* is not reflected in a narrative integrity, and has escaped the notice of half a millennium of Chaucerians. It is scarcely self-evident.

And yet. There is much supportive material for the interpretations I give each tale, interpretations which produce a linear movement and thematic coherence. I have cited that supportive material—perhaps too much in some cases, perhaps too little in others—in an effort to indicate that many of the blocks from which this interpretation is built have been lying around for some time and are more or less commonly held notions. To this end, in fact, I have quoted particulars consonant with my own views from even those whose broader conclusions I reject. But what must finally validate this view of the *Tales* is not the weight of critical opinion, or even critical consensus on greater or smaller matters, but its own internal consistency: does it make good vi

sense? Does reading the *Tales* as a dialectic, one tale answering the previous, work? Does reading the whole as a metaphysical and artistic pilgrimage away from the inn, the secular world, the naturalistic art and ribald chaos of the *Miller's Tale*, toward the saint's shrine, the New Jerusalem, the didacticism and sober religiosity of the *Parson's Tale*—does this explain things about the poem which might otherwise remain puzzling? Does this study open for others the kinds of avenues previous scholarship has opened for me?

This remains to be seen. For my own part, I can only acknowledge those whose work has come before, the giants on the shoulders of giants whose names fill notes and index. For their specific assistance in reading and commenting upon this manuscript, I am indebted to Dr. Peter Heidtmann, Dr. Arnold Henderson, and Ms. Lisa Rodgers. My students have taught me much, Mrs. Laura Sweetland especially among them. Finally, I am indebted to Bradley University, which provided a grant which supported this study, and to Pamela Mueller and Frances McCarthy who typed so ably the final manuscript.

CHAPTER I

PRELIMINARY CONSIDERATIONS

More than any other major work of English poetry, Chaucer's *Canterbury Tales* have provided almost infinite opportunity for critical digression. Generations of copyists with their cumulative errors of substance and accidence have produced a variety of texts; the work becomes an object for exercises in textual analysis and multi-text editions. Chaucer is "the father of English poetry"; it becomes a mine for social and literary historians. Chaucer is manifestly well versed in theology, philosophy, and the science of his age; his work is an ore from which are refined medieval theology, philosophy, and science. The poet was something of a political figure; his characters become historical personalities and his plots historical events disguised behind allegorical narratives. And perhaps most important of all, the poem divides nicely into a number of discrete parts that lend themselves to individual analysis; we discuss the *Knight's Tale*, or the *Friar's Tale*, or the prologue to the Parson's tale, or maybe the Knight's and Miller's tales as a matched set, or a marriage group of tales, but rarely if ever do we consider the *Canterbury Tales*. What, we wonder when all is said and done, is the *Canterbury Tales* about? We are still not sure.1 And yet, it seems to me, the *Canterbury Tales* demand as much or more consideration as a thematic unity than Sidney's *Arcadia* or Masters' *Spoon River Anthology*.

Only recently, in fact, have we come to consider the *Canterbury Tales* a more or less unified, consciously structured whole, rather than a collection of individual tales prefaced with an interesting but in many respects conventional prologue and rounded off with a largely irrelevant postscript. In part it is a matter of viewing one tale as a direct or indirect answer to another tale or tales; beyond that it is a matter of considering groups of tales to be a discussion of one central theme.2 More recently criticism has come to focus on themes which permeate the whole, and most recently—although very guardedly—on the work as a unified poem. Writing in 1955, Ralph Baldwin was obliged to argue at some length the case for unity in the *Canterbury Tales*, and even his case was strongly qualified:

This study proposes a stylistic analysis of the narrative art of *The Canterbury Tales*. Its scope is the beginning and the ending of the Tales, with such transitions as are necessary to yield wholeness and aesthetic pattern to the idea of pilgrimage; the procedure is the structure-analytical method urged above.

It is accepted that *The Canterbury Tales* is not a whole, not an achieved work of art, but rather a truncated and aborted congeries of tales woven about a frame, the Pilgrimage from London to Canterbury. Although there is a closely articulated beginning, the *General Prologue*, and this beginning has, in turn, a beginning, a middle, and an end, the middle of the entire work reveals that the plan as presented by the Host is not even one-half realized on the outward journey, and as this study should demonstrate, no return talefest is even attempted...It would appear then that an ending is nonexistant, because the pilgrimage is never brought back to the Tabard, the fund of stories never equates with the explicit number ordained by Harry Bailey, and the *motifs* released at the outset are never artistically concluded, never resolved....

But this apparent lack of balanced composition in the *Tales* would appear to result not from the surface tell-as-you-go tone, nor yet because it is a medley of "trifling faits divers," but rather because it is incomplete.3

Paul Ruggiers, Baldwin's successor in studying the *Tales* as a coherent whole, agrees that "Chaucer fails entirely to put together a unified plot in any conventional sense," and while proposing to examine the encyclopaedic middle of the tales themselves sees that middle as "centers of interest suspended between two poles," an "examination of the choices available to man."4 He is, moreover, content to see these points as essentially unrelated in any linear fashion and will in the course of discussion treat the tales not in sequence but under two general headings ("Function: Comedy and Irony" and "Function: Romance") which obscure sequential relationships. Some tales are for all practical purposes ignored. Similarly, Bernard Huppé, who has considered at some length the implication of pilgrimage as a motif in the *Canterbury Tales*, concludes, "The interplay between the literal and spiritual meanings [of pilgrimage] provides the thematic touchstone by which the gallery of pilgrims may be judged."5 Pilgrimage as a spiritual journey, pilgrimage as an entertainment—the two interact as balanced opposites until resolved in the Parson's sermon. Trevor Whittock alone reads the *Tales* in sequence, but he too guards himself carefully:

> Certainly I would suggest Chaucer had a more definite overall scheme than Pound [in the *Cantos*], and some of the themes to be found in different tales are as deliberately related by echoes and cross references as Pound's themes are. Provided dogmatic assertions are avoided, there can be little harm and much reward in seeking for unifying devices in Chaucer's poem.6

However—despite the work of Ruggiers and Baldwin, Huppé and Whittock—John Lawlor can write, "Any discussion of the coherence of the *Tales* should properly begin, and may perhaps end, with the plain recognition that the work is unfinished,"7 a clear indication of his willingness to see lack of completion as structural incoherence. In 1971 Donald Howard could correctly observe that most Chaucer criticism assumes more tales were to be added to the extant collection and a return journey supplied to what the poet had already written. For his part, Howard is willing to concede that what exists is all that was to have existed or all we need to have, since the essential principle of the *Tales* is "a controlled lapse from one remembered world into another remembered world," and poet Chaucer in effect "tells it as it comes into his mind."8 The position hardly implies a definite overall scheme on the poet's part.

The almost universally held assumption that the *Canterbury Tales* is a congeries of rather randomly selected individual stories, or a loose unity with definite beginning and ending but a vaguely defined middle is based on two largely unexamined assumptions: that Harry Bailey's plan was of necessity Chaucer's plan (see, for example, Baldwin's remarks quoted above), and that Chaucer the poet was given to tiring of poems and leaving them incomplete. Both seem reasonable enough at first glance, but neither will withstand close examination.

That the Host proposes a round trip—two tales per pilgrim going and two more returning, dinner at his place—is indisputable. And Chaucer the pilgrim does assent to this arrangement as he, with the others, assents to Harry's governance. But the unmistakable replacement of the Host as governor by the Parson as the group nears Canterbury, coupled with a shift from realistic narrative (reflective of a physical pilgrimage) to supraliteral narrative (reflecting an allegorical or spiritual pilgrimage), makes it clear that Harry is not the only pilgrim to have plans for the journey and suggests, I believe, that in the final analysis Harry's decree, like his authority over the pilgrims, is subject to a higher law which may alter it significantly. The priorities—and the alterations—are recognized by the Host himself who, at a point when Chaucer had written nowhere near the 120 tales necessitated by Harry's plan, can say "Now lakketh us no tales mo than oon" (X, 16), and again, when his projected social round trip from and to the Tabard has obviously been superceded by a one-way spiritual journey to the New Jerusalem, "Fulfilled is my sentence and my decree" (X, 17). Harry's plan is that of a London tavern keeper; the Parson's plan is God's plan. Precisely what poet Chaucer had in mind is unclear, but it would be unwise to assume he ever actually intended over a hundred tales and later "for some unexplained reason" changed his mind, as the standard explanation runs. Quite probably Chaucer foresaw at the outset that whatever schema he might outline for both his work and his life (the two are not entirely independent) would be in the end subject to divine Providence. In point of fact there is plenty of evidence to suggest that two tales per pilgrim going and coming was never Chaucer's intention. First, of course, there is the manifest improbability of a fifty-year old Chaucer completing such an undertaking even by using slightly revised extant pieces like the Knight's and Clerk's tales. Second, there is the obvious point that no pilgrim tells two, let alone three or four tales. The Cook may come close, although I do not believe the *Manciple's Prologue* is to be read literally; and besides, he is excused there for his *tale*—singular. Chaucer was then thinking in terms of one tale per pilgrim. Finally, as Howard points out, no account of a pilgrimage before 1484, fictional or historical, treats a return journey in any depth, and few even mention it.9

The assumption that Chaucer was less than religious about finishing poems rests on incontrovertible evidence: the *House of Fame*, the *Legend of Good Women*, the *Cook's Tale*, those references to "us women" in the Shipman's narrative, the discrepancy between "the company of nine-and-twenty" and a count of those pilgrims actually described in the *General Prologue*, Chaucer's failure to provide links between several tales. And yet medieval narrative was not difficult to finish, and Chaucer had already produced complete, well integrated, unified poems by the time he began the *Canterbury Tales*. One concludes, then, that when the poet left something incomplete, he did so not because it was fragmented beyond hope or because he had lost interest in his narrative, but because the work was not taking him where he wanted to go thematically, or because he had changed his mind about his goal. The measure of the *Parliament of Fowles* is not the smoothness of transition from one fragment to the next, but Chaucer's success (or lack of success) in symbolically assimilating various manifestations of love under the aegis of Nature in the conclusion of that poem. The measure of unity in the *Canterbury Tales* is not smooth transitions from one tale to the next, but thematic and aesthetic coherence among the tales. Or, since the work is frankly exploratory and dialectic (much like the *Parliament*), the measure of unity in the *Tales* is what I have chosen to call movement throughout the pilgrimage.

I am with those who hold that the *Canterbury Tales* is a spiritual as well as, perhaps more than, a literal journey, and that the pilgrimage has a specific metaphysical and spiritual beginning and ending. We need not make the work "an allegory of the Way to Truth"10 in the sense that *Pilgrim's Progress* or *Piers Plowman* are allegories to realize that Chaucer's pilgrims proceed from an inn to a temple,11 from submission to the profane and thoroughly secular Harry Bailey to submission to the holy Parson, from the enlightened but essentially a-Christian philosophy of the *Knight's Tale* to the Christian affirmation of the Parson's sermon...and this kind of movement is allegorical in the broadest sense of that term. It is this position I wish to develop in this book, particularly as it affects our reading of the broad middle of the *Tales*. For Chaucer does not simply set out one spring morning and end up some few days later, either as a pilgrim or as an artist; throughout the *Tales* we can see him in progress along *his* pilgrimage (narrative, metaphysical, and aesthetic) working out with a more or less devout heart philosophical and artistic stances for himself through the mouthpieces provided by his assorted pilgrims, developing and discarding attitudes and ideas, recasting and modifying his position as he progresses erratically toward a spiritual and artistic New Jerusalem.

By the close of the fourteenth century, pilgrimage was more than a theological commonplace, more even than a literary and visual motif. The notion of Augustine's *Civitas Dei peregrinans* (*City of God*, XVIII, 51), and the attendant notion of mortal man as pilgrim from Eden to a new Eden through a world beset with the snares of the world, the flesh, and the devil—these had developed into a full fledged medieval genre, the pilgrimage of life.12 Discounting the obviously pagan influenced Anglo-Saxon poems, discounting the confessional *Confessions* of St. Augustine, discounting the dramatic morality plays, discounting even the Arthurian *Quests del Saint Graal* and the devotional *Scale of Perfection*, we are left with a number of theological odysseys of no mean literary value: Langland's *Piers Plowman*, Dante's *Comedy*, Dequileville's remarkable *Peleringe de la Vie Humaine*, Jean de Courcy's *Chemin de Vaillance*, and—of course, Chaucer's *Canterbury Tales*. While the purest form of the genre is obviously the narratives of Deguileville (widely popular throughout the fourteenth century) and his successor de Courcy (less well known), the appearance of pilgrimage as a structuring device or dominant motif in the work of Dante, Langland, and Chaucer suggests that the pure form may well function as a key to the unity of these more literary poems. Dante's *Comedy*, of course, is so carefully organized as to force reading the poem as a unified whole; *Piers Plowman* and the *Canterbury Tales* are less structured and, therefore, more easily mistaken. And yet the most striking feature of Deguileville's work, I suspect, is precisely its lack of structure. The Dreamer in this pilgrimage travels a crooked path indeed, a path always explicable in terms of theology and human nature, but a path jumping ahead and falling behind by leaps and bounds. Early in the poem (or relatively early, since its initial five thousand lines are taken up with an exposition of the twelve articles of faith and the seven virtues), the Dreamer finds himself equipped with the whole armor of god, confronting the fork in the road which, given the right choice, could lead him to quick grace and an easy salvation. But, like Piers rending his pardon and Chaucer turning petulantly from the theology of the Man of Law to the experience of the Wife of Bath, the dreamer tosses off his armor and, following youth and idleness, rushes off down the wrong path. So near, and yet so far. Over the course of the remaining seven thousand lines, the Dreamer approaches nearer to, then farther from the grace he seeks, arriving with his death at a vision of Mercy, dispatching prayer and alms to prepare a place for him. Now the *Pelerinage de la vie Humaine* as a source for the *Canterbury Tales* is one of the great unwritten works of Chaucerian scholarship: parallels between Chaucer's work and Deguileville's are nothing short of remarkable, as the most casual scansion of even Lydgate's translation will demonstrate—and, as Chaucer's "A.B.C." reveals, the English poet was more familiar with this poem than he was with many of his supposed sources.

But the French poem is most important for what it tell us of broad medieval notions of pilgrimage, both as a literary motif and as a genre. First, and most significantly, we note that the pilgrim's movement is erratic: he proceeds by fits and starts, coming close to his goal more than once before his ultimately successful entrance. The movement of pilgrim from sin to grace, from this world to the next, is rarely if ever as direct, as progressive, as—in literary terms—structured as Dante's movement in the *Comedy*. We note second the poem's primary concern is with the state of the pilgrim's mind as he proceeds through a series of metphysical stances before arriving at his final state of grace. No matter now literalistic or supraliteralistic external narrative may appear, it is invariably a reflection of the pilgrim's mind at a given point in space-time. We note third that the pilgrim is instructed constantly on his journey, and although he may at any time throw off what he has learned and go running after Youth or Idleness or Venus, what he learns is accretive and ultimately necessary for his salvation. We note finally, if we read carefully, that a concern for time, for death, for aging is important to the pilgrim, increasingly so as he proceeds from youth to age, from folly to wisdom. Each of these observations—and I do not think this a contrived or prejudiced reading of Deguileville's poem—is reflected in Chaucer's work: the social, metaphysical, and aesthetic development of his pilgrimage is erratic (indeed, the antepenultimate tale of Apollo and his crow represents in many respects an almost fatal regression on Chaucer's part); the metaphysical and aesthetic positions found in various prologues and tales reflect the developing spiritual condition of poet Chaucer and his pilgrims as the pilgrimage proceeds; what Chaucer and pilgrims and Host learn is accretive and does serve to bring them ultimately to a state of grace; age and time and death are omnipresent concerns—of the Host, of pilgrims like the Reeve, of poet and pilgrim Chaucer. In fact, nothing supports a reading of the *Canterbury Tales* as linear, allegorical pilgrimage so much as a reading of other medieval linear allegorical pilgrimages!13

Such a reading of the *Tales* immediately raises the autobiographical problem, since the focus of the poem is not a Dreamer who clearly is the poet, or on a Will who is clearly Everyman, but a community of pilgrims among whom the poet represents only a minor (and most irregular) figure. To what extent can we read the figure of Chaucer behind his pilgrims, behind his persona, behind his poem? An age which has directed considerable energies to reading each tale as a dramatic extension of the pilgrim who tells it is likely to object strongly to such an autobiographical proposal. Speaking of the narrator of the *Tales*, for example, George Kane has written,

> The first reason why the author of a fourteenth-century narrative poem was present in his poetry was because he delivered it orally, if not in all instances at least often enough for this

circumstance to form in him an attitude to his public, which he conceived of as an audience, and thus to affect his tone...There are two other circumstances which would induce a poet to identify himself with his narrator. The first is the absence, in fourteenth-century England, of any convention of detached, impersonal narrative. A tale implied a teller; and this was, by implication as well as by his vocal use of the first person, the poet. The second is that any considerable poet of the time would be writing for a coterie, that set of people, comprising his patrons and their associates, to whom he read, and thus in effect presented and published his work.14

The first of these reasons may explain Chaucer's involvement in the *Tales* as reporter, as naive observer; the second and third suggest that Chaucer as poet has a much stronger commitment to participation in his work. In the structural device of the *Canterbury Tales* the poet has hit upon the solution to a problem which plagued him all his artistic career: finding a form to contain the antitheses he constantly struggled to reconcile, the antitheses which never really came together in the *Parliament*, which wrecked the *House of Fame*, which managed only the unity of "dynamically balanced opposites"15 in *Troilus and Criseyde*. One can almost see Chaucer discovering the potential for dialectic in the structure of the *Legend of Good Women*, a commissioned piece, then dropping that poem in haste and excitement as he begins the *Canterbury Tales* in an effort to define, isolate, and confront propositions which, in other structures, had proven elusive. In the end, it seems to me, some tensions are resolved, some attitudes flatly rejected, some positions found attractive but untenable—but over the course of the *Tales* each is given its hearing. The progress of the Canterbury pilgrimage is more than a dynamic in which one story grows out of another, or social class "becomes the motive power of the whole narrative scheme";16 it represents a dialectic within the mind of Chaucer the thinker and artist. To be sure the dialectic is contrived, Chaucer's progress is erratic, the pilgrim wanders; but dialectic and thus clear linear movement exists in the *Tales*.

The most obvious form of movement through the *Tales* is the various social developments of the physical pilgrimage: the early emergence of host Harry Bailey as a temporal ruler over the human community and his gradual eclipse late in the pilgrimage by the Parson, its spiritual lord (a process already commented upon by both Baldwin and Ruggiers, but not as sudden a development as either would have us believe); the instruction of both Host and pilgrim Chaucer by other pilgrims and by developments on the journey itself; the early disintegration of social harmony into social discord under the leadership of Harry, and the subsequent restoration of that harmony late in the pilgrimage. All of this is more than a series of developments on a literal pilgrimage, however: the changes are emblematic of metaphysical developments that occur over the course of the journey. It is altogether fitting, for example, that Harry Bailey, lord temporal whose governance encourages spite and malice and the waste of precious time, should provoke social disharmony despite his demands for order. And it is natural that as pilgrim poet and human community look toward the end of their symbolic pilgrimage, they should turn from a temporal to a spiritual guide; such is indeed the thrust of the journey's education of all concerned, Harry himself included. We might also expect that once the pilgrims reach some degree of spiritual awareness, their confessions will become increasingly sincere and genuine harmony will replace the discord which marked the pilgrimage's early stages: a kiss of peace between the quarreling Host and Pardoner instead of scurrilous and debasing hostilities between a drunken Miller and a choleric Reeve or a wrathful Summoner and a greedy Friar. As a man's character determines his visage, so his spiritual condition determines his action, so the spiritual condition of Chaucer's pilgrims manifests itself in their tales and actions, so Chaucer's metaphysics find reflection in narrative developments.

This means, of course, that we must attend carefully to Chaucer's developing metaphysics as revealed in the tales of each individual pilgrim. Over the course of the *Canterbury Tales* Chaucer concerns himself with more than the charity which Alan Markman sees as the core of his poem;17 he presents a series of statements on the nature of order and disorder on both the macrocosmic and microcosmic level (a concern not only of the Knight's and Miller's tales, but of most of the other tales as well); on the tragic or comic or tragicomic reality of human experience (a topic closely related to but distinct from the issue of order and disorder); on game and earnest; on the relationship between intent (a function of human will) and realization (a function of the divine will), a problem posed overtly by the Friar in his tale but implicit in the vast majority of tales, both as self-contained works of art and as dramatic monologues spoken by pilgrims; on the matter of marriage (which is, like music, emblematic of divine order); and on the role and nature of homiletics in spiritual enlightenment and artistic creation. In these concerns we may frequently ascend to a level of awareness behind the consciousness of the pilgrims themselves: probably the Knight does not recognize his tale as a comment more on order in the cosmos than on courtly behavior; certainly the Miller does not consciously see his fabliau as an assertion of disordered human affairs, although each tale may reflect the point of view and experience of its teller. In tracing these concerns through the *Canterbury Tales* we observe the mind and thought of Chaucer as artist, wrestling with problems of his own (problems which have concerned him since early in his literary career), writing them out as it were in the speeches of his Canterbury pilgrims, progressing haltingly but inexorably toward the position ultimately delineated by his Parson. Concerning Chaucer's House of Fame, *Sheila Delany* has written,

> In earlier chapters I have noted that at certain points in the *House of Fame* the experience of the Narrator—who is himself a poet—closely approaches Chaucer's...Such passages do not, of course, mean that the *House of Fame* is an autobiographical allegory which can be connected at every point with some fact of Chaucer's life. They do suggest, however, that Chaucer used the work to explore some artistic problems with which he was directly concerned.18

Much the same might be said of Chaucer's later work: the *Canterbury Tales* show the poet exploring metaphysical problems at arm's length.

And there are aesthetic matters too, which will also concern us here. Subsequent criticism has, I believe, laid to rest Tatlock's contention that Chaucer "took his poetry with a lack of constant seriousness that is in part characteristic of the Middle Ages and in part of himself."19 We have come to see the philosophical importance of even his comic tales, and recently we have come to realize that Chaucer often consciously dealt with problems of aesthetics. It is in this highest sense that Chaucer is himself participant in his fictional pilgrimage. His numerous references to art and aesthetic theory indicate he is far more conscious an aesthetician than Mroczkowski asserts, nor is Chaucer's aesthetic position limited to the naturalism implied by the close of the *General Prologue*. Such an assumption leads directly the faulty conclusion that in closing the *Canterbury Tales* "Chaucer had to find a way of living with the impossible paradox that to be true to his art was to be false to his convictions."20 The pilgrimage is artistic as well as metaphysical and social for poet Chaucer, who concerns himself continually with an issue of crucial importance to himself and to his age: what is the artist's role in (what develops to be) a Christian cosmos? The answer, Chaucer sees, depends upon one's view of society and his perception of reality: as his cosmology changes, so does his art. In fact, after initially considering both aesthetic and metaphysical problems concurrently, Chaucer appears to divide the question (at the *Man of Law's Tale*), resolving first the problem of order (cast in the traditional marriage metaphor of fragments III through V), then the matter of aesthetics (fragments VI and VII). In the *General Prologue* what we would call today a realistic or naturalistic aesthetic predominates both in the type of poetry Chaucer writes there and in the apology he makes for what is to come ("I must tell what I saw or else falsify my material"). Implicit in the other tales, however, are a variety of alternatives: satire in *Thopas*, moral didacticism in the Monk's tales, allegory in the *Clerk's Tale*, an aesthetic which denies aesthetics in the Nun's Priest's fable. And explicit in the Parson's prologue and tale is an aesthetic which denies fictive art—"Why sholde I sowen draf out of my fest,/Whan I may sowen whete, if that me lest?" (X, 35-36)—and leads directly and unavoidably (if from a modern perspective somewhat lamentably) to the retraction of some earlier tales and termination of Chaucer's narration. The middle of the *Canterbury Tales* is a dialectic in which metaphysical and aesthetic positions develop in response to the success or failure of earlier positions to create a linear progression rather than a series of random points suspended between two poles. We observe a relatively ordered process of developments, some more clear than others, some a concern more of prologues and epilogues than of tales proper. Not every tale furthers the progress of each of Chaucer's concerns, and the line of Chaucer's movement is far from arrow straight or plumb line true. Some of Chaucer's weaker tales, in fact, do not appreciably further social, metaphysical, or aesthetic developments; not coincidentally they are those the poet himself appears to have been most uncertain about: the *Squire's Tale*, the *Shipman's Tale*, the Cook's fragment. Finally, since conception of the Canterbury pilgrimage in all its dimensions preceded execution of the poem itself (just as the writing of individual tales preceded in most cases the writing of the links which join them), thematic movement of the tales is supported only sporadically by developments in the narrative of the pilgrimage *per se*. Nevertheless, through the whole of the Canterbury pilgrimage movement proceeds, sporadically forward.

At this juncture two obvious objections present themselves and demand an answer: first, the tales prove an odd mix of Chaucer's genius, some of them Italian pieces of his younger days, some clearly products of his artistic maturity. And while the chronology of Chaucer's work is far from certain, in no order of the *Canterbury Tales* do they appear in their most probably order of composition.21 How, then, is it possible that one tale answers another philosophically or aesthetically? Is a dialectic possible when its component parts are separated by some two decades? The answer, I believe, is yes in Chaucer's case and in the case of any artist whose central thematic concerns do not change considerably in his lifetime. The issues that Chaucer confronts in the *Canterbury Tales* are those which concerned him throughout his artistic career. What is new is the opportunity the *Tales* afford to explore various possibilities in separate tales. The possibilities exist in a thesis-antithesis relationship one to the other, although the whole is more construct than accident. Like the steps of a scholastic argument (which, incidentally, the *Canterbury Tales* is not), the tales represent a certain contrivance: what appears to be a linear progression in which one position emerges out of another is actually the result of considerable cutting and fitting, revision and renovation that is far less spontaneous than it appears. While the dialectic is sincere, it is also contrived, and such contrivance would certainly admit to the inclusion of pieces originally written at virtually any time during the artist's life. Like the builders of medieval cathedrals, Chaucer was not adverse to using pieces of older material when they fit.

The second objection is more difficult to deal with, partially because it is more complex and has engaged the attention of an army of scholars for nearly a century now, partially because ultimately it is incapable of resolution, especially at a distance of five hundred years from Chaucer's poem. Is it possible to imagine linear progression in a series of tales as disordered as the *Canterbury Tales* appear to be? How can we speak of dialectic development when we're uncertain whether the *Man of Law's Tale* is followed by the Wife of Bath's or the Shipman's? Any interpretation of the *Canterbury Tales* which posits a linear progression from one tale to the next demands support for the order of the *Tales* it presupposes, and the critical disarray over this matter suggests no agreement is possible. Indeed, at that point a couple of decades ago when unanimity had nearly been reached, opinion favored an order of the *Tales* which incorporated the so-called Bradshaw shift and placed all of fragment VII between II and III.22 What justification can be found for the Ellesmere order?

It seems to me there are three considerations which would lead us finally to prefer the Ellesmere order to any other. The first is simple: that order has the overwhelming support of the most and best manuscripts.23 Conversely, the Chaucer Society order, embodying the Bradshaw shift, has the support of a single manuscript in combining II and VII, a manuscript which, incidentally, places the combined II-VII between V and VIII, and VI between VIII and IX.

Furthermore, the evidence which supports the Bradshaw shift—and, indirectly, provides license to all subsequent rearrangement—assumes unquestioned a literal pilgrimage and Chaucer's studied fidelity to the particulars of the standard, fourteenth century London to Canterbury road. Pratt summarizes the reasons for reordering the *Tales* as follows:

> That Chaucer has a definite plan for the order of the Fragments is revealed by various kinds of internal evidence, including the mention of towns by the Pilgrims' Way, the reality and precise locations of which were clear and obvious to the poet and his audience. The Ellesmere (or group a) order of the Tales has long seemed unsatisfactory because it distorts the geographical order of allusions to towns, and Chaucer would not deliberately have alluded to Sittingbourne (Fragment III) before Rochester (Fragment VII) on the way from Southwark and Greenwich to Boughton-under-Blean and Canterbury.24

Reordering finds further support in the epilogue to the *Man of Law's Tale* (often regarded as genuine but cancelled) which appears to introduce the *Shipman's Tale*, and we are off into essays, treatises, whole dissertations on the order of the *Canterbury Tales*. But the case for the Bradshaw shift is, in fact, weak, as Donald C. Baker has shown25 and other recent critics seem to recognize.26 In the first place, the *Canterbury Tales* contain enough examples of obvious unrevised inconsistencies to support Robinson's suggestion that the Rochester-Sittingbourne inconsistency is but an uncorrected oversight on Chaucer's part. In the second place, the Summoner's reference to Sittingbourne (III, 845-48) reads "and I beshrewe me,/But if I telle tales two or thre/Of freres, er I come to Sidyngborne,/That I shal make thyn herte for to morne." This need not imply proximity to the town, and it need not imply that these two or three tales will be immediately forthcoming; in fact "tales two or thre" may refer to the Host's plan for two tales per pilgrim going and coming, and mean nothing more than "two or three tales before we arrive in Canterbury." In the third place, rearrangement of the *Tales* to straighten out geographical references causes difficulties in references to time, thereby necessitating (or allowing, as one's predilections run) further reordering—all of which is rejected by Pratt in his nearly final statement on the matter. Moreover, it is altogether unclear just what Chaucer intended to do with what has become the *Shipman's Tale*. The consensus of present opinion is that it was in fact once the Wife's tale and was intended to lead off fragment III, which would then have followed the *Man of Law's Tale*. At the very least, those feminine references in the *Shipman's Tale* clearly indicate the poet was unsure of where the tale belonged, and the entire matter was quite up in the air. It may finally be observed that whatever advantages may be gained from introducing the so-called marriage group (fragments III to V) with the *Nun's Priest's Tale* (the end of fragment VII) are undercut more than a trifle by the difficulty of explaining the Nun's Priest's apparent defensiveness about the Wife at a time when the Wife has not yet spoken:27

> But for I noot to whome it myght displese,
> If I counseil of wommen wolde blame,
> Passe over, for I seyde it in my game.
> Rede auctours, where they trete of swich mateere,
> And what they seyn of wommen ye may heere.
> Thise been the cokkes wordes, and nat myne;
> I kan noon harm of no womman divyne.
>   (VII, 3260-66)

Most important, the Ellesmere order has a thematic validity of its own (as this book will demonstrate), and—just as significantly—the apparent confusion in geographical references may be explained in a manner which will obviate the need for reordering. We have already seen that Harry Bailey's plan for the pilgrimage was not, in all likelihood, Chaucer's plan, although the assumption appears at first glance reasonable enough. Already Donaldson has noted the supraliteral action of the closing scenes in the *Parson's Prologue*:

> Over the fictional pilgrimage, which has for many
> years been the reflection of his own mind and
> which now becomes its reflection in a more
> personal sense, there comes something of the chill
> and urgency of late afternoon....Already a kind of
> darkness that makes recognition difficult seems to
> have come over the pilgrims. Where are they? At
> the end of a little nameless village that is surely
> neither on the road to Canterbury nor on the road
> back, but on a road that leads to a city far from
> England. The Host speaks to the parson as if he
> had never seen him before, recognizing only the

priest and knowing nothing of the man. In this
suddenly alien and lonely world we must hurry to
get in that last, virtuous tale. Why is it the last?
Not because the grand plan that Chaucer devised
has been brought close to completion, but because
a grander one of a greater Creator is hurrying to its
end.28

Suppose that the Parson's sermon was no death-bed appendage of
Chaucer's but the logical completion of a movement that has been
taking place throughout the whole of the *Tales*. Recall the
quasi-allegorical action of the Canon's Yeoman's and Manciple's
prologues. Recall for a moment that a sense of urgency has
pervaded the pilgrimage almost from its beginning. Recall the
confusing references to Sittingbourne and Rochester. May it not
be that the transition from real geographical pilgrimage to unreal
allegorical pilgrimage has been more gradual than Donaldson
suggests, and that the references to physical geography are not
determinative of the order of the tales at all? If geography has
become so distorted by the Parson's prologue that we find
ourselves, like Gawain in the great fourteenth century alliterative
romance, out of the real and into the suprareal, how can we be
certain just where we passed through the looking glass? The
answer is, of course, that we cannot, and that there is no reason for
reordering all of the tales to accommodate a realistic geography
which Chaucer has manifestly dropped somewhere between the
real Tabard Inn and the imaginary Bob-up-and-down.29 The
possibility of a non-realistic reading of the Canterbury pilgrimage
is, I maintain, a quite reasonable explanation for any
inconsistencies in geography and chronology in the order of
Chaucer's tales, and the more one supports a symbolic
supraliteralistic reading of the poem, the more he obviates the
need for realistic chronological accuracy. If geography and
chronology might render unreliable an order which supports a
thematic reading of the *Canterbury Tales*, so a thematic reading
may obviate the need for strict chronology.30 And I would suggest
that Chaucer, like most other medieval poets, was interested far
more in thematic statement than in chronological, geographical, or
arithmetic accuracy.

FOOTNOTES TO CHAPTER I

1 In 1963 Robert Payne complained, "we have had nearly no criticism of the *Canterbury Tales* in toto as they actually exist." (*The Key of Remembrance* [New Haven: Yale University Press], p. 150.) For his part, Payne is content to see the *Tales* as "a mass of amplifying material" (p. 155), "a collection of experiments in separating the individual elements in earlier poetry" (p. 169).

2 In addition to Kittredge's well known marriage group in fragments III through V, Alan Gaylord has proposed a group of tales in fragment VII on story-telling. See "Sentence and Solaas in Fragment VII of the *Canterbury Tales*," *PMLA* 82 (1967), 226-35.

3 *The Unity of the Canterbury Tales* (Copenhagen, 1955), p. 15.

4 *The Art of the Canterbury Tales* (Madison: University of Wisconsin Press, 1965), p. xiv. But note Arnold Hauser's comments on the gothic style, relevant here: "Now, a gothic building is not merely a mass in movement; it mobilizes the spectator, too, and turns an act of enjoyment into a process *with definite direction and gradual accomplishment*" (italics mine). *The Social History of Art* (New York: Knopf, 1952), I, p. 242.

5 *A Reading of the Canterbury Tales* (Albany: State University of New York Press, 1967), pp. 15-20.

6 *A Reading of the Canterbury Tales* (Cambridge, Eng.: University Press, 1968), pp. 33, 34.

7 *Chaucer* (New York: Harper & Row, 1969), p. 109.

8 "The Canterbury Tales: Memory and Form," *English Literary History*, 38 (September, 1971), 321.

9 p. 326.

10 John Findlayson, "The Satiric Mode in the Parson's Tale," *Chaucer Review*, 6 (1971), 104. Findlayson argues that the *Tales* are *not* such an allegory, because if they were, Chaucer would have made his allegorical meanings explicit.

11 The significance of the inn, at which a pilgrim on the road of life traditionally seeks comfort, ought not to escape us. See Gerhart Ladner, "Homo Viator: Alienation and Order," *Speculum*, 42 (1967), 236, 37.

12 See Siegfried Wenzel, "The Pilgrimage of Life as a Late Medieval Genre," *Medieval Studies*, 35 (1973), 370-88.

13 A gesture in this direction has already been made by Edmund Reiss, "The Pilgrimage Narrative and the Canterbury Tales,"

Studies in Philology, 67 (1970), 295-305. Reiss begins by arguing that pilgrimage "and the level it represents provide the *raison d'etre* for the stories told: while the tales have meaning in relation to teach other, they provide most of all a way of expressing the developing pilgrimage; and when between the tales we return to the explicit pilgrimage, it is to a narrative level that takes on meaning and point because of the tales." But Reiss fails to develop the point and concludes "on the other hand, this tale [the Parson's] may be seen as a prologue to a return to London, that is to this world." If so, of course, the pilgrimage has moved nowhere, has remained a social diversion.

14 *The Autobiographical Fallacy in Chaucer and Langland Studies* (London, 1965), pp. 10, 11.

15 Sanford B. Meech, *Design in Chaucer's Troilus* (Syracuse, New York: Syracuse University Press, 1959), p. 18.

16 Przemyslaw Mroczkowski, "Mediaeval Art and Aesthetics in the *Canterbury Tales*," Speculum, 33 (1958), 218.

17 "The Concern of Chaucer's Poetry," *Annuale Mediaevale*, 7 (1966), 90-103.

18 *Chaucer's House of Fame: The Poetics of Skeptical Fideism* (Chicago: University of Chicago Press, 1972), p. 109.

19 *The Development and Chronology of Chaucer's Works* (1907; rpt. Gloucester, Mass: Peter Smith, 1963), p. 47.

20 Robert M. Jordan, "Chaucer's Sense of Illusion: Roadside Drama Reconsidered," *English Literary History*, 29 (1962), 33. This is close to the conclusions reached by Alain Renoir, "Tradition and Moral Realism," *Studia Neophilologica*, 35 (1963), 199-210, and G.D. Josipovici's "Fiction and Game in the Canterbury Tales," *Critical Quarterly*, 7 (1965), 185-97.

21 In *Development and Chronology* Tatlock suggests something like the following order for those tales which can be dated: *Knight's Tale, Physician's Tale, Clerk's Tale* and *Monk's Tale, Melibee* and *The Wife of Bath's Tale, Man of Law's Tale, Merchant's Tale.*

22 See Robert A. Pratt's definitive "The Order of the Canterbury Tales," *PMLA*, 66 (1951), 1141-67; and also Donald C. Baker's admission in his brilliant "The Bradshaw Order of the Canterbury Tales," *Neuphilologische Mitteilungen*, 63 (1962), 247.

23 See Robinson, p. 889 and Huppé, p. 3.

24 "The Order of the Canterbury Tales," p. 1141.

25 "The Bradshaw Order" (above).

26 Huppé, Whittock and Corsa favor or lean toward the Ellesmere
   order; Ruggiers (to judge from the order of his "Function:
   Romance" tales) favors the Bradshaw shift.
27 It is possible to explain this as a reference to the Prioress,
   especially in light of the potential pun in "wommen divyne."
   But the Prioress we meet in both *General Prologue* and the
   Prioress' Tale is scarcely a woman to elicit the Nun's Priest's
   reaction.
28 E. Talbot Donaldson, *Chaucer's Poetry* (New York: Ronald
   Press, 1958), pp. 948, 49.
29 For a full discussion of the search for Bob-Up-and-Down, see
   Henry Littlehales, *Some Notes on the Road from London to
   Canterbury*, Chaucer Society, Series II, No. 30 (London: N.
   Trubner, 1898), 36-38. Largely for want of a more likely
   candidate. Chaucerians have been content to identify Bobbe-
   up-and-doun with Harbledown (also Herbaldoun and
   .lcbbadonne) or with Up-and-Down Field.
30 The inconsistency between "nyne and twenty" of *General
   Prologue* 24 and an actual head count of those pilgrims listed
   by Chaucer is to be explained in terms of the numerological
   significance of twenty-nine (see Chapter 5). Certainly in this
   case Chaucer sacrifices arithmetic consistency in the literal,
   realistic pilgrimage to thematic concerns on the symbolic level.

CHAPTER II

FRAGMENTS I AND II: DIALECTIC

Like so many poets of all ages, Chaucer gives us a very clear indication of what he intends to do with his poem right at its start—in the initial eighteen lines, in fact. The dualities of that frequently-memorized section of the *General Prologue* have been pointed out by other readers on more than one occasion: a natural impulse which pushes and a sacred impulse which draws pilgrims toward Canterbury; sexual and religious elements wrestling with each other for control of the prologue; the sacred and profane commingled—or, rather, the profane yielding gradually to the sacred as the elaborate, high-styled set piece rolls to its rhetorical conclusion.1 It is, in fact, this last—the movement in these lines *from* the world's natural animalism (that engendering of fish, flesh, and fowl taking place in lines 1-11) *to* to the religiosity of the saint's shrine—which foreshadows generally the development of Chaucer's entire work, as the *Canterbury Tales* moves from a literal or historical pilgrimage through familiar English countryside to an allegorical pilgrimage of the spirit, from the secular philosophizing of Knight's and Miller's tales to the Parson's Christian doctrine, from the road to English Canterbury to the road to a New Jerusalem, from a largely naturalistic aesthetic to a symbolic aesthetic directly related to religious considerations. Indeed, the *General Prologue* contains in condensed form all the various movements of the entire Canterbury pilgrimage. Significantly, points of departure and arrival are not unrelated, either in the *Prologue* or the *Tales* as a whole: it is a natural, generative impulse which launches man on his spiritual pilgrimage through this world toward the next, and it is a natural impulse which directs all men—indeed, all creation—from the mundane toward the divine. Certainly it is reasonable for a man to seek healing for physical or spiritual illness, and fallen from a state of grace, dying from birth in a spiritual disease, man seeks almost instinctively the grace embodied in the blessed martyr's shrine and the Parson's sermon. "So priketh hem nature in hir corages."

The second sentence of Chaucer's prologue involves a considerable drop from the elevated rhetoric of those initial

eighteen lines, an abrupt change of scenery as our minds leave the
saint's shrine for the tavern, and we find ourselves being
introduced to Chaucer himself, the poet, ready to go on his
pilgrimage—physical, metaphysical, artistic—"with ful devout
corage." Since E. Talbot Donaldson's well known essay of two
decades ago, most readers of the *Tales* have viewed the narrator
presented in the *General Prologue* as something of a persona, or at
least a pose.2 Indeed, given some of the remarks made by pilgrim
Chaucer in the *General Prologue*, and some of the remarks made
about poet Chaucer in the *Man of Law's Tale*, and the two tales
told by pilgrim Chaucer later on the journey, the point is difficult to
argue, although the limited point of view of this persona is
regularly and vigorously violated both in the *Prologue* and
elsewhere.3 The only real debate seems to be over the acumen of
Chaucer the pilgrim: is he naive and credulous as Donaldson,
Huppé, and others see him, or is he shrewd and clever as Bronson,
Lumiansky, Major and still others would have him?4 Certainly
pilgrim Chaucer functions as an instrument of irony, as proponents
of the shrewd narrator point out. But this strikingly modern usage
of the narrator in no way necessitates a shrewd and clever persona;
in fact the irregularity of Chaucer's use of his pose may suggest
precisely the opposite: aware that a credulous narrator, insisted
upon at every moment of the *Tales*, would be as monotonous as a
completed *Sir Thopas*, Chaucer restricted his use of the pose. It
seems to me that we may also reject Duncan's notion that Chaucer
"left the Narrator, as a personality, so vague and so undeveloped
that the reader's interest is at once centered not on him or the
sources of his knowledge, but on the matters the Narrator himself
is interested in: the situation and the other pilgrims."5 Had
Chaucer sought such an effect, he might better have dropped the
persona entirely.

We are left pretty much where we began: with Donaldson's
naive, credulous, literal-minded narrator. A reporter and an
agreer. A yes man. "The dull standard of common sense,"
Garbaty calls him, "personification of the social average."6 And
here, I believe, we are on to something, for the Chaucerian
narrator is neither more nor less obtuse or shrewd than most of the
rest of the pilgrims gathered at the Tabard Inn about to begin their
pilgrimages. He suffers from what we might call occluded moral
vision the likes of which caused Gawain to view the green chapel,
scene of his spiritual regeneration, as "the corsedest kirk that euer
I com inne," which causes the Friar's summoner to insist upon his
own damnation when given every conceivable opportunity to avoid
it, which prevents the Wife from realizing that she herself

exemplifies all the vices attributed to women by the anti-feminist clerics she so vociferously attacks, which renders the Pardoner helpless to resist that final and disasterous invitation to Harry to come forward and receive pardon. Over the course of this spiritual pilgrimage the moral vision of pilgrim Chaucer and the others will become clearer;7 for the present, however, the narrator can applaud the Monk's assertion of his own will against the divine, view Friar and Knight alike as virtuous and admirable, wax unabashedly enthusiastic in his praise of Prioress' femininity and Monk's verility, describe the Summoner as "a gentil harlot and a kynde" (1.647) and the Shipman as "a good felawe" (1.395). Chaucer can do this because he describes pilgrims "as it semed me" (1.39), and in the *General Prologue* at least the narrator does not see clearly. The occluded moral vision leads easily to errors of judgment and that unthinking approbation which mark pilgrim Chaucer's reaction to many of his peers:

> And I seyde his opinion was good,
> What sholde he studie and make hymselven wood,
> Upon a book in cloystre alwey to poure,
> Or swynken with his handes, and laboure,
> As Austyn bit? How shal the world be served?
> Lat Austyn have his swynk to hym reserved!
> (183-88)

To pilgrim Chaucer, the Monk's arguments seem perfectly reasonable; after all, how is world served? When you're sitting in a tavern drinking your beer—a socially normative state, incidentally—things look different than they do when you're about to enter the shrine of a saint. Your morality is different, and that causes you to see things differently and form corresponding attitudes and judgments. John Swart has observed that "the generic concepts by which Chaucer seems to reguate the appearance of his pilgrims are indicated by two main qualities, on one side what the character represents, his responsibility, on the other side the way in which he discharges his duties, and his personal attitude."8 The same tension is present in the poet's presentation of himself as he attempts to describe fellow pilgrims as they appear to him.

"Moral realism," Donaldson calls this sort of reporting.9 Its attendant aesthetic, reportorial realism, appears late in the *General Prologue* as Chaucer's excuse for presenting, inter alia, "the tales of Caunterbury, thilke that sownen into synne":

> For this ye knowen al so as wel as I,
> Whoso shal telle a tale after a man,

He moot reherce as ny as evere he kan
Everich a word, if it be in his charge,
Al speke he never so rudeliche and large
Or ellis he moot telle his tale untrewe,
Or feyne thyng, or fynde wordes newe.
He may nat spare althogh he were his brother;
He moot as wel seye o word as another.
Christ spak hymself ful brode in hooly writ,
Eek Plato seith, whoso kan hym rede,
The wordes mote be cosyn to the dede.
Also I pray yow to foryeve it me,
Al have I nat set folk in hir degree
Here in this tale, as that they sholde stonde.
My wit is short, ye may wel understonde.

(730-46)

The wit of Chaucer the pilgrim is, as we have seen, a function of his role as personification of the social average, and therefore—at the outset of the pilgrimage—very, very short. In his first explicit aesthetic statement of the *Canterbury Tales*, Chaucer commits himself as poet to a realism determined largely by his persona: that is, the occluded vision of the persona results in an aesthetic advanced by the persona, but Chaucer as artist—not persona—is ultimately responsible for the content of the Miller's, Reeve's, Cook's (and Friar's and Summoner's) Tales. What persona reports must be created by poet. And as persona is made to see distorted reality as a manifestation of his spiritual blindness, poet is compelled to create that distorted reality. The passage is complex and perplexing, and may be read in several ways. In one sense this is just one of Chaucer's many jokes; in another sense this is Chaucer's obvious attempt to finesse a potentially delicate situation. But the retraction of those tales Chaucer is here justifying, which comes at the end of what is in one sense Chaucer's artistic pilgrimage, and the denial of this aesthetic of reportorial realism implicit in that retraction, make it difficult to view this statement as either joke or finesse. In light of Chaucer's retraction (which is, as we shall see, a direct outgrowth of considerable deliberation on aesthetic theory and practice) we are forced to view these lines of the *General Prologue* as serious statements about art, sincere insofar as the initial position of any contrived dialectic is sincere, the first stance of Chaucer the poet toward his art. It is a stance which brings poet and persona very close, and suggests that for all the obvious contrivance of the naive pilgrim, the two are at this point not far distant. No, Chaucer the poet is not blind to the shortcomings of Prioress and Monk, but he may at this point be committed to a realism which is the artistic equivalent of that excuse used by his persona to justify the Monk: how shall the world be served? The moral realism of Chaucer's persona and the aesthetic realism used to justify some forthcoming tales are related in that both place emphasis on appearances and externals. The one is, as Chaucer will discover in his personal pilgrimage, as pernicious as the other.

Thus far we have seen pilgrim-as-he-is (in contrast to pilgrim-as-he-ought-to-be) and poet-as-he-is (in contrast to poet-as he-ought-to-be), the duty discharged measured against the responsibility, to borrow Swart's terminology. Chaucer has managed, rather delicately I believe, to portray himself as deficient both in his public role as pilgrim personification of societal norm, and in his very private role as artist. What of the rest of this fellowship? Is it, like Chaucer, devout of heart but oblivious to the spirituality of this journey? Granted the fellowship is described by an unreliable reporter; granted the events of the pilgrimage are created by an artist whose commitment to a fictional realism makes his art suspect; granted the descriptions of the *General Prologue* peel like an onion until there's nothing solid, concrete left—still I think we can agree that the Canterbury pilgrims are a fellowship badly in need of grace, of instruction, of reawakening and regeneration. Not only that the vast majority of them are as individuals unregenerate (if frequently unconscious) sinners, but that the fellowship itself is all awry. The Host informs us that he's not seen such a merry company at his inn this whole year (1. 764), yet we find them not a tale's ride from the Tabard and they're quarreling among themselves. Moreover, they will quarrel the better part of the road to Canterbury, venting petty jealousies and drunken irrationalities that are the mark of fellowship without charity. Those pilgrims specifically described as most capable of a jovial trip seem invariably to be those most out of tune with the pilgrimage's spiritual nature and those most out of harmony with their fellow pilgrims. The Wife of Bath,—"in felaweshipe wel koude she laughe and carpe" (1. 474). Yet she's lived a life of constant strife, falls all out of charity whenever anyone else goes to the offering before she, is a wanderer by the wayside who has spent her life on repeated pilgrimages to (the Old) Jerusalem and like Parzival at the Grail Castle failed singularly to grasp just what those pilgrimages were all about. The Shipman, "a good fellow," drowns those who cross him. The companionship of Summoner and Pardoner smacks of sexual perversion, emblemized by their grotesque harmonizing on a love song. The Miller, "a janglere and a goliardeys" (1. 560) whose cacophonous bagpipes lead the fellowship out of town, is in fact the very drunkard whose acrimonious insistence on his own way destroys the fellowship's tenuous order in the pilgrimage's second tale. These examples could be multiplied, but the point is obvious: here is a fellowship (the word is used twice within seven lines as Chaucer describes their arrival at the Tabard) desperately in need of spiritual regeneration and the aid of whatever help the blessed martyr might offer "whan that they were seeke." This is not to suggest that the company is any more unregenerate than the rest of the human community. It is only to emphasize its condition in departing from the Tabard Inn. Only the Parson and his brother the Plowman, whose work bears fruit in the theologically proper sense, and perhaps the Clerk, whose sparse speech leads only to virtue, can be credited with moral virtue, spiritual health, a sense of rectitude and awareness. And in the fellowship of the *General Prologue*, they are silent, minority voices.

The dominant voice, apart from that of pilgrim Chaucer of course, belongs to Harry Bailey, who makes his appearance just before the close of the *Prologue*. Curiously, we are introduced to Harry immediately after Chaucer's espousal of verisimilitude and realism in the statement quoted above, an aesthetic with which the Host is closely associated, the defects of which he himself best exemplifies. Being literal-minded, narrow, superficial, and generally low class, Harry fixates on the worst aspects of "the real things of life": sexuality, vulgarity, obscenity, profanity, abuse, and—very occasionally—the slightest bit of sentimental piety or practical, down-to-earth information. Despite his protestations of taste, we may be certain that his choice for the prize dinner would not be the tale "of best sentence and most solaas." In fact, in the obvious inadequacies of Harry's critical judgments and his consistent antagonism toward a homiletics which Chaucer causes ultimately to triumph, we see Chaucer's own rejection of the aesthetics of realism for the same reason the Parson prefers wheat to chaff, for the same reason Plato expelled poets from his Republic. "Realism" becomes illusion once one becomes aware of higher reality, as the *is* becomes the *ought*, as discharged duty comes to accord with responsibility. Art, then, becomes not a mirror to reflect existing reality, but a construct enabling the artist to measure and transform existing reality by providing a vision of that new reality to persons heretofore blind to it. The higher reality, of course, is spiritual, as the higher morality is Christian, as the higher aesthetic is largely homiletic; but Chaucer's pilgrimage begins with things of this world, with *is* instead of *ought*, with realism in its various manifestations.

And a thoroughly worldly, realistic, secular rule, Harry Bailey is.

It has often been noted that an inn keeper is a perfectly appropriate occupation for one who presides over the early stages of any pilgrimage: what could be more emblematic of the transitory nature of that journey than an inn, who more emblematic of these lords temporal than the innkeeper to whom we pay our few pennies for a night's rest and a quick supper before moving on? Certainly Harry's role is significant in this respect. But his primary importance lies not so much in his occupation as in the position of leadership to which he, with the assent of all pilgrims present, elevates himself. "A semely man oure Hoost was withalle," Chaucer recalls, "For to han been a marchal in an halle" (751-52). It is not thirty lines later that Harry, to entertain the pilgrims, to wile away the hours, to provide the company with some diversion, has ascended to that position, a position he will insist jealously upon through most of the *Canterbury Tales*:

> And if yow liketh alle by oon assent
> For to stonden at my juggement,
> And for to werken as I shal yow seye,
> To-morwe, whan ye riden by the weye,
> Now, by my fader soule that is deed,
> But ye be myrie, I wol yeve yow myn heed!
> Hoold up youre hondes, withouten moore speche.
> (777-83)

Harry is, let it be noted, an elected monarch in accordance with the best medieval political theorists.10 He is also absolute: the pilgrims are to stand at his judgment, do as he says, work his will in all things. Whoever argues will pay the costs of the entire company's round trip. And Harry reasserts his position again and again, both here in the *General Prologue* and throughout the remainder of the *Tales*:

> And whoso wole my juggement withseye
> Shal paye al that we spenden by the weye.
> (805-6)

> Whoso be rebel to my juggement
> Shal paye for al that by the wey is spent.
> (833-34)

> "Sire Knight," quod he, "my mayster and my
>   lord,
> Now draweth cut, for that is myn accord."
> (837-38)

Of course the Host's obsession with being ruler, governor, judge, and general figure of authority is part of Chaucer's development of

his character. But we ought to note too that pilgrim Chaucer is
more than willing to grant him the position he assumes:

> This thyng was graunted, and oure othes swore
> With ful glad herte, and preyden him also
> That he woulde vouche sauf for to do so,
> And that he wolde been oure governour,
> And of oure tales juge and reportour,
> And sette a soper at a certeyn pris,
> And we wol reuled been at his devys
> In heigh and lough; and thus by oon assent
> We been acorded to his juggement.
>
> (809-17)

Even the Knight, Harry's social superior, accepts his command
and is obedient to his will. The Hosts's own address to the Knight
as "my mayster and my lord" is but a social convention, since it
was at Harry's own insistence that cuts are drawn and he may very
well fix them anyway. There can be no doubt as to just who's in
charge here: Harry has installed himself as the secular ruler, the
governor, the guide, the judge of this human fellowship for what
he expects to be the duration of the pilgrimage. This much the
language of those closing lines of the *General Prologue* makes
clear.

As rule, Harry imposes upon the group his plan for the
pilgrimage and his own brand of mirth and comedy. In return for
absolute authority, he promises—upon pain of his head—a good
time. Stories. Games. "Sentence and solaas," he claims, will be
the twin criteria for judging best tale, but we can imagine what he
really has in mind (and just in case we can't, we need only look to
the Cook's prologue, or the tales of the Friar and Summoner for
some good clues). *Solaas*—in the form of pietistic tale, bawdy
story, or a good fight—is far more important than *sentence*,
because it kills time better. You don't get bored, even if you don't
get instructed. In all of this, of course, Harry is an ideal choice as
secular ruler, thorough in his secularity and persistent in his
blindness to any and all spiritual concerns, the likes of which will
ultimately dethrone him, revise dramatically his plans for the
pilgrimage, upset his judgments, abrogate his self-granted
prerogatives, deny his brand of art. He is the only pilgrim who
leaves the Tabard Inn with purely secular motives (most probably
a brief vacation from his shrewish wife, although he also has his
eye on that dinner at the Tabard they'll all have together upon
their return); he is not the sort to lead the pilgrims *into* Canterbury
at the far side of their journey, but he is certainly an appropriate
governor here in the mundane, workaday world, at the beginning

of this pilgrimage.

What is interesting, however, is the ironic foreshadowing artist Chaucer implants in those closing lines of the *Prologue*: "by my fader soule that is deed," Harry swears in line 781, promising mirth and revelry. In the midst of beginning, the finality of death; in the midst of secular jocularity a glimpse of things to come. *Respice finem*. But Harry is not concerned with either souls or death. He gathers the pilgrims "togidre alle in a flok," Chaucer tells us, bringing to mind the Parson and his flock, and herds them out of town for fun and games without a moment's reflection on the eschatology implicit in his oath.

THE KNIGHT'S TALE

First cut falls to the Knight. Chaucer is uncertain whether the draw was a result of "aventure, or sort, or cas," and his uncertainty about the draw is more than matched by readers' uncertainty about this first tale—do things happen here by accident, or destiny, or chance? Everyone has a theory; no one can agree wholeheartedly with anyone else. And then there is the Knight himself—people can't even agree about him.11

All of this is not surprising, for the matter of cause or accident broached so casually in pilgrim Chaucer's remarks of the *General Prologue* is the thematic center of artist Chaucer's tale, and this tale is put in the mouth of a pilgrim especially constructed to tell it. As Lumiansky, among others, has noted, the tale is clearly a reflection of its teller, and any attempt to explain it must be colored by one's view of the Knight himself.12 In Chaucer's portrait of the Knight in the *General Prologue* we discover much of the subtle ambiguity so characteristic of Chaucer, ambiguity which frequently leaves us in doubt as to a pilgrim's actual character. This knight is worthy and he is wise. He loves chivalry, truth, honor, liberality, and courtesy. He is a faithful servant of his lord in battle, has ridden in that service both in Christian and heathen lands, and is everywhere honored for his worthiness. In three lists he has slain his foe. His armor is dirty. On the surface, this portrait is flattering—so much so that some have been tempted to read it as a thinly veiled compliment to John of Gaunt or other friends of the poet.13 Thomas Hatton has gone so far as to claim Chaucer's "audience could hardly fail to see the program of the Order of the Passion [supported by none other than John of Gaunt] reflected in the Knight's portrait."14 Muriel Bowden talks about "the 'ideal'

nature of the Knight,'' and her admiration is evident throughout
her discussion of his personage.15 John Swart takes the Knight to
represent ideal nobility as the Parson represents an ideal
commoner and the Clerk represents an ideal bourgeoisie.16 "A
completely ideal figure," states F.N. Robinson flatly.17

But others are not so convinced. In their study of the *Knight's
Tale* already cited, Brooks and Fowler register some reservations
about the Knight as a person: he shares Theseus' virtues and his
vices, specifically service to Mars, "a certain jovial secularity and
stoicism of attitude," a belief in Fortune, genuine reservations
about lesser deities.18 Jeffrey Helterman is also unconvinced of
the Knight's status as "a completely ideal figure.". He reads the
Knight as a man still in process of becoming:

> Although it is conventional to go on a pilgrimage
> after the successful completion of a military
> endeavor, Chaucer may be suggesting, through
> the fact that the Knight is still dressed for battle,
> that his task is not complete. In *The Squire of Low
> Degree*, the hero is told that his battles are
> incomplete unless they are followed by a
> pilgrimage. The Knight's haste indicates that
> despite his many victories and "sovereyn prys" he
> is still seeking for something—something not to be
> found on the field of battle.19

And Charles Mitchell, in an extraordinarily sensitive study, has
ar ued that although the Knight is *worthy* and *wise*, he is not
necessarily *good*, and Chaucer never once applies the adjective to
him.20 Certainly the Knight is virtuous in that he fulfills the
obligations imposed upon him by his role and social status, and
there is no denying that he had "foughten for oure feith at
Tramyssene." But there is nothing particularly Christian about his
virtue, and in one case at least he had fought for heathen as well as
Christian lords.21 The whole notion of virtue is, to begin with,
suspect in the *General Prologue*, tainted by pilgrim Chaucer's easy
approbation of any and all pilgrims; *worthy* is tainted by its use in
describing the Merchant. This is not to say Chaucer is being ironic
in describing the Knight as *worthy* and virtuous in the broadest
sense; it is only to say that the descriptions of pilgrim Chaucer
need careful assessment. Most of the Knight's virtue derives from
martial prowess and courtesy. Courtesy is not a Christian virtue,
and as the pretensions of the Prioress make clear, it is at best an
ambivalent quality. Martial prowess is in most cases not a
Christian virtue, especially when proffered to both heathen and
Christian lords. Especially when it involves killing your foe in three

lists or engaging in fifteen mortal battles. Especially when it involves service in partially commercial enterprises like the campaigns at Satalye and Lyeys.

Now this is not to say the Knight is a bad fellow. He is not. He is, in fact, a *good man* . . . but he has his limitations, and those limitations must be recognized. He is a paragon, but a secular paragon. He serves *a* lord, but not necessarily *the* Lord. His clothing, dirtied from service to various lords, suggests St. Paul's whole armor of God largely by way of contrast. His reverence is for truth *as he sees it*, honor, and courtesy, not for Christian service and godly religion. Indeed, it may be his easy submission to a-Christian, secular rule, emblemized by his willing and unquestioning submission to Harry's governance,22 that necessitates the pilgrimage upon which he finds himself.

The Knight is, however, an intelligent fellow and thoughtful, one who has meditated upon the world as revealed to him by his experience. This much accounts for the infusion of Boethian philosophy into his tale, which is the major alteration Chaucer made in translating it from Boccaccio's poem. The tale amounts to a long, philosophically reflective romance which concerns itself superficially with the world of chivalric behavior and feats of arms, but which takes as its real thematic center several subjects which have concerned Chaucer throughout his artistic career and (through the personages of other pilgrims) will concern him throughout the *Canterbury Tales*: the possibility of ordering human experience, the nature of universal order (or disorder), the intelligibility of celestial order to the human mind, the relationship between freedom of human will and deterministic forces. His conclusions are suspiciously reminiscent of those reached at the close of *Troilus and Criseyde*: men's lives are considerably, perhaps entirely determined by destinal forces they can only dimly comprehend, but those forces are themselves capricious and unpredictable (here a significant difference between the *Knight's Tale* and *Troilus and Criseyde*); he survives who best rolls with the punches. Virtue, as Theseus is made to observe, consists of making do with a necessity imposed by celestial order . . . which, we see in the workings of the tale's celestial hierarchy, is largely disorder.23 Ultimately the entire tale dissolves into random accident, coincidence, and disorder which, given its constant striving for pattern and order, creates a curious ambivalence reminiscent of that surrounding that Knight's own character. This ambivalence is further reflected stylistically in what Paul Ruggiers has accurately described as "the free admixture of styles, the presence of comic stringencies within passages of considerable solemnity, the adducing of personal attitudes, not found in Boccaccio which from time to time ruffle the surface tone," what Bernard Huppé calls "rhetorical sinking," and what Paul Thurston has termed "artistic ambivalence" in the tale.24

The tale's deterministic disorder, Chaucer's attempts to penetrate the celestial cloud which veils its workings from human sight, and the tale's philosophical resolution to the problems it poses are all centered in the person of Duke Theseus. Palamon and Arcite are peas in a pod; Emily is just "there." It is on Theseus that our attention is (quite properly) focused; he is a complex figure who plays several roles. In one sense he is the Knight's own spokesman, a projection of the Knight into his tale. In a much more legitimate sense he is Chaucer's self projected into this romance.25 In the context of the fiction itself, he is on the one hand a powerful mortal whose will is frustrated again and again by whatever powers there be, and on the other a figural representation of those same gods. The strands bear unraveling, for when disentangled they prove very similar. Any one individually and all collectively will take us to Chaucer's first important philosophical statement in the pilgrimage toward Canterbury.

First, and perhaps most important, Theseus is a man—"lord and governour, and...conqueror." He is a man very much like the Knight, a man who loves chivalry, battle, truth and justice, and most of all order. But like the Knight, although perhaps more manifestly, Theseus evidences certain inconsistencies of character which suggest his chivalry is not all it's made out to be. His order, for example, is constantly subverted from without and changed from within. One set of rules governs in one circumstance, another in the same circumstance a few months hence, or in an analogous but different situation. It is in keeping with Theseus' passion for justice and decency that he rush off and level Thebes to punish a king who refused proper burial to his enemies; on the other hand, it's all well and good for looters to ransack the battle field, despoiling the still warm (and, we learn, still living) bodies of those Theseus has vanquished. One year the tournament between Palamon and Arcite is to be a battle to the death; the next year Theseus has changed his mind;

> Wherfore, to shapen that they shal nat dye,
> He [Theseus] wol his firste purpos modifye.
> No man therfore, up peyne of los of lyf,
> No maner shot, ne polax, ne short knyf
> Into the lystes sende, or thider brynge;
>
>   (2541-45)

In one line the good Duke concludes shortly, "Ye shal be deed, by myghty Mars the rede!" Sixty lines later he's changed his mind: "I yow foryeve al hoolly this trespaas" (1818). He may be courteous, as in his most generous offer to cleanse Thebes; or he may be discourteous, as in his refusal to allow Palamon and Arcite ransom, or his failure to consult Emily, the tournament's prize, about whom she'd like to marry (turns out she'd just as soon remain a virgin—but no matter; the Knight informs us, somewhat unchivalrously, women follow fortune and she's bound to love a winner!). His vaunted wisdom proves incapable of accurately perceiving any agent of destiny beyond Fortune, to whom he most frequently ascribes responsibility for events here on earth: even that final Boethian speech on first causes never manages a full Boethian view of things with the concomitant affirmation it might afford. It leads him to assert an order which is largely unknown and unknowable, which guarantees only death to the king as well as to the page, which allows man only to make virtue of necessity. And his will, which asserts itself constantly, is just as regularly changed. In at least four separate instances (refusing to release Palamon and Arcite from prison, condemning them to death in the lines quoted above, decreeing a tournament to the death, and deciding that Emily will go to the winner of that tournament), Theseus' decree is not as fixed as he would have us believe. The Duke may be attractive as a mortal man—his willingness to excuse the brothers for helping themselves in love and in distress, coupled with his reminiscences on his own service to the god of love certainly make him attractive as well as human—but like human beings he is inconsistent. Usually he's chivalrous, but sometimes he's not. He is wise, but his wisdom has its limitations. His pity runs easily as his heart is gentle, but that pity is not to be counted on: sometimes it flows, sometimes it does not. And being turned on, it may turn off. Or vice versa. You never really know.

One reason Theseus is inconsistent is that he's merely mortal; another reason is that his own will is constantly being frustrated by whatever powers control his life, so that he must constantly revise his plans to accommodate what cannot be avoided. The harmony of his homecoming is disrupted by weeping and wailing women, disorder caused by Fortune's false wheel (925). Theseus' plan, his will (the word appears frequently throughout the tale), is that Palamon and Arcite will each gather a company of knights, fight for Emily, and he "To whom that Fortune yeveth so fair a grace" shall win her (1861). Fortune, the Duke believes, is the imponderable, but as events work out his will is frustrated even in this: he to whom Fortune gives grace to win the tournament is not he who gets to marry Emily. We are reminded of just that fact in lines 2657 following:

> I wol be trewe juge, and no partie.
> Arcite of Thebes shal have Emilie,
> That by his fortune hath hire faire ywonne.

In the end Theseus is reduced to a long speech which asserts a fixed order ordained by Jupiter the king, against which man may not rebel and in harmony with which the wise man lives his life. You can't see it, but it's there, Theseus informs the assembled multitude:

> Thanne is it wysdom, as it thynketh me,
> To maken vertu of necessitee,
> And take it weel that we may nat eschue,
> And namely that to us alle is due.
>
> (3041-44)

Of course Theseus is not the only mortal whose will is frustrated by the gods; Palamon and Arcite find their sworn brotherhood undone by Love, "a gretter law, by my pan,/Than may be yeve to any erthely man" (1165, 66): surely no one is more upset than Arcite when his plans to win and wed are thrown into disarray by Saturn's fury; even the will of the Knight, who informs us again and again that his intent is to tell a short tale and get right to the point, is manifestly thwarted by whatever muses control the telling of the tale.

But while Theseus and other mortals in this tale are mere men subject to destinal controls above and beyond their understanding, Theseus at least is on several occasions a figure for these forces. He is the human counterpart of Jupiter, and as such he is regularly described as a god, or in situations which make him appear a god. The company of kneeling women who greet him on his homecoming, the kneeling figures of Palamon and Arcite who address him in that bloody field as "lord and judge" (1729) and make their confessions to him, the two companies of knights arranged below his chair in the royal lists—all these suggest those depictions of Christ in Judgment, seated above balanced companies of damned and elect in those tympanum scenes so familiar to any medieval church-goer:

> Duc Theseus was at a wyndow set,
> Arrayed right as he were a god in trone.
> The peple presseth thiderward ful soone

Hym for to seen, and doon heigh reverence,
And eek to herkne his hest and his sentence.
(2528-32)

Like the gods, Theseus is powerful, revered, worshipped. Like the gods he imposes order—or what he hopes will be order—on chaos.

And like the gods, Theseus finds his order disintegrating into chaos. This is, in fact, the final irony: that while Theseus should find himself so much like the gods at the very moment he is frustrated by the gods, the gods should find themselves so mortal, so confused, so frustrated themselves by—by what? By the working out of events, by their own squabbling, by accident and chance. Theseus, as spokesman for a divinely appointed order, has made quite a point of this order: it's there, he says, beyond fortune and accident, a destiny wrought by Jupiter which appoints to every living creature its beginning and end, which works harmony in the firmament and among the elements:

Ther nedeth noght noon auctoritee t'allegge,
For it is preeved by experience,
But that me list declaren my sentence.
Thanne may men by this ordre wel discerne
That thilke Moevere stable is and eterne...
What maketh this but Juppiter, the kyng,
That is prince and cause of alle thyng,
Convertynge al unto his propre welle
From which it is dirryved, sooth to telle?
And heer-agayns no creature on lyve,
O no degree, availleth for to stryve.
(3000-4, 35-40)

The problem is, it's not there. In fact, Chaucer has taken great pains to show his readers the workings of destiny as it operates in this tale. First, of course, there are those disasters depicted on the walls of every temple constructed by Theseus, everything from broken sleep and sighing and foolishness and bawdry in the temple of Venus to the vengeance of Diane on Acteon to madness and wrath and suicide and murder in the temple of Mars. Such are the rewards of all who serve these gods! Then there is the treacherous message of Mercury given to a sleeping Arcite: "To Atthenes shaltou wende,/Ther is thee shapen of thy wo an ende" (1391, 92). Arcite runs off to Athens with the best of expectations, only to find himself done in by the gods who sent him there. But most important there is that long glimpse of the gods at work, controlling the lives of mortal men, recounted in lines 2438-78. Venus and Mars have accidentally made contradictory promises, and the gods squabble among themselves. King Jupiter tries his best to calm them down, but he can do nothing. Finally it is Saturn, one of the underlings, who assumes control of the situation and finds a solution: he will kill off Arcite, the winner, so that loser Palamon can marry the girl. Lo, the end of prayer to these gods! Lo, the nature of divine will which controls mortal affairs! Lo, the order which governs this world! To settle an argument among petty (and very human) gods, men die unjustly, for as virtually every reader of the *Knight's Tale* realizes, Arcite's reward is in no way connected with his moral character. Moreover, if "Destiny proper is represented first by the three divinities to whom the rivals and Emilye appeal; then by Saturn, who settles the issue among the divinities; and ultimately by a Divinity—'the sight avove' (1672), 'the Firste Moevere' (2987)—beyond all divinities,"26 then the entire scheme of things, bottom to top, is awry. Death is no longer a necessity from which "man may yet snatch the assurance of a gracious cooperation with the forces of nature,"27 it is a bad joke played by jealous and indifferent gods upon mortals. Well might Egeus complain, "This world nys but a thurghfare ful of wo,/And we been pilgrymes, passynge to and fro" (2847,48). In this philosophical romance the earthly pilgrimage is confused, directionless, benighted, and ultimately tragic.

The forces of destiny in this tale resemble mortals in their confusion; mortal agents of order find disorder undermining their efforts at every step of the human pilgrimage. The randomness of life is seen most clearly not by Theseus, but by Arcite in a speech which immediately follows his accidental release from prison:

> Allas, why pleynen folk so in commune
> On purveiaunce of God, or of Fortune,
> That yeveth hem ful ofte in many a gyse
> Wel bettre than they kan hemself devys?
> Som man desireth for to han richesse,
> That cause is of his mordre or greet siknesse;
> And som man wolde out of his prisoun fayn,
> That in his hous is of his meynee slayn.
> Infinite harmes been in this mateere.
> We witen nat what thing we preyen heere;
>
>   (1251-60)

We move through clouds of night, drunk as a mouse, mistaking good for bad and bad for good, thoroughly confused. Palamon, in his cell far from Arcite, has similar feelings:

> What governance is in this prescience,
> That giltelees tormenteth innocence?
>
>   (1313-14)

One can only imagine the reaction of Palamon and Arcite if they actually knew the true causes behind those events which unfold late in the tale. In fact, the order sought by everyone in this tale, assumed to be beneficient by Theseus and malevolent by both Palamon and Arcite, simply does not exist. From the paintings on those temple walls to the actual convocation of the gods, every objective look at the workings of destiny suggests disorder under a facade of order, random in the guise of justice. The "Boethian test case" (Paul Ruggiers) collapses. The harmony of Palamon and Emily's emblematic marriage (Robertson) and the "blisse, richesse, and heele" of the couple are specious. As valiantly as the Knight struggles for a beatific vision, the view of the universe taken by the tale is tragic, and the condition of man presented by its teller is also tragic.

This, then, is the philosophical beginning of the Canterbury pilgrimage, Chaucer's first statement on the nature of things. It is learned, relying heavily on his translation of Boethius. It is as sweet as the trappings of the chivalric world and its elaborate rhetoric can make it. But in the final analysis it is profoundly unsettling: all the gold enameling (and there is much gold in this tale, rhetorical and otherwise) will not cover the fact that the world is but a confused thoroughfare of woe, and death the end of every worldly sorrow. While the Knight is no fool, and has a conscious sense of both this world and man's pilgrimage through it, his position is far from the Christian affirmation of the *Parson's Tale*: one ends in death, the other in life. One is sold, fixed, certain; the other is for all its determinism ultimately uncertain: "His spirit chaunged hous and wente ther,/As I cam nevere, I kan nat tellen wher" (2809, 10).

It is with the Parson's sermon that the *Knight's Tale* is most frequently compared: at one end of the pilgrimage the Knight's chivalric romance, at the other the Parson's homily on penitence and salvation. Like the beginning and end of any medieval work, these two tales claim special attention because of their positions; they are more conspicuous and therefore more important than the middle tales. And they will afford numerous points of contrast: the Knight is prone to rhetorical elaboration and the gold enameling mentioned earlier, which the Parson explicitly avoids; the Knight tells a philosophical romance while the Parson shuns the chaff of narrative; the Knight's philosophy is not explicitly Christian, his deities frankly pagan, while the Parson's dogma is entirely and unabashedly Christian; the order of the *Knight's Tale* is apparently specious, while that of the *Parson's Tale* represents the

greatest certainty in all the *Canterbury Tales*;28 the Knight's
romance, perhaps because of its uncertainty, seems dark, even
tragic, while the Parson's sermon is for all of its sense of sin comic
in the theological sense. Their obvious points of contrast and our
certainty about their positions in the order of the *Canterbury
Tales*29 have led readers concerned with unity in the poem to focus
their attention on the poles represented by Knight and Parson, and
slight the middle. The *Knight's Tale*, however, is followed not by
the Parson's tale, but by the Miller's and the Reeve's; it is in fact
by progressing through these and other fictional constructs that
artist and pilgrims arrive ultimately at the position of the
Parson.30 While the *Knight's Tale* and the *Parson's Tale* may be
paired off against each other with profit, one cannot ignore the
relationships of each with other tales in their respective
proximities.

THE MILLER'S TALE

The aesthetics of the *Knight's Tale* are those of any standard,
serious medieval work of art: it is a narrative which offers
implicitly the "sentence and solaas" requested by Harry Bailey at
the close of the *General Prologue,* if only a reader will take the
time to reflect on things. No matter as far as aesthetics are
concerned that whatever solace the tale might offer is constructed
on sand; here is story and theme. In the person of Theseus we have
an example; in the ruminations of himself and his father and in the
frequent soliloquies of Palamon and Arcite we find overt moral
sententiousness. Except for its somber colors and a-Christian
philosophizing, it is the sort of tale of which, with few minor
modifications, Saint Augustine would have approved. The other
pilgrims see it as a noble story and worthy to commit to memory,
although I rather suspect they see only the surface of things. I
suspect also that the Knight is not entirely satisfied with his
statement, since it is in the final analysis an affirmation of
uncertainty and accident (in fact, his very presence on this
pilgrimage may suggest a certain dissatisfaction with his position
and a search for something more certain); and I also suspect that
artist Chaucer is dissatisfied with the view of things he's taken in
the *Knight's Tale*. The Miller's requital of the Knight is in effect
Chaucer's requital of Chaucer.

The aesthetics of the *Miller's Tale* are very different from those
of its predecessor; it is the medieval equivalent of anti-story.
While it certainly does not deny narrative or realism as other tales

will, it does deny analysis and meaning, the "sentence" which in
the medieval mind justified serious narrative. Moreover, the
realism of the tale itself and the reportorial realism of Chaucer's
retelling of it are more dangerous than the telling and retelling of
the Knight's romance, since both posit reality only in things, in
externals, whereas the Knight at least acknowledged a
neo-Platonic reality of ideas. The Miller's morality, as has been
frequently pointed out, is the morality of practicality and
opportunism. We would say that God helps him who helps himself,
but in the cosmos of the *Miller's Tale* God, although often
mentioned, is not a force to be reckoned with (an ironic contrast to
the Knight's cosmos, in which the Christian god is entirely absent,
but god-as-first-mover is omnipresent). As Paul Ruggiers puts it,
this is "the world of contrivance and deception, of situations and
actions generating their own special kind of morality and their own
justice."31 The same thing might also be said of the action in
Chaucer's frame: Knight's and Miller's tales interact almost
undirected by outside intervention, two realities battling each
other, neutralizing each other, generating their own justice.
Chaucer simply reports.

The relationships between Knight's and Miller's tales have
been carefully examined on several occasions;32 what such close
examination unmistakably reveals is that the pair is a well matched
set with numerous parallels and studied contrasts. The Miller,
after all, tells a tale with which he "wol now quite the Knyghtes
tale" (3127). And to a certain extent it is true that the stories are
matched contrasts, both in the ways already suggested and in the
mock courtly wooing of Alisoun by a pair of lovers (Nicholas a more
active Arcite, Absolon a more mannered Palamon), the vigor and
high spirits of the fabliau as a genre (a sharp contrast to the stasis
and sobriety of the romance which preceded it), the absence of
overt sententiousness and didacticism (indeed, the only
philosophical advice the Miller has to offer is that one ought not to
wax overly philosophical), the parody of the noble fellowship of the
Knight's Tale in the fellowship of this second Noah (1. 3539), and
the attitude taken by a superstitious carpenter toward providence
and destiny. It is not without significance, for example, that handy
Nicholas is a student of astrology, that it is his study of the stars
and moon (and Mars and Venus?) which supposedly has revealed
to him the impending flood. There is no flood, of course, just as
there is none of the kissing Absalon anticipates so deliciously:
"My mouth hath icched al this longe day;/That is a signe of
kissyng atte leeste" (3683, 84). When Nicholas talks about sun and
moon and flood, he's blowing steam:

"Now John," quod Nicholas, "I wol nat lye;
I have yfounde in myn astrologye,
As I have looked in the moone bright,
That now a Monday next, at quarter nyght,
Shal falle a reyn, and that so wilde and wood,
That half so greet was nevere Noes flood.
This world," he seyde, "in lasse than an hour
Shal al be dreynt, so hidous is the shour.
Thus shal mankynde drenche, and lese hir lyf."
(3513-21)

Lies, all lies—but there is precisely the point: the "forces" of destiny are but materials to be manipulated by enterprising clerks in pursuit of a fey young wench. Certainly they never produce anything of consequence of their own power. Charles Muscatine has written of the functionalism of fabliau description:

Particularizing detail is most often brought in with
a view towards practical utility in the action.
Where a house is placed by a river, someone is
thrown into that river. Where there is an especially
cold winter, there is a very hot fire, and the fire is
used to heat an implement at the climax of the
story. An action set in September, when berries
are ripe, involves a hungry priest who gets caught
in a berry bush. So it goes with description
generally.33

So it goes with all the astrological learning of the *Miller's Tale*, with God and with biblical lore, with Nicholas' studies: they are functional, there to be used. Beyond being functional, the forces of destiny in this tale become nominal: they have no real existence. In this the tale reflects the Miller's own philosophy as expressed in his prologue: man ought not to be overly inquisitive about God's providence...about destiny, in other words. The Knight, with his concern for discovering a knowable, fixed, objective order in the cosmos was just plain off base. In the tale itself, John claims such pursuits will bring a man to distraction:

This man is falle, with his astromye,
In some woodnesse, or in som agonye.
I thoughte ay wel that it sholde be!
Men sholde nat knowe of Goddes pryvetee.
Ye, blessed be alwey a lewed man
That noght but oonly his bileve kan!
So ferde another clerk with astromye;
He walked in the feeldes, for to prye
Upon the sterres, what ther sholde bifalle,
Til he was in a marle-pit yfalle;
He saugh nat that.
(3451-61)

In the prologue to the tale, Robin asserts that such pursuits will
make a man unduly suspicious:

> An housbonde shal nat been inquisityf
> Of Goddes pryvetee, nor of his wyf.
> So he may fynde Goddes foyson there,
> Of the remenant nedeth nat enquere.
>
> (3163-66)

In all likelihood, however, serious pursuit of astrology will bring a
man to neither insanity nor suspicion; it will merely expend his
energies needlessly. That sort of knowledge simply doesn't exist,
as Nicholas well knows. You manufacture your own destiny as the
situation demands, without intereference from the gods. In
explaining motivation and first causes, then, neither the Miller nor
his clerk leaves any room to Fortune or Destiny or the other agents
of Boethian control which fill the *Knight's Tale*. Where the
philosophical Knight repeatedly prefaced the unfolding of
elements in his narrative with causal ascriptions to Fortune, the
Miller makes it quite clear that Nicholas alone is responsible for
most of what goes on in his tale. Action is a function of character,
and adept manipulation of people, and the human will. The rest
simply happens because it happens to happen: "And so bifel it on
a Saterday. . . ."
  But in the final analysis, the Miller's morality of opportunism
and the Knight's morality of enlightened philosophical speculation
lead to very similar conclusions: chaos, somber in the first tale,
humorous in the second. It doesn't matter that the Knight assumes
divine control of mortal affairs; events of the *Knight's Tale*
proceed as much by accident and happenstance as events of the
Miller's Tale. One might even argue that Nicholas, the pragmatist,
is much more successful at controlling his world than Theseus the
philosopher: it takes him but a moment's thought to accomodate
the unexpected appearance of John, whereas Theseus required the
"lenghte of certeyn yeres" to adjust to Archite's accidental death.
The end of each tale, however, is chaos, and significantly enough,
chaos begins to intrude into the framework of the pilgrimage itself
with this tale. Harry has chosen Dan Piers, the Monk, to follow the
Knight, but the rude and drunken Miller disrupts his order. As
Charles Owen has noted, "the patterns of decorum and of
obedience to the Host are shattered,"34 just as the patterns of
order and obedience postulated in the *Knight's Tale* proved
specious and untenable, and the order of the Miller's fabliau will
prove little more than a momentary balance of kinetic accidents.
Having arrived at a philosophical conclusion in the *Knight's Tale*,

artist Chaucer assimilates that position into the framework of the *Canterbury Tales* and proceeds to develop the position more fully in his next tale. In this sense the Miller's prologue and tale grow directly out of the *Knight's Tale*. The differences between the two—that one purports to tell us about the principles of order which govern the nature of things, while the other denies the existence of such workings—are superficial, in that neither has anything definite or concrete to say about order. At the conclusion of both tales (and we might add the *Reeve's Tale* here) the company of pilgrims is nowhere near salvation, and, more important, the very possibility of salvation seems remote. One might even argue that the Miller's story, like the Knight's, is in essence tragic: no one is left in a state of prosperity, except insofar as the various humors to which the male characters have proven addicted (vices, W. F. Bolton calls them in his reading of this tale35) have been purged, and purgation of affectation, lechery, pride, and superstition cannot help but leave them saner and—in the last analysis—healthier. We may take the Miller's word for it Absolon "fro that tyme that he hadde kist hir ers,/Of paramours he sette nat a kers;/For he was heeled of his maladie." And we can assume, I think, that Nicholas' blistered seat will dampen his ardor and undercut his pride, and that old John has learned a bit about jealousy and superstition from his broken arm and the villagers' jeers. Alison remains, of course, Alison: the woman there to be used. She is not cured, since she was not sick. But if we interpret the males' return to sanity as a measure of prosperity, then the tale may be comic; otherwise we have three characters who begin in a sort of prosperity and end in the misfortune of dirtied lips, a scalded ass, and a broken arm.

The most important distinction between Knight's and Miller's tales, then, is not in their attitudes toward order and disorder, but in the implications of the reportorial realism to which Chaucer consigned himself at the close of the *General Prologue*. It's all well and good to retell as accurately as possible a tale like that of Palamon and Arcite; who's to object? In such a context Chaucer's objective realism seems innocent enough. But in the prologue to the *Miller's Tale*, as William Brown has pointed out, Chaucer uses the argument he made earlier in an attempt "to evade moral and social responsibility for his actions by claiming beforehand the amoral role of the reporter."36

> What sholde I moore seyn, but this Millere
> He nolde his wordes for no man forbere,
> But tolde his cherles tale in his manere.

M'athynketh that I shal reherce it heere.
And therefore every gentil wight I preye,
For Goddes love, demeth nat that I seye
Of yvel entente, but for I moot reherce
Hir tales alle, be they bettre or werse,
Or elles falsen som of my mateere.

(3167-75)

Of course Chaucer was evading similar responsibility in the
Knight's Tale, but since the Knight's content more closely accords
with what we would call a morally and socially responsible
position, there was little moral and social responsibility to evade.
The validity of a realistic aesthetic, Chaucer seems to imply, the
acceptability of this "mirror held up to nature" excuse depends on
what you're holding a mirror in front of. Hold it up to the Knight's
world, and that's one thing; hold it before the Miller's, with its
denial both of the possibility and of the necessity for knowing, and
with its debasement of character and action, and you've got
something else entirely. Chaucer's position vis-a-vis the aesthetics
of realism becomes more desperate with the *Miller's Tale*. With
the Reeve's and Cook's tales, it becomes altogether untenable.

THE REEVE'S TALE

I have dwelt so long upon the philosophical and aesthetic
dangers of the *Miller's Tale* that one unfamiliar with the story
might think it more than a bit depressing. It is not; it is, in fact, one
of the funniest things in our English tongue. And in its light tone
and purgation of assorted male humors, in its keen and obvious
delight in simple physical exercise (sexual and otherwise), the tale
manages what we moderns would call redemptive social value. If
you skipped lightly through the Miller's (and Chaucer's)
performance without taking offense and without thinking too
much, you might find very little to complain about. It is up to the
Reeve's Prologue and *Tale* to make clear the deficiencies implicit
in the Miller's view of things; it is in the Reeve's performance that
we discover that whatever redemptive social value the *Miller's
Tale* appeared to have is more a product of the particularities of his
plot and style than a function of his philosophical and aesthetic
position, that his values are specious, that his position is
untenable.

The measure of Robin, the Miller, was to be taken, were we alert
to it, in his character as revealed in the *General Prologue* and the

prologue to his own tale. He is a drunken agent of disorder, loud and brash but not what we'd call a "mean drunk," confusing the virtue of a saint's life with the scurrility of his own fabliau ("I wol telle a legende and a lyf, he has promised), infusing the pilgrimage with social disharmony as his bagpipes infused it with musical cacophony at the company's depature from the Tabard. He is the fury, creating chaos in Harry's ordered world. But it's a good-natured disorder, at least on the surface of things, and when the tale is finished, there is little complaining. True that time is being wasted in all these fun and games, and in Robin's requital of the Knight a game has begun which can generate nothing "thrifty." But, given the character of the Miller, the youth and enthusiasm of his pair of lovers, we cannot object overly much. One suspects, to judge from the craft lavished on this tale, that Chaucer enjoyed it very much.

The Reeve and his tale are another story. His age makes time appear a far more valuable commodity than it heretofore seemed, and the bawdy sex-farce of the fabliau more objectionable. His characters lack the vitality and hence the attractiveness of Alison and Nicholas.37 And in his mouth the entire notion of requiting, whatever it meant consiously or unconsciously to the Miller, degenerates to simple vindictiveness.38 Again Chaucer gives us the man's measure in his sketch of the *General Prologue* and the prologue which prefaces his tale. He is a con man, bilking his young lord of more than a few pence annually by the simple expedient of lending him his own goods and winning both thanks and more tangible expressions of gratitude. He is choleric: quick to anger and slow to cool. He is feared by bailiff and herdsman alike, for he is clever and powerful. And he is old.

It is precisely his age, I suspect, which makes his tale so unpleasant, because it is his age which makes his subject inappropriate. A young cocksman is a rake, a hellion, a rogue. An old cocksman is a dirty old man. Moreover, the Reeve's insistence on his age brings to our minds the end of man's pilgrimage through life, the end of this pilgrimage, the spirituality which ought to mark both. And suddenly the ribaldry of the *Miller's Tale* seems a waste of precious time, a fruitless game, an embarassment.

> Gras tyme is doon, my fodder is now forage;
> This white top writeth myne olde yeris;
> Myn herte is also mowled as mynre heris,
> But if I fare as dooth an open-ers,—
> That ilke fruyt is ever lenger the wers,
> Til it be roten in mullok or in stree.

We olde men, I drede, so fare we:
Til we be roten, kan we nat by rype;

(3867-75)

Even the images in which the Reeve couches his complaint are
unpleasant. While the Reeve's meditation may cause Host Harry
to become impatient for the next tale ("Sey forth thy tale, and tarie
nat the tyme," Harry commands, "It were al tyme thy tale to
bigynne"), while it may cause the Reeve himself to reflect
momentarily on past sins and future follies, it causes us to consider
more eschatological matters and provokes an impatience with both
the Reeve's folly and Harry's games—and, I might add, with the
aesthetic and philosophy of the Miller to be continued less
attractively by the Reeve. For the *Reeve's Tale* is but a
continuation of the Miller's brand of art. "Oure wyl desireth folie
ever in oon," Oswald tells us, and "wyl ne shal nat faillen, that is
sooth" (3880, 87). Inappropriate, foolish as even he realizes it to
be, he will answer the Miller "right in his cherles termes" (3917).

So Oswald tells another fabliau, this one about a corrupt Miller,
and his wife and daughter, and John and Aleyn, two clerks who
have them both (respectively) "bolt upright." Absent in the tale
are the Miller's rhetoric, the high spirits of his tale, the clever
machinations and ingenious preliminaries of Nicholas' intrigue,
the rollicking good humor of the *Miller's Tale*. In the Reeve's
fabliau, we skip preliminaries and the action of both halves of the
plot proceeds unadorned by rhetorical elaboration. Characters are
not developed, and they are particularized only insofar as demands
of plot necessitate. The Reeve recounts Symkin's wife's ancestry,
because this is knowledge necessary to our understanding of both
his and her pride. And we are informed that the couple has two
children: a daughter of twenty (thick and well grown), and a baby.
Both will be important in Symkin's discomfiture. But apart from
the fact that Symkin and wife are proud, and daughter is plain, and
baby simply is, we do not learn much about them. Certainly there
is nothing to endear them to us, nothing comparable to Alison's
animal vitality or John's touching solicitude. Then, these
characters in place, we are hurriedly introduced to John and
Aleyn, two yokels from Cambridge, characterized primarily by the
simple device of dialect. Not a hundred lines into the tale the first
half of the Reeve's fabliau is underway. Events proceed quickly to
their logical end, without any of Oswald's characters eliciting the
slightest drop of our sympathy.39

Not only are the gulls painted unattractively, the heroes of this
adventure are far from inventive (their plan to catch the thieving

Symkin fools no one for a moment, while Aleyn's seduction of Molly amounts to sneaking up on her before she sees him coming, and John has the wife by the simple expedient of moving a cradle). Handy Nicholas would run circles around the entire company. And the atmosphere of this tale is generally smuttier than the atmosphere of the *Miller's Tale*. It is true the previous tale saw Nicholas farting and pissing out of Alison's bedroom window, but this tale goes the Miller one or two better:

> This millere hath so wisely bibbed ale
> That as an hors he fnorteth in his sleep,
> Ne of his tayl bihynde he took no keep.
> His wyf bar hym a burdon, a ful strong;
> Men myghte hir rowtyng heere two furlong;
> The wenche rowteth eek, *par compaignye*.
>
> (4162-67)

Enough to keep poor John and Aleyn up all night! And where the villagers contented themselves with verbal abuse of old John in the *Miller's Tale*, the close of the *Reeve's Tale* finds Aleyn and John beating Symkin "ful weel" before they let him be. This is, then, a dirtier, more brutal, generally less artistic effort, and we come away less amused.

Also less amusing are the Reeve's treatment of holy church and courtly behaviour, both satirized in the *Miller's Tale*, both debased further here. Nicholas' "Love me quick or I shall die" was an amusing parody of the language of courtly love, and a rather appropriate adaptation of the Knight's mode of thought and behaviour to the Miller's world of direct action. But Aleyn's insincere aube, sung by a country simpleton to a thick, well grown wench, is pointless and therefore artless.40 The satire of clergy inherent in the Miller's presentation of Absolon was light and amusing; the satire of clergy in the father of Symkin's wife is sharp and bitter:

> This person of the toun, for she [Molly] was feir,
> In purpos was to maken hire his heir,
> Bothe of his catel and his mesuage,
> And straunge he made it of hir mariage.
> His purpos was for to bistowe hire hye
> Into som worthy blood of auncetrye;
> For hooly chirches good moot been despended
> On hooly chirches blood, that is descended.
> Therefore he wolde his hooly blood honoure,
> Though that he hooly chirche sholde devoure.
>
> (3977-86)

One gets the distinction impression that this parson would like to give Molly much more than her dowery. He is a bad fellow, so much so that M. Copland has called him "the evil genius of the tale," the wellspring of pollution as it were.41 Surely he is more venal than Absolon ever thought of being.

On the one hand, then, Chaucer speaks through the Reeve to *show* the Miller's realism more unpleasant than we might have thought it. And, we might add, this unpleasantness is enhanced by the fact that of the two, the Reeve's world is probably more real than the contrived microcosm of the *Miller's Tale*. If reportorial realism amounts to an art which mirrors *this* kind of reality, we are simply not interested; here is neither "sentence" nor "solaas." On the other hand, however, Chaucer comments directly on the nominalist position taken in the *Miller's Tale*—this in Symkin's anti-intellectual remarks to the clerks lodged in his house for the night:

> Myn hous is streit, buy ye han lerned art;
> Ye konne by arguments make a place
> A myle brood of twenty foot of space.
> Lat se now if this place may suffise,
> Or make it rowm with speche, as it youre gise.
>   (4122-26)

Reality is what you make it, what you call it. Symkin is joking here, but the joke has significance beyond its immediate context. In his tale the Miller created a world of nominal reality, his answer to the philosophical speculations of the Knight, a world which has been perpetuated in the *Reeve's Tale* as Oswald answers Robin "right in his cherles termes." It is, let us admit, the world of fabliau, and as much a result of these tales' generic and stylistic ancestry as anything else. But in jokes like this and Nicholas' casual use of destinal powers, in which the old carpenter superstitiously believes but which Nicholas knows have no real existence—in places like these Chaucer insists explicitly on the metaphysics implicit in what we might call the strict utilitarianism of the fabliau as a genre. The fact that such a nominalist metaphysics is here a joke in an unpleasant tale suggests to me at least that Chaucer is rejecting it as he previously rejected the ineffectual Boethian philosophizing of the Knight. In fact, the nominalist position seriously considered and explicitly asserted will not reappear in the *Canterbury Tales*.

THE COOK'S TALE

The Reeve's denial of absolutes, his debasement of holy church in the person of his parson, his generally scurrilous tale, and Chaucer's reportorial realism which allows him to repeat unedited elements from the worst aspects of the fallen world—all these render particularly ironic or significant, depending on point of view, Oswald's closing comments: "And God, that sitteth heighe in magestee,/Save al this compaignye." Where, we might ask, has this God been throughout the tale? Why, given Oswald's age, is he so intent on willful folly, so ignorant of this God in high majesty? But we do not ask these questions because we recognize instinctively that this formula is an appendage tacked on unthinkingly to the fabliau; the Reeve doesn't really mean it, although Chaucer may have intended it as an ironic reminder of the spiritual nature of his pilgrimage and the Reeve's need of spiritual regeneration. Clearly Chaucer must work his way out of both metaphysics and aesthetics if the pilgrimage is to proceed to a fruitful conclusion.

First, however, he takes the opportunity to show clearly where this sort of art is leading, and to develop further the character of Harry Bailey:

> The Cook of Londoun, whil the Reve spak,
> For joye him thoughte he clawed him on the bak.
> "Ha! ha!" quod he, "for Christes passion,
> This millere hadde a sharp conclusion
> Upon his argument of herbergage!...
> But God forbede that we stynte heere;
> And therfore, if ye vouche-sauf to heere
> A tale of me, that am a povre man,
> I wol yow telle, as wel as evere I kan,
> A litel jape that fil in oure citee."
>
> (4325-29, 39-43)

How quickly the pilgrimage has disintegrated from the thoughtful philosophizing of the Knight to the bawdy requital of the Miller to the dirty vindictiveness of the Reeve, and now to "a little joke" from Roger the Cook. Roger's oaths, his obvious enthusiasm for a base art used to base ends, and what little Chaucer gives us of his tale all make perfectly obvious the fact that time will continue to be wasted so long as the pilgrimage is in the hands of characters like Robin and Oswald and Roger.

What is most interesting, however, is the Host's assent to all this nonsense. "I graunte it thee," answers Harry to the Cook's request for permission to tell his little joke; "looke that it be good," he warns. When last we saw Harry in the *Reeve's Prologue* he was speaking "as lordly as a kyng" (3900), telling the Reeve to quit preaching and get on with his tale. An odd set of values, this, which objects to Oswald's meditation on the sins of old age as a waste of time but approves what is obviously to be a pointless and probably artless joke from the Cook. We gain insight here into Harry's literary sensibilities and the quality of his rule, and on neither case does he appear a desirable ruler. He aligns himself closely with debased realism, with game (in which, he argues somewhat speciously, we may often times say truth), and with whatever agents of disruption and misrule happen to intrude into his plans. From the Miller's drunken interruption to the Reeve's requiting to the Cook's joke: if that's the way things work out, then Harry is more than willing to make virtue of necessity and accomodate himself. His governance, then, is non-governance, his artistic taste minimal. He emerges as embodiment of the *Tales'* secularism in its most unattractive aspects.

The *Cook's Tale* marks for Chaucer an end to what I've called the realistic aesthetic and the nominalist metaphysics. What might have appeared a viable alternative to the Knight's ineffectual theorizing, indeed, what began a direct outgrowth of the Knight's position, has proven itself equally ineffectual. Moreso, in fact. For the *Knight's Tale* was the most heroic of the pilgrimage's a-Christian metaphysical constructs and not entirely unattractive in its honest attempts at wrestling order out of chaos. It had a purity of motive and a high seriousness of intent which has been lost to the Reeve's and Miller's and Cook's nihilistic denial of values and hierarchies, and to the Host's affinity for game instead of earnest.42 We are at something of a dead end, and Chaucer faces a dilemma similar to that which confronted Perkyn's employer. And Chaucer's decision is that of the employer: "Wel bet is roten appul out of hoord/Than that it rotie al the remnaunt" (4406, 7). Chaucer drops the tale *in medias res*, lets it go "with sorwe and meschaunce!" The *Man of Law's Tale* will take a dramatically different approach to the problems which have confronted pilgrims and artist in fragment one.

THE MAN OF LAW'S TALE

The introduction to the *Man of Law's Tale* contains the most explicit and the most emphatic insistence on time we have thus far encountered in the *Canterbury Tales*, foreshadowing in many respects the prologue to the *Parson's Tale* just as the affirmation of God's Providence which is the Man of Law's thematic center foreshadows the affirmation of God's good order found in the Parson's sermon. A subtheme in the *General Prologue* and *Reeve's Prologue*, time dramatically becomes the focus of attention in the opening lines to this introduction. Harry, "though he were nat depe ystert in loore," is bright enough to determine through rather simple mathematical calculations involving some possibly significant numbers43 that it is ten o'clock, April 18. Both time and date are significant. April 18 will put us in Lent—late Lent, perhaps even Holy Week—the season of pilgrimage and spirituality, a time when mortals on this pilgrimage through life turn their thoughts momentarily to Christ who died for their sins. Implicit in the season and Chaucer's reference to April 18 are all the motifs of death and rebirth, the need for and seeking of grace, the general religiosity of those opening lines of the *General Prologue*. Of course these concerns have been in the back of our minds since this poem began, and they've obviously been on the pilgrims' minds as they head down to Canterbury—although we and they may have forgotten them in the ribaldry of that last trio of fabliaux. Now Chaucer chooses to remind us again of both the season and the point of this pilgrimage. He does so immediately prior to a tale of Christian devotion and at 10:00 a.m., the hour of mass, time for religious meditation.

Probably Harry does not need his shadow to tell him the hour; no doubt chapel bells along the route would have brought to his mind both time and date had he never glanced down out of the bright sun. It is not surprising that he turns momentarily serious, looks briefly to things eschatological, and with an uncharacteristic insight which is directly in contrast to his remarks on time in the Reeve's Prologue warns the pilgrims about the dangers of time wasted:

> Now, for the love of God and of Seint John,
> Leseth no tyme, as ferforth as ye may.
> Lordynges, the tyme wasteth nyght and day,
> And steleth from us, what pryvely slepynge,
> And what thurgh necligence in oure wakynge,
> As dooth the streem that turneth nevere agayn,
> Descendynge fro the montaigne into playn.
>
> (16-24)

After noting that Seneca laments the loss of time more than loss of gold, an interesting gloss on the gold motif recurrent throughout the *Canterbury Tales*, Harry concludes his exhortation to the pilgrims with "Let us nat mowlen thus in ydelnesse." The admonition, its direct and indirect source aside, is thoroughly Christian, the sort of thing these pilgrims have heard before and will no doubt hear again from their clergymen: life is a pilgrimage of uncertain duration, and man must remain vigilant and work against the coming of the night. Be not idle. Such a thought, such an admonition, is appropriate to the journey in progress, the season of the church year, the hour of the day.

But Harry is no clergyman, and cast in the mouth of one whose interest has proven to be primarily in unthrifty game, it seems more than a bit ironic. Moreover, the Host follows this brief sermon, fraught with Christian overtones, with a more typical and far less Christian assertion of his own will and temporal lordship:

> Ye been sybmytted, thurgh youre free assent,
> To stonden in this cas at my juggement.
> Acquiteth yow now of youre biheeste;
> Thanne have ye do youre devoir atte leeste.
>
> (35-38)

These lines represent more than a characteristic attempt on Harry's part to speak to a pilgrim in his own language (a pretentious habit the Host exhibits repeatedly throughout the pilgrimage); they are an assertion of his own power and right to govern at the very moment in the day, at the very season of the year he should be most cognizant of higher governing forces. It is in light of this assertion of human will and power that we must qualify all Harry has just said about time misspent: we conclude that Harry speaks more from habit than conviction when he worries about wasting time, and that he really has no sound notion of what constitutes time well or badly spent. It may very well be that the Host draws no connection between the tightness of time and assertion of his own human will.

The Man of Law, however, recognizes the connection and the implications of Harry's demand for submission. He is particularly alert to the implications of "thurgh youre free assent," which he hastens to qualify. He has not wished to bind himself to any temporal lord, he replies, except "for swich lawe as a man yeveth another wight" (43). That much Harry may assert, as is his right; but as numerous characters in the *Man of Law's Tale* discover, human law is circumscribed by a higher law, and the governance of Harry and the Sultan and Alla by a higher governance. As the wills of each character in the tale are subject to divine will, so Harry's own will should and eventually will become subject to divine providence. It is to the Man of Law's credit, student of temporal and divine law that he is, that he recognizes early in the pilgrimage this fact.

Following this interchange Chaucer, in one of those perplexing
violations of fictional point of view so common to the *Canterbury
Tales*, interjects himself as artist into his poem. The Man of Law
knows no thrifty tale except one he once heard from a merchant
gone many years now. Seems Chaucer has already told them all:
"And if he have noght seyd hem, leve brother,/In o book, he hath
seyd hem in another." Tales of love and lovers more than Ovid
knew, the story of Ceyx and Alcyone in his youth, the legends of
Cupid—all these and more Chaucer has already taken. Now this is
an odd remark, and for reasons more than that just mentioned. For
one thing, the Man of Law lists only tales of love—no mention of
what Chaucer in his retraction will call "othere bookes of legendes
of seintes, and omelies, and moralitee, and devocioun," of the
Consolation of Philosophy, even of that great affront to the God of
Love (see *Legend of Good Women*, G 264ff.) the *Troilus and
Criseyde*. For another thing, the Man of Law's list is, so far as we
can tell, inaccurate: he attributes to Chaucer stories which were
either never written or have been lost. And so this remark has
been variously interpreted: The Man of Law is showing off his
interest in matters beyond the law, but being superficial and
pretentious he muffs the job; Chaucer is giving his listeners a
sneak preview of tales to be added to the *Legend of Good Women*;
the Man of Laws knows exactly what he's talking about and we've
simply lost the tales of Dianire, Hermone, Hero, Eleyne, Briseide,
Laodamia, and Penelope; the Man of Law's list comes from Ovid,
not from Chaucer; and so forth.44 It may be that the remarks,
coupled with the reference to Gower (which has also puzzled critics
for some time now), are nothing more than a joke on Chaucer's
part: "Chaucer has written very nice love stories, nothing like
those scurrilous stories in Gower's *Confessio Amantis*," the Man
of Law informs us not half a page after Chaucer has finished three
tales more amoral in content, metaphysics, and aesthetics than
anything the Moral Gower ever contemplated in his life. It is more
likely, however, that Chaucer is using these lines at an important
juncture in this pilgrimage to remind us that the journey involves
not only fictional characters and the poet's various *personae*, but
his own self. Behind the fiction of the literal pilgrimage, behind
the dialectic of contending ideas advanced by Miller and Reeve
and Knight, stands artist Chaucer sorting out, weighing, testing,
affirming or rejecting attitudes, metaphysics, aesthetics of his
own. Here, at a moment when everyone from the Host to the Man
of Law looks ahead to the pilgrimage's end, Chaucer too looks back
and then ahead at his own career as artist. it is significant that
although the Man of Law's list is far from accurate, it does not

include anything which Chaucer in his retractions will find
satisfactory poems. In this the poet pictures himself as worse than
he in fact is; the same effect is to be had from the lines about
Gower. Glancing back over his life's work and the distance he has
already traveled on this Canterbury pilgrimage, dissatisfied with
the road he has thus far traversed, ready for a fresh start, Chaucer
asks the obvious question: "But of my tale how shal I doon this
day?" (90). The answer to this question involves a new perspective
on some of the problems which have troubled pilgrims and artist
over the course of the previous fragment.45

The *Prologue to the Man of Law's Tale* proper poses further
critical puzzles, the major one being what, if anything, links these
remarks on wealth and poverty to the tale itself, the minor puzzle
being what, if anything, links the *Prologue* with the *Introduction.*
If the *Introduction, Prologue,* and *Tale* are all intended as
characterization of the Man of Law, it might be argued that these
lines blaming poverty and praising wealth are but part of the
Man's pretensions and a mere reflection of his social status. But I
see a certain casual attitude on Chaucer's part that suggests to me
at least that his attention here is focused on concerns other than
characterization. For one thing, the two motifs of this *Introduction*
are not fully integrated with each other on any level other than that
I have pointed out; and neither relates very easily to the matter of
poverty and wealth. For another thing, the Man of Law promises a
piece in prose, when he delivers a piece in rime royal. For a third,
Chaucer's translation of Trivet probably antedated the *Canterbury
Tales* by some years, or at the very least dates from a time when
the full Canterbury scheme had not yet emerged in Chaucer's
mind.46 Chaucer's hurried revision, which caused the
prose/poetry lapse (is it possible that the *Tale of Melibee* was
initially intended for the Man of Law?), the peculiarities of the
introduction to the tale, the poet's emphasis on spiritual concerns
appropriate to time and date—all argue a preoccupation with
concerns other than characterization.47 Furthermore, as we soon
shall see, the Man of Law's remarks posit wealth as one of God's
blessings, poverty as a curse, so that his true concern here is not so
much with the world's good as with divine rewards and
punishments. And such a concern, while not a particularly useful
characterizing device, is certainly congenial with the theme of his
tale. It would appear that Chaucer, mindful of the allegory of his
pilgrimage and the common metaphor of a day as a human
lifespan, has noted season and hour, written an introduction and
prologue appropriate to day and hour, and borrowed an extant tale
suitable to hour and season and—more or less—to introduction

and prologue. Characterization is a minor, perhaps non-existent concern.

The *Man of Law's Tale* itself exhibits numerous and obvious parallels with the *Knight's Tale*. These are on the one hand structural (both are multi-partite romances) and on the other hand thematic. References to Fortune, the stars and planets, other agents of Boethian determinism, destiny and providence abound in the Man of Law's tale. Typical are the narrator's remarks on the Sultan's decision to marry Constance and his apostrophe upon her departure for Turkey:

> Paraventure in thilke large book
> Which that men clepe the hevene ywriten was
> With sterres, whan that he his birthe took,
> That he for love sholde han his deeth, allas!
> For in the sterres, clerer than is glas,
> Is writen, God woot, whoso koude it rede,
> The deeth of every man, withouten drede,
>
> (190-96)

> O firste moevyng! cruel firmament,
> With thy dirunal sweigh that crowdest ay
> And hurlest al from est til occident
> That naturelly wolde holde another way,
> Thy crowdyng set the hevene in swich array
> At the bigynning of his fiers viage,
> That crueel Mars hath slayn this mariage.

> Infortunat ascendent torouous,
> Of which the lord is helplees falle, allas,
> Out of his angle into the derkeste hous!
> O Mars, o atazir, as in this cas!
> O feible moone, unhappy been thy paas!
> Thou knyttest thee ther thou art nat receyved;
> Ther thou were weel, fro thennes artow weyved.
>
> (295-308)

But Constance is not without divine aid: Mary mother of God, plays a role faintly reminiscent of that played by Saturn in the *Knight's Tale*, as she "Hath shapen, thurgh hir endelees goodnesse,/To make an ende of al hir [Constance's] hevynesse" (951, 52) and intervenes more or less regularly to "heelp hire right anon" (920). Here, in fact, is precisely the difference between the Knight's and Man of Law's tales, the crucial distinction which makes the *Man of Law's Tale* more than a simple re-establishment of Boethian order after the disestablishment of the Knight's order by Miller and Reeve. In the Man of Law's version of things, agents or destiny are themselves subject to divine control and intervention; in fact, it appears that God and the planets are at times antagonists, the one actively promoting Constance's incessant misfortune, the other just as actively and far more effectively shielding her with His providence.48 "Lord of Fortune," the Man of Law calls Christ in line 448; the will of Christ, invariably triumphant, is mentioned specifically again and again (e.g., lines 511, 567, 636). Moreover, the goodness of God is a constant, and stems from "endless [and therefore reliable] goodness" rather than fickle caprice.49 This crucial difference profoundly alters the tone of Chaucer's narrative: instead of the Knight's dark pessimism and the chaos and confusion which overturn Theseus' order, we discover in the *Man of Law's Tale* a somewhat superstitious optimism predicated on unshakable faith and an assertion of Christian comedy which is in no way undercut. For the faithful, the Man of Law asserts, God's order is fixed and it is easily known and it is beneficient. The only requirement is that man subject his will to the will of Lord Jesus Christ "that of his myght may sende/ Joye after wo, governe us in his grace,/ And kepe us alle that been in this place!" (1160-62).

Will and intent play important roles in this tale, as they will in the overall movement of the *Canterbury Tales* and in Christian theology. As we have seen, the will of Christ is omnipresent, and as virtually everyone who has had occasion to comment on this tale has noted, the bulk of Chaucer's additions to his source amount to specific references to Suzanna, David, Judith, Jonah, and others whose unqualified submission to divine will and subsequent divine support in time of danger render more credible Constance's own submission and support. For her part, Constance represents an absolute denial of human will, complete passivity.50 Throughout the tale, the will of God is contraposed against the will of men: the intent of the Sultan and his mother, the will of the knight who would love Constance, the desire of the sailor who would rape her, the intent of evil Donegild. Just as consistently their assertiveness is juxtaposed against Constance's submissive passivity. And just as consistently, of course, divine providence rescues the passive Constance by frustrating human intent and whatever malevolent machinations the planets may have concocted. For the Christian, the fruit of faith (and "fruit" begins to creep into Chaucer's vocabulary with increasing regularity beginning with this tale) is not "sodeyne wo, . . . successour/To worldly blisse, spreynd with bitternesse" (421, 22; a distant echo here of the *Knight's Tale*) but the joy and gladness promised by the Man of Law in those closing lines of his tale. In a tale of profound Christian morality, then, the Man of Law answers questions raised by the Knight and the ensuing fabliaux concerning the nature of order in the cosmos and in human experience.

But however sound the position may appear theologically, it has its weaknesses. While perhaps more reassuring than the *Knight's Tale* and the *Miller's Tale* in its insistence on the goodness and dependability of divinely appointed and controlled order, it is unsettling in another respect: mundane manifestations of God's goodness and order are regularly miraculous. "Chaucer encourages us," Paul Ruggiers writes, "to see the impingement of the supernatural on the life of creatures."51 But despite the Man of Law's (or, more properly, Chaucer's) attempts to make Constance natural and lifelike, her example valid, her situation and predicament universal, the fact remains that she is no more human than the Patient Griselda, the likes of whom is not to be found on this earth, the Clerk advises us. Moreover, Constance is not human in that she does not develop: she is perfect when the tale begins, throughout the tale, and when it ends. Her character is fixed by an almost allegorical narrative which tries paradoxically to be literalistic.52 Block has suggested an "irreconcilable dualism" between Chaucer's attempts at piety and his realism, and in this he is correct.53 A tension exists between the Man of Law's demand that we recognize Constance as a normal human being, and our awareness of the fact that God does not work for us he worked for her. Such must have been the reaction of Chaucer's pilgrims, for even in an age of faith, the experience of most people was that whatever pies were to be had must have been delivered in the sky because there were certainly precious few on earth. The reckoning which concerns the Man of Law both in his tale and in his prologue comes not on earth but in heaven, not now but later. The inaccurate conjoining of heavenly reward and earthly prosperity which forms the basis of this tale also forms the basis of a link between the prologue on poverty and the ensuing tale. The Man of Law connects earthly well being, the goods of this world, with a state of spiritual grace, and vice versa: Constance trusts God and she is rewarded with longevity and happiness here on earth, in this life, as a mortal. The wealthy man trusts God and is rewarded with more wealth; by implication the poor man's status reflects his own state of gracelessness:

> Herkne what is the sentence of the wise:
> "Bet is to dyen than have indigence";
> "Thy selve neighebor wol thee despise."
> If thou be povre, farwel thy reverence!
> Yet of the wise man take this sentence:
> "Alle the dayes of the povre men been wikke."
> Be war, therfore, er thou come to that prikke!
>   (113-19)

Here is the Puritan ethic some several centuries before our Puritan fathers! In time the clerk will concern himself with rectifying this particular misconception, and with defining properly the nature of spiritual and temporal conditions in his own Christian allegory. For the moment, however, the position of the Man of Law, affirmative in all its implications but well outside the realm of human experience, remains unanswered, its inadequacies glaring but unresolved.

The tale's thematic defects are related to its artistic defects in that the aesthetics of the tale are such as to insist on a literalism which is probably incapable of reconciliation with the tale's didactic purpose, and unachievable within the confines of the saints' life or the romance as genres. This aesthetic defect will also be remedied by the Clerk, who will drop all pretense to realism and insist on allegory (only to undermine his own denial of literalism in a post script), and ultimately by the Parson, who will refuse any literal narrative, denying the reality of this world, and discarding the chaff of narrative for the wheat of doctrine. Curiously the Man of Law makes a remark about wheat and chaff which directly foreshadows the Parson's position, and we ought not to miss it: "Me list nat of the chaf, ne of the stree./Maken so long a tale as of the corn" (701, 2). Such a parallel can serve only to direct attention to contrasts between his and the Parson's aesthetic practice, and reveal the inadequacy of the former.

The measure of the Man of Law's defective art is to be found in Harry Bailey's reaction to his tale, recorded in that problematical epilogue not found in so many manuscripts of the *Tales*. Like the *Introduction*, the *Epilogue* poses problems, not the least of which is the apparent introduction of the *Shipman's Tale*...when in no manuscript save one does the *Shipman's Tale* follow the Man of Law's!54 Once again one gets the distinct impression that Chaucer's mind was on things other than the fiction of his pilgrimage. For while the *Epilogue* makes little sense as an introduction to the next tale, it makes plenty of sense in terms of the time of day and season of the year we mentioned earlier, and the sudden infusion of spirituality which has marked the pilgrimage at 10:00 this Lenten morning. Harry's reaction to that tale, his exchange with the Parson, and the Shipman's refusal to be taught are all in perfect keeping with the reading we have been giving the *Tales*.

Harry is impressed by the Man of Law's effort. His superstitious piety is aroused, as we might expect it to be. But hailing it as "a thrifty tale for the nones," and demanding another of the Parson, he both swears and reasserts his own authority:

"Sir Parisshe Prest," quod he, "for Goddes
    bones,
Telle us a tale, as was thi forward yore.
I se wel that ye lerned men in lore
Can moche good, by Goddes dignitee!"
(1166-69)

In two quick lines Harry reveals the superficiality of his piety and the fact he's missed entirely the Man of Law's point about temporal and divine governance. The Priest reproves his oath and denies his authority, pointing out his disease ("what eyleth the man, so synfully to swere?"), a spiritual disease which requires a spiritual pilgrimage begun in the *General Prologue* before Harry arrived upon the scene. The Parson will not play by the Host's rules; in fact, he will not even play the Host's game. Harry's reaction is predictable: a scornful attack on the pilgrim's character and methods. "This Lollere heer wil prechen us somwhat!" he snorts. He is joined by the Shipman, who also objects: "heer schal he nat preche;/He schal no gospel glosen here ne teche" (1179, 80). To do so would spoil the game, "springen cokkel in our clene corn" (1183). Both the Shipman and Harry have a mistaken view of weeds and corn, of game and earnest appropriate to their perverse characters, but here both are in a sense correct. Here, at this hour and in this place the Priest will not preach, primarily because—to borrow a phrase—his hour is not yet come. At 10:00, the hour of the mass, we have approached the realization to which the Priest will ultimately bring us. We have heard the most religious of the tales of the early Canterbury pilgrimage. But the route of this pilgrimage is the route of life, of the whole day, and all three—life, day, pilgrimage—are now just beginning. Few if any mortals remember their Maker in the days of their youth, mass or no mass, Priest or no Priest, and Chaucer and his pilgrims are no exceptions. Neither pilgrims nor artist will turn again to the Priest and the grace and comfort he might afford until journey's end. There he will appropriately preach, and be willingly heeded by pilgrims, Host, and artist alike. For the moment, however, other positions remain to be explored. Time for more merry tales, if not from the Shipman, then from other pilgrims. The truly comic tale, the true good news of the gospel, will have to wait.

FOOTNOTES TO CHAPTER II

1 The seminal work in this regard is Arthur Hoffman, "Chaucer's Prologue to Pilgrimage: The Two Voices," *English Literary History*, 21 (1954), 1-16.

2 E. Talbot Donaldson, "Chaucer the Pilgrim," *PMLA*, 69 (1954), 928-36. For a recent summary of critical positions on the issue, and an attempt to reconcile two opposing camps, see Thomas Garbaty, "The Degradation of Chaucer's 'Geffrey'," *PMLA*, 89 (1974), 97-104.

3 See especially Edgar Duncan, "Narrator's Points of View in the Portrait-Sketches, Prologue to the *Canterbury Tales*," *Essays in Honor of Walter Clyde Curry* (Nashville, 1955), pp. 77-101.

4 Ruth Nevo, "Chaucer: Motive and Mask in the 'General Prologue'," *Modern Language Review*, 58 (1963), 1-9; Bernard Huppé, *A Reading of the* Canterbury Tales (Albany: State University of New York Press, 1964), pp. 21-28; Kemp Malone, *Chapters on Chaucer* (Baltimore: Johns Hopkins Press, 1951), p. 38; Bertrand Bronson, *In Search of Chaucer* (Toronto: University of Toronto Press, 1960), pp. 25-31; R. M. Lumiansky, *Of Sondry Folk* (Austin: University of Texas Press, 1955), pp. 83-95; John M. Major, "The Personality of Chaucer the Pilgrim," *pmla*, 75 (1960), 160-62.

5 "Narrator's Points of View," p. 92.

6 "The Degradation of Chaucer's 'Geffrey'," pp. 98-99.

7 Baldwin observes (p. 24) that spring, the season of this particular pilgrimage, was used in the middle ages to represent psychological as well as religious reawakenings, and may be so used by Chaucer. Certainly Chaucer the narrator, as presented in the *General prologue*, is in need of psychological and perhaps even physiological regeneration. Here Baldwin and I agree. But I cannot agree with his explanation of the narrator's obvious admiration of coruption: "there could be no misanthropy because there could be no 'deophoby'—in contemning His [God's] creatures, you contemn Him in His creation. In no other secular writer is, to my knowledge, the discrimination between sin and the sinner so well observed as in Chaucer" (p. 39).

8 "The Construction of Chaucer's General Prologue," *Neophilologus*, 38 (1954), 130. Swart includes poet Chaucer in his group of "hardened sinners" described in the Prologue, more because of "his doubt of the value of 'authority,' even that of the church" (p. 129), than his artistic creation or mistaken judgments.

9 "Chaucer The Pilgrim," p. 935.

10 The major works in this regard are the *Polycraticus* of John of Salisbury (1159), *De Legibus et Consuetudinibus Regni Angliae* of Henry de Bracton (1250-58), Aquinas' *Summa Theologica* (1169-72), and William Ockham's *Dialogus* (1334-48). Even Salisbury, the conservative, insists on the election of monarchs. See *The Statesman's Books of John of Salisbury*, trans. John Dickinson (1955; rpt. New York: Russell & Russell, 1963), p. 350.

11 The variety of opinion on this tale is, in fact, bewildering. Helen Storm Corsa, in *Chaucer: Poet of Mirth and Morality* (South Bend, Indiana: University of Notre Dame Press, 1964) views the Knight's "clear statement about the nature of human existence" as "thoroughly optimistic, completely cherful in essence" (p. 106). Douglas Brooks and Alastair Fowler, focusing on astrological elements of the tale in "The Meaning of Chaucer's *Knight's Tale,*" *Medium Aevum*, 39 (1970), reads the tale as "meant to convey something of the order underlying the unpredictable changes of human destiny," "the Knight's secular vision of seven ages and planetary guardians" (p. 142). In *"The Knight's Tale:* Incident, Idea, Incorporation," *Chaucer Review*, 3 (1968), Merle Fifield suggests the tale embodies Chaucer's definition of "Fortune and man's proper attitude toward Her in a unification of organized incident, character, and idea which defies Her" (p. 106). But William Frost, in "An Interpretation of Chaucer's *Knight's Tale,*" *The Review of English Studies*, 25 (1949), 290-304, has argued that the tale affirms order and harmony, as well as Christian faith and chivalric standards. Bernard Huppé, in *A Reading of the Canterbury Tales* (Albany: State University of New York Press, 1964), sees the tale as a "high comedy" designed to lead the Knight's son "from courtly folly back to an ideal of Christian chivalry" (p. 54), This is close to the reading of this tale given by D. W. Robertson, Jr. in *A Preface to Chaucer* (Princeton: Princeton University Press, 1962), in which the romance is considered an exemplification of the disasterous effects of cupidinous love (p. 466). Charles Muscatine, however, reads the tale as a statement on "the experience of the noble life, which is itself the subject of the poem and the object of its philosophical questioning"; *Chaucer and the French Tradition* (Berkeley: University of California Press, 1966), 186. Paul Thurston, in *Artistic Ambivalence in Chaucer's Knight's Tale* (Gainesville: University of Florida Press, 1968), reads the tale as "A work of art satirizing the hallowed institutions of the

chivalric tradition and their literary and supposed societal foundations'' (p. ix). The tale, incidentally, has also been read as allegory and simple romance narrative.

12 ''Chaucer's Philosophical Knight,'' *Tennessee Studies in Literature*, 3 (1952), 47-68. See also Frost, Fowler, Corsa, Fifield, Muscatine, and Thurston, above.

13 John Manly suggests members of the Scrope family as ''approximate models'' for Chaucer's Knight. See ''A Knight Ther Was,'' *Transactions of the American Philological Association*, 38 (1907), 89-107.

14 ''Chaucer's Crusading Knight, A Slanted Ideal,'' *Chaucer Review* 3 (1968), 86.

15 *A Commentary on the General Prologue to the Canterbury Tales* (New York: MacMillan, 1948), p. 67.

16 ''The Construction of Chaucer's *General Prologue*,'' *Neophilologus*, 38 (1954), 130.

17 Chaucer, *Works*, p. 652.

18 p. 141.

19 ''The Metamorphoses of The Knight's Tale,'' *English Literary History*, 38 (1971), 505.

20 ''The Worthiness of Chaucer's Knight,'' *Modern Language Quarterly*, 25 (1964), 66-75.

21 The speculation of Manly, recorded in Robinson (p. 652), that the Knight's pilgrimage follows immediately his return from Lithuania, which turned Christian in 1386, is interesting in its attempt to avoid confronting the unpleasant probability that he had served a heathen lord in that campaign. The same may be said of arguments that the lord of Palatye was bound to the Christian King Peter, so that in serving him the Knight was really serving a Christian, not a heathen prince.

22 Interestingly, pilgrims like the Clerk and Man of Law qualify their submission to the Host: ''For swich lawe as a man yeveth another wight,/He sholde hymselven usen it, by right,'' says the Man of Law in II 43, 44. ''I am under youre yerde;/Ye han of us as *now* the governance,'' says the Clerk (IV 22, 23, italics mine).

23 Robertson's position that the tale affirms the actions of Theseus which are 'directed toward the establishment and maintenance of those traditional hierarchies which were dear to the medieval mind'' (*A Preface to Chaucer*, p. 265) has been effectively refuted by both Joseph Westlund in ''The *Knight's* Tale as an Impetus for Pilgrimage,'' *Philological Quarterly*, 43 (1964) and Merle Fifield (''The *Knight's Tale:* Incident, Idea, Incorporation'').

24 *The Art of the Canterbury Tales,* p. 152; *A Reading of the Canterbury Tales,* p. 50; and *Artistic Ambivalence in the Canterbury Tales* respectively. All are at odds with Charles Muscatine (*Chaucer and the French Tradition*) who sees, stylistically at least, only order in the *Knight's Tale.*

25 That the *Knight's Tale,* in one form or another, had already been written when the schema of the *Canterbury Tales* was just beginning to take shape in Chaucer's mind is one of the few universally held assumptions about this tale, and ought not to be forgotten. It is Chaucer's tale before it is the Knight's.

26 William Frost, "An Interpretation of Chaucer's *Knight's Tale,*" 290.

27 Paul Ruggiers, *The Art of the Canterbury Tales,* p. 165.

28 John Findlayson, however, sees the sermon as partially satiric, finding Chaucer's character "rather pedantic, and hence not infrequently tedious," and the tale far from morally and ethically normative. But the ambivalent, partially satiric mode of the *General Prologue,* which he cites as support for this position in that it sets a tone for all the *Canterbury Tales,* is so far from the *Parson's Tale* as to make the relationship tenuous indeed. See "The Satiric Mode and the Parson's Tale," *Chaucer Review,* 6 (1971), 94-116.

29 Baldwin, I believe, has shown conclusively that the Parson was to have told the final tale of the pilgrimage as the company enters Canterbury-become-the New Jerusalem. See *Unity of the Canterbury Tales,* chapter five.

30 For an excellent study of relationships among the Knight's, Miller's, Reeve's, and Cook's tales, see Charles Owen, "Chaucer's *Canterbury Tales:* Aesthetic Design in Stories of the First Day," *English Studies,* 25 (1954), 49-59.

31 *The Art of the Canterbury Tales,* 55.

32 See *The Art of the Canterbury Tales,* 55-57; Bernard Huppé, *A Reading of The Canterbury Tales,* chapter 3; Charles A. Owen, Jr., "Chaucer's *Canterbury Tales:* Aesthetic Design in Stories of the First Day"; and William C. Stokoe, Jr., "Structure and Intention in the First Fragment of the *Canterbury Tales,*" *University of Toronto Quarterly,* 21 (1952), 120-27.

33 *Chaucer and the French Tradition,* p. 60.

34 "Aesthetic Design," p. 51.

35 "The Miller's Tale': An Interpretation," *Medieval Studies,* 25 (1962), 83-94.

36 "Chaucer's Double Apology for the *Miller's Tale,*" *University of Colorado Studies: Series in Langugage and Literature,* 10

(1966), 15-22. It is difficult to agree with Paul Ruggiers (*The Art of the Canterbury Tales*, p. 54) that Chaucer's defense here is "a defense by the poet of all comedy," unless we assume that comedy is somehow more real than tragedy. But comedy is *not* inherently more realistic than tragedy, it is merely baser. What Chaucer defends is not content but manner of presentation, not comedy but realism.

37 This observation has become almost a commonplace of Chaucer criticism. See especially M. Copland, "*The Reeve's Tale*" Harlotrie or Sermonyng?" *Medium Aevum*, 31 (1962), 17: "To put it crudely in order not to linger, whereas we feel Simkin and his wife as decidedly unlovely characters, all the characters in *The Miller's Tale* are by comparison 'rather nice' and therefore the less punishable."

38 Also nearly a commonplace, but see especially Sheila Delany, "Clerks and Quiting in the *Reeve's Tale*," *Medieval Studies*, 29 (1967), 351-56.

39 It is difficult to feel sorry for Symkind's daughter, Molly. She's a plain enough lass to begin with, obviously acquiesces to Aleyn knowing full well he'll be off with the morning light, and probably enjoys herself immensely. This night may, in fact, be the high point of her love life.

40 See Robert E. Kaske, "An Aube in the *Reeve's Tale*," *English Literary History*, 26 (1959), 295-310.

41 "Harlotrie or Sermonyng?" p. 22.

42 William Brown reaches a similar conclusion. "What Chaucer never fails to appreciate is that moral and artistic judgment can neither be abandoned nor suspended with impunity. The progression of stories in the first fragment of the *Canterbury Tales* is so arranged as to illustrate exactly the point" ("Chaucer's Double Apology," 17).

43 The sun is 45 degrees above the horizon. Since 4 and 5 total 9, and 9 is emblematic of imperfection (cf. the *Parson's Prologue*), Chaucer may be alluding here numerologically to the spiritual condition of his company of pilgrims.

44 See especially Carleton Brown, "The Man of Law's Headlink and the Prologue of the *Canterbury Tales*," *Studies in Philology*, 34 (1937), 8-35; Bernard I. Duffey, "The Intention and Art of *The Man of Law's Tale*," *English Literary History*, 14 (1947), 181-93; Robert E. Lewis, "Chaucer's Artistic Use of Pope Innocent III's *De Miseria Humane Conditionis*," *PMLA*, 81 (1966), 485-92; and William Sullivan, "Chaucer's Man of Law as a Literary Critic," *Modern Language Notes*, 68 (1953), 1-8.

45 Alfred David has noted this same thing: "The Man of Law's problem—what story to tell next—is also Chaucer's. Ultimately all the prilgrims are personae of their creator, and the tales they choose are ones he has chosen for them...By introducing a discussion of his former works into the frame story of a new work still in its formative stage, Chaucer prompts us to compare his previous achievements with the task on which he is currently engaged. He takes stock of what has gone before and perhaps looks ahead to what is still to come." "The Man of Law vs. Chaucer: A Case in Poetics," *PMLA*, 82 (1967), 217. David's interpretation of this tale and mine are very similar, and, I believe, more sophisticated than other readings of the *Introduction* and *Tale*. It is, nevertheless, still possible to read both as nothing more than Chaucer's characterization of the Man of Law—Thomas Pynchbeck, if Manly is correct—as a pretentious, vain individual. Cf. Sullivan, above.

46 For a full and characteristically brilliant discussion of date, see J.S.P. Tatlock, *The Development and Chronology of Chaucer's Works,* London: 1907 (reprinted Gloucester, Mass.: Peter Smith, 1964), chapter 5 section 6. Tatlock favors a date around or after 1390, arguing that the tale implies a familiarity with *all* of Gower's *Confessio Amantis*, assuming that Chaucer borrowed from Gower and not vice versa, denying that the tale's style and sophistication betray the Chaucer of an earlier period. Tatlock does note, however, that Skeat, Pollard, Hales, and Ker all favor a date earlier in Chaucer's career.

47 Other critics have noticed this apparently hurried, careless revision. Lewis (above) writes, "the connections between Introduction and Prologue, on the one hand, and between Prologue and Tale, on the other, are somewhat artificial, possibly because the three-part sequence was put together hurriedly (as indicated by Chaucer's failure to cancel 'speke in prose')" (p. 488); John Yunck has gone so far as to suggest the Man of Law was not intended to tell this tale: "The introduction makes it clear that the Man of Law was not originally connected with a verse tale (96), and there is certainly nothing about that suave pilgrim, either in his introduction or in the General Prologue, which would lead us to expect the religious intensification to which Chaucer has submitted Trivet's old story. The original teller would seem to have been a religious, and one who professed to take his vocation seriously. My own guess, in a world in which proof is not forthcoming, is that Chaucer at one time had the Prioress in mind." "Religious Elements in Chaucer's *Man of Law's*

Tale," *English Literary History*, 27, no. 4 (December, 1960), 260.

48 See Yunck, p. 259; and Duffey, 189ff; and Ruggiers (*The Art of the Canterbury Tales*), p. 171.

49 The Help of God, Robert T. Farrell points out, was in fact a traditional and important series of images well known in the medieval church, and is consciously used by Chaucer in the additions he makes to Trivet (the stories of Daniel, Jonah, the Hebrews passing through the Red Sea, and the miracle of the loaves and fishes, lines 463-504). See "Chaucer's Use of the Theme of the Help of God in the *Man of Law's Tale*," *Neuphilologische Mitteilugen*, 71 (1970), 239-43.

50 Cf. Yunck, 250: "We can best begin with an important basic change which Chaucer introduced into the religious nature of the heroine. He carefully excised only one religious element from his source: the aggressive sanctity of Trivet's Constance, that sort of militant self-assured, often unpleasant proselytizing fervor not uncommon in the early saints' lives; an element which he allowed to remain, for example, in the Second Nun's retelling of the life of St. Cecilia."

51 *The Art of the Canterbury Tales*, p. 172.

52 See both Block and Duffey on the attempts of Chaucer to make Constance life-like; but note Duffey, "She is definitely not made perfect through suffering, as he [Root] would have us believe; she was rather carefully made perfect to begin with" (186).

53 "Originality, Controlling Purpose, and Craftsmanship in Chaucer's *Man of Law's Tale*," *PMLA*, 68 (1953), 598.

54 Robinson's edition, p. 696.

CHAPTER III

FRAGMENTS III THROUGH V: THE MATTER OF ORDER

The *General Prologue* and tales of framents I and II seem to deal with all the various concerns of Chaucer's Canterbury pilgrimage, social, philosophical, aesthetic. In this respect and in the completion of narrative links among tales this block of tales is the most complete unit of Chaucer's poem, with the possible exception of the unit comprised of fragments VIII through X (to be examined later). Between fragments II and VIII the *Canterbury Tales* become architectonically and thematically confused: important narrative links are missing, assignment of tales to tellers is at times dubious, and the thematic wholeness we have observed thus far is often absent. The confusion is not as total, however, as previous scholarship has assumed. Fragments III through V appear to constitute a relatively coherent subdialectic focusing not so much on marriage, as Kittredge had it, as on the order for which marriage is a metaphor. The human will and its relation to marriage, social order, and art is another major concern of Chaucer. Matters of aesthetics and social order, while frequently treated, are secondary concerns of the artist. For their part, fragments VI and VII seem to dwell almost exclusively on matters of aesthetics, the problem of order having been largely settled with the *Franklin's Tale*. Within these two blocks of tales—the one focusing on order, the other on art—we observe movement nearly as orderly as that found in the poem thus far, and a resolution (separately) of issues treated concurrently in the tales of I and II.

THE WIFE OF BATH'S PROLOGUE AND TALE

Whatever order of the *Canterbury Tales* Chaucer did or did not have in mind, was or was not working toward, the *Man of Law's Tale-Wife of Bath's Prologue* sequence has, as Bernard Huppé has noted, a logic to it stronger than any logic for a *Man of Law's Tale-Shipman's Tale* sequence.1 The Man of Law has painted an abstracted and utterly submissive woman who must certainly have offended the Wife and evoked some sort of response from this concrete, living, breathing, fighting, loving female. His world was

the world of idea; hers is the world of empirical reality. He built
upon theory; she will assert experience. He offered an orthodox, if
over-simplified, theology; she will quarrel with theologians from
St. Paul to Jerome to her own fifth husband. There is, however, a
distinct break between the tales of the Man of Law and the Wife of
Bath: the discussion of marriage which the Wife begins progresses
on a plane radically different from the discussion which precedes
it. On the surface of things, this marriage debate may appear to be
a digression, a substitution of marriage for God's order as the focal
point of the debate among the pilgrims (and the dialectic within
Chaucer's mind). But the real distinction is artistic: marriage
becomes a metaphor for order (as the Clerk makes abundantly
clear, although the metaphor has appeared earlier in the
Canterbury Tales and was, by Chaucer's day, a commonplace),
and instead of a metaphysical digression we have a metaphoric
indirection. Even the Wife's discussion of marriage, for all her
emphasis on experience and facts and figures, must be viewed
metaphorically.2 And Chaucer's art changes here in another
respect: the confessional nature of the Wife's prologue and tale,
while certainly appropriate to a spiritual pilgrimage and to some
extent a development of the tale-as-reflective-of-teller we have
seen in Knight, Miller, and Reeve, is unprovoked and unexpected.

In fact, with the Wife's prologue and tale the pilgrim's self and
the pilgrim's fiction become virtually indistinguishable. Others
have been able to dissociate their own persons from their tales, no
matter how much tale may have reflected social status or
philosophical temperament; in a way unmatched by any pilgrim
other than the Pardoner, the Wife *is* her prologue and tale . . . so
much to that the tale itself, a Breton lay, seems nothing more than
a further development of certain aspects of its teller's character.3
That character has proven one of the most controversial on the
pilgrimage. Like Falstaff, she is most certainly a vice (or
compendium of vices); like Falstaff, she so overwhelms a reader as
to appear a virtue.4 At the very least she is one of Chaucer's less
objectionable vices. This variety of opinion concerning the Wife,
however, reflects not so much uncertainty about who she is and
what she represents, as a variety of attitudes *toward* what she
represents. Her severest critics view her from a theological and
moralistic perspective; those who find her most attractive view her
invariably from a human point of view. One's reaction to the Wife,
more than to any other pilgrim, tells more about one's self than
about the Wife.

This is very much a result of Chaucer's own artistry: she is
created as a loud, unabashed spokesman for the human position in

all its temporality, enthusiasm, misunderstanding, incapacity, and carnality. If one cannot accept the carnal and the temporal, then the Wife appears grotesque and damned; if one finds a place for the merely human in the scheme of things (as Chaucer most certainly wanted to with at least half of his devout spirit), then the Wife is still a grotesque but scarcely condemned. Chaucer, being human and a poet first and a theologian second, finds her character and position attractive, especially at this juncture, although he is not oblivious to and will not let us ignore the deficiencies in both her character and epistemology.

In answering the Man of Law, the Wife siezes immediately upon the major defect of his tale: its inapplicability to the human condition, its remove from normal experience. Experience, not authority, leads to understanding: this is the keystone of Alison's epistemology, and she informs us immediately of her bias:

> Experience, though noon auctoritee
> Were in this world, is right ynogh for me
> To speke of wo that is in mariage;
>
> (1-3)

The fabliaux have suggested that experience is preferable to abstract philosophizing, especially when you want to get things done, but they have also suggested that experience demonstrates the limits of human understanding and the inefficacy of manipulation. In fact, they reduced all reality to a nominalist nothing. Where the Miller and the Reeve derived from their experiences only a faith in the temporary utility of manipulation and a superstitious reluctance to inquire too deeply into their wives' secrets,5 the Wife insists on universals at every oppotunity. The argument central to her pologue is predicated on a general biblical directive that man be fruitful and multiply, although ironically we have no record of her own vigorous attempts having born fruit other than the strife and discord which mark all her marriages, marriages all founded on false premises and disordered hierarchies. The thrust of the Wife's tale is the dogma that *all* women desire sovereignty "As wel over hir housbond as hir love" (1039). To these universals, Alison claims, she has been lead by experience, although the initial two hundred lines of her prologue indicate her wisdom is well butressed with "auctoritee," misread and misinterpreted in every case. Marginal glosses to the *Canterbury Tales*, for example, become particularly heavy at the Wife's prologue and indicate a heavy reliance on St. Jerome, the Vulgate, and the storehouse of medieval anti-feminist literature.6 Robert Miller has shown that her tale relies not only on Gower's

Tale of Florent and *The Marriage of Sir Gawain and Dame Ragnel*,
but on "a group of stories involving a transformed woman, and
often illustrating the power of the virtue of Obedience, which
appear in the medieval collections of exempla...."7 Here certainly
is authority of sorts, as well as the Wife's experience.

Ironically, however, the Wife misrepresents authority to make it
conform to experience. Miller's exampla, for example, involve the
transformation of bauty into deformity in order to illustrate the
depravity of women and encourage obedience to the monastic ideal
of chastity. A typical story, from Odo of Cheriton, involves "the
devil in the guise of an Ethiopian woman, so foul and stinking that
he [the monk] could not stand to look at her and repelled her from
him. But she spoke to him, saying: 'I am she who appears in hearts
of men as a lovely lady; but because of your obedience and labor
God will not permit me to harm you, but only to make known to you
my stench!'"8 The Wife, of course, turns things around: in her tale
deformity is illusion and physical beauty truth. The biblical
admonition that man be fruitful and multiply is inapplicable to the
Wife, because she is interested in carnal pleasure, not
multiplication. Solomon is cited as a multi-wived paragon of
wisdom; in fact, the foolishness of Solomon in his old age was
proverbial.9 And the Wife's gloss on John 4:9 is ingenious:10

> Let hem [the virgins] be breed of pured
>   whete-seed,
> And lat us wyves hoten barly-breed;
> And yet with barly-breed, Mark telle kan,
> Oure Lord Jhesu refresshed many a man.
>   (143-46)

The ultimate misreprsentation comes in that passage just cited,
with Alison's confusion of the gospels of Mark and John.
But misreprsentation is precisely the point of her prologue and
tale when read as confession. She who appears so pleased with a
life of sexual adventure is in reality a somewhat pathetic and even
tragic figure who has endured a life of sexual misadventure and
use as an object instead of a person.11 While confessing at one
moment to following her desires, she refers at others to making "a
feyned appetite" (417) and laments her lost youth. She who
purports to desire dominance yields it at the first opportunity, even
though she has lost hearing in one ear to gain it:

> After that day we hadden never debaat.
> Gode helpe me so, I was to hym as kynde
> As any wyf from Denmark unto Ynde,
> And also trewe, and so was he to me.

I prey to God, that sit in magestee,
So blesse his soule for his mercy deere.

(822-27)

She who claims to desire easily dominated men reveals herself to love most men who give her the toughest battle:

I trowe I loved hym best, for that he
Was of his love daungerous to me.

(513-14)

The woman who survives three old husbands just to accumulate property gives it all away to a fifth for love (although she regrets it later). The realist is at heart a romantic; the burgher has pretentions to gentility. Alison tells finally not the *Shipman's Tale*, with its commercialism of sex, its marital and extra-marital prostitution, but a romantic Breton lay set in the never-never land of King Arthur. Clearly Alison suffers from a variety of illusions and delusions, about her own self and about the world around her. Experience has led her to misread the nature of things with rather unfortunate results. She had had five (or more precisely, four and a half) unhappy marriages, so that she has become an authority on the "wo that is in mariage." She has been on an assortment of pilgrimages which have served only to return her to her starting point: pleasures of the flesh, a striving for physical dominance, the accumulation of property, property, property, and the search for another husband. Magnificent, heroic, attractive as Alison may appear, these are the fruits of her view of life and her approach to marriage. Practically, then, neither character nor epistemology work for any protracted length of time.

Chaucer is very careful to make us understand this point, for he undercuts Alison's position virtually every step of the way. It is the Wife's intent to preach feminism and experience; it is her practice to rely heavily on (distorted) authority, to demonstrate the inadequacy of experience as a means to knowledge, and to prove by example the validity of the anti-feminists' attacks. In point of fact, Alison exemplifies every point made by Jerome, Theofrastus, John of Salisbury, and their sect against women in the book which has precipitated this entire performance:12 she is a creature of pride, lust, verbosity and vanity, she is unfaithful as a wife, and she manifestly interferes with a clerk's study.13 This much we all see: it is part of the joke Chaucer and his audience both appreciated. "Ye been a noble prechour in this cas," says the Pardoner sarcastically (165). "This is a long preamble of a tale!" jokes the Friar. What we may not see is that the Wife's frustration is a direct result of her assertion of her own will, which has allowed her to follow the inclination of her stars and brought her to her Martian-Venusian complex. God puts things in man's judgment, Alison tells us (68), and she has been willful enough to retain that power instead of following the good advice of her hag and submitting in turn to the Lord. She is in this respect the exact antithesis of Constance of the *Man of Law's Tale*. Alison has more fun, is the more endearing character. But she pays the price for her willfulness: for the woman whose trust is in God, He will intervene to hold destiny and the stars in abeyance; to one who asserts her own will in such matters, however, no such reprive is available. To cast the matter in Boethian terms, Alison yields herself to the powers of destiny and is thereby made subject to them:

> For certes, I am al Vernerien
> In feelynge, and myn herte is Marcien.
> Venus yaf me my lust, my likerousnesse,
> And Mars yaf me my sturdy hardynesse;
> Myn ascendent was Taur, and Mars therinne.
> Allas! allas! that evere love was synne!
> I folwed ay myn inclinacioun
> By vertu of my constellacioun;
>
> (609-16)

Moreover, will not only causes the Wife's downfall, it causes her refusal to be corrected:

> But al for noght, I sette noght an hawe
> Of his proverbes n'of his olde sawe,
> Ne I wolde nat of hym corrected be.
>
> (659-61)

When we meet her, age has caught up with Alison; she is a physical and spiritual grotesque who has degenerated to the extent that, for all her insistence on 'real' experience, she can find reality only in projections into Arthurian romance and rambling reminiscences of her youth. Neither, it proves, is any more substantial than the world of Constance, objection to which precipitated this insistence on human experience.

In addition to providing a measure of the invalidity of Alison's empiricism, her reminiscences and projections function as a first step in her spiritual regeneration. In a very real sense, both prologue and tale are confession.14 This element, new to the *Canterbury Tales* with this tale, is introduced by Chaucer into his pilgrimage at a time when tale and teller have become virtually indistinguishable. In telling their tales the pilgrims confess; through confession they are purged, prepared for assimilation into the New Jerusalem. Alison's famous remark, "The flour is goon, ther is namoore to telle;/The bren, as I best kan, now moste I selle" (477, 78) is but one of several points in the course of her prologue and tale at which she half-consciously realizes her predicament. She notes that she always wants what she can't have, that she loved those who were most difficult to manage, that she longs for the good old days when knighthood was in flower. To some extent she becomes aware of her own fantasies and pretensions. She is far from total regeneration, as her closing lines indicate; but Chaucer is also, at this point in his pilgrimage, far from regeneration. Nevertheless, a process of confession has begun: the pilgrims confess themselves in their tales, and Chaucer, working out metaphysical and aesthetic positions through his mouthpieces, confesses himself in his poem. The process bodes well for the future. Alison is on yet another pilgrimage, looking for her sixth husband. In the sixth age, the sixth hour, Robertson reminds us, comes Jesus Christ.15 This pilgrimage will not return to the Tabard, but end at the saint's shrine in Canterbury.

THE FRIAR'S AND SUMMONER'S PROLOGUES AND TALES

In the prologues and tales of the Friar and Summoner, Chaucer suspends for a moment his consideration of order metaphorically packaged in the institution of marriage, and investigates a subtopic which has raised itself in the Wife's confession: the matter of human will and its relation to both art and order. The subject fascinates Chaucer, and he returns to it later in the *Tales* in the Pardoner's performance and the *Prioress' Tale*. What is the relation of art to will, to intent? Does honest art require honest motivation? Do bad people necessarily produce bad art? And disorder? I believe Chaucer answers affirmatively, at least insofar as art exists not for its own sake (a notion Chaucer would have found alien and absurd) but as a mode of communication between artist and audience. Inevitably, Chaucer discovers with the Friar and Summoner, the unbridled human will must invariably produce social disorder and distortion of human character. We suspect this in the Wife of Bath; we become certain of this after the Friar's and Summoner's prologues and tales.

The disintegration of the social fabric of this pilgrimage has been proceeding apace since the Miller's drunken interruption of Harry back there at Southwark, stayed only momentarily with the *Man of Law's Introduction*, begun again with the endlink of that tale. There, we will recall, the Host selected the Parson to speak next, then changed his mind about the man, insulted him, and allowed the Shipman's objection to nullify his initial decision. Not two hundred lines further we find the Pardoner interrupting the Wife of Bath with his curious remark about wedding a wife, and Alison requesting " 'Abyde,...my tale is nat bigonne'." At the conclusion of her prologue begins the quarrel between the Friar and Summoner. Friar Huberd remarks pleasantly enough, "This is a long preamble of a tale!" (831). No malice intended; Huberd is merely voicing what everyone else is thinking. And then the Summoner, in a clumsy attempt to buy into the humor, makes a less innocent comment:

> "Lo," quod the Somonour, "Goddes armes two!
> A frere wol entremette hym evermo.
> Lo, goode men, a flye and eek a frere
> Wol falle in every dyssh and eek mateere.
> What spekestow of preambulacioun?
> What! amble, or trotte, or pees, or go sit down!
> Thou lettest oure disport in this mannere."
>   (833-39)

The Summoner is not as verbal as Huberd, and he lacks the Friar's sophistication. His tone is all wrong, his joke falls flat, and instead of amusing the other pilgrims he succeeds only in angering Huberd, who promises to tell a tale or two of summoners to make the folk laugh in this place. Rising to the bait, the Summoner promises a tale or two "er I come to Sidyngborne,/That I shal make thyn herte for to morne." Harry Bailey orders both to shut up and let the Wife tell her tale.

And they've been at it, this pair, all through the Wife's tale: while she has been antagonizing the Clerk, Huberd has been silently antagonizing the Summoner. No nasty words "as yet," but obviously a storm is brewing that will make the Miller-Reeve exchange appear polite by comparison. A drunken Miller is one thing; villainy from the worthy, noble Friar is something different. Even Harry is surprised:

> Oure Hoost tho spak, "A! sire, ye sholde be hende
> And curteys, as a man of youre estaat;
> In compaignye we wol have no debaat.
> Telleth youre tale, and lat the Somonour be."
>   (1286-89)

It is precisely the social status of the Friar which makes this altercation so significant, for if anyone would have observed the social niceties, the decorum of civilized society, we would expect it to have been Huberd. But works are the fruit of will, of intent, Chaucer implies, not of wealth (the Wife) or status (Huberd). Base intent must invariably precipitate discord, no matter how civilized one appears. We see this in the person of Harry Bailey, the most wilfull of all Canterbury pilgrims, who, not fifty lines after requesting Huberd to let the Summoner be and ordering "Pees, namoore of this!" (1298) is urging the Friar to lay it on and "telleth forth, thogh that the Somonour gale;/Ne spareth nat, myn owene maister deere" (1336, 37). Despite his position and his pretensions, Harry is as much an agent of discord as anyone else.

And we see the fruits of bad intent in the persons of both the Friar and the Summoner. Indeed, the very word *intent* appears some seven times in the *Friar's Tale* (in which intent forms the folcrum on which all the tale's concurrent ironies turn), and twice in the *Summoner's Tale*, in which it is of equal thematic importance. Chaucer suggests that intent has much to do with the fruit of one's labor; that evil intention often blinds one to reality; that bad intent breeds misaction, bad art, chaos, and disorder—the most salient features of the interchange between these two pilgrims. In the tales we see artist Chaucer working toward a notion he will develop later: that his own intent as artist has something to do with the kind of art he produces, an aesthetic which leads diretly to the dictum that to be a good artist one must first be a good man. This notion, in turn, is implicit in the ironies of these two tales themselves, in the Summoner's insistence that for the offices of the church to be at all efficacious those performing them must be holy and good (cf. his tale, 1709-60), and in Chaucer's confession and retraction at the end of the *Canterbury Tales*. But most of all in these two tales we see Chaucer realizing that base intent will out, that it must precipitate misaction and disorder because it involves an assertion of human will against the divine. That, first and foremost, is the lesson of the Friar's and Summoner's prologues and tales.

The key to both is, as most modern readers recognize, irony in all of Professor Ramsey's many modes.16 It pervades both prologues and tales to an extent heretofore absent from the *Canterbury Tales*, and has recently attracted its fair share of critical attention.17 On the one level, each tale itself contains self-contained ironies: the poor Thomas' fart is ironic requital for the Summoner's friar's own blasts of hot air preached all too extensively at this all too short-tempered mortal; it is ironic that Huberd's summoner should precipitate his own damnation while attempting to extort a few pence from some honest widow with the line "Nay, olde stot, that is nat myn entente." On another level it is ironic that the Friar's summoner resembles the Summoner on the pilgrimage, and that the Summoner's friar resembles Friar Huberd. But the irony most central to Chaucer's aesthetic and

metaphysical point is this: in both prologues and tales, both the
Friar and the Summoner reveal more of themselves than they do
about their antagonists, and thus ironically blacken not so much
their adversaries but their own selves. Donald C. Baker has
observed that Chaucer often uses rhetorical exemplary figures as
characterizing devices: "that is, he causes a character to reveal
much about himself, about others, and about the tale that he tells,
by the use that the character makes, consciously or unconsciously,
of the *exemplum*, or by the contrast of his *exempla* with his or
others' actions."18 Baker concerns himself primarily with the
Friar's use of *exempla* to demonstrate what he thinks of the Wife's
overly rhetorical speech, to give a traditional coloring to his devil,
and to demonstrate the abysmal ignorance of his antagonist, and
with the Summoner's use of exempla "in very nearly the same
manner." What is more interesting is the way each tale causes "a
character to reveal much about himself" which he would just as
soon hide. The mud slung in these exempla so distinctively reflects
the peculiar moral deformities of Friar and Summoner
respectively, that each pilgrim succeeds primarily in
demonstrating what an unpleasant fellow he himself is, and how
disgustingly similar apparently different manifestations of vice
are. More than anything else, the pair reveals that base intent, no
matter how technically impressive the art, invariably turns upon a
base artist.

It is the Friar's intention to tell "of a somonour swich a tale or
two,/That alle the folk shal laughen in this place." Richard Passon
closes an essay on intention in this tale with the observation that
the "most telling piece of irony is that the uncharitable 'entents' of
the Friar himself, in reciting his spiteful tale and preaching his
pointed sermon, is the very thing that we are made most aware of
through his hypocritical prayer at the end."19 He is most certainly
correct, but we are aware of the Friar's moral weaknesses long
before the close of the tale. As the tale unfolds we note some
interesting features of Huberd's summoner, his devil, and his
narrative which comment not so much on his adversary as upon
himself. He reveals himself to be not only hypocritical and
insincere, but pompous and malicious (Baker), incontinent,
wrathful, avaricious, diabolical, and deaf to all warnings about his
own impending undoing by the Summoner...everything, in short,
he accuses the Summoner of being.

The major concerns of the Friar's summoner, for example, are
greed and lechery, concerns he takes to be central to the lives of all
summoners. "A somonour is a rennere up and doun/With
mandementz for fornicacioun," Huberd informs us early in his

prologue. This particular summoner bends every effort to punish fornicators, witches, boasters, and userers, "But certes, leechours dide he grettest wo;/They sholde syngen if that they were hent..." (1310, 11). Now within the tale itself this emphasis on lechery is ironic in that it foreshadows the accusations this summoner will bring against the poor but honest widow who undoes him; in the context of other tales, the remark about such a con game being the "fruyt of al his rente" (1373) foreshadows a similar phrase used by the squire in the *Summoner's Tale* to describe Thomas' gift. But here the focus on lechery serves to recall the portraits of the *General Prologue*. True the Summoner was described as "lecherous as a sparwe" (626), but there is a perversion to his sexuality and an unpleasantness to his features absent in the Friar's summoner. In fact, the Friar's fictional creation recalls his own sexuality more than his adversary's. The Friar, let us recall, was described by pilgrim Chaucer as "a wantowne and a merye" who has made full many a marriage of young women "at his owene cost," presumably because of their pressing need for husbands. He is "unto his ordre...a noble post," skilled in dalliance and wooing women (*General Prologue*, 233-39). The Summoner reminds us of this Friar's fondness for women too: "Peter! so been the wommen of the styves...yput out of oure cure!" he exclaims early in the *Friar's Tale* (1332, 33). Surely we see in Hubard's venomous attack on the Summoner as a prosecutor of lechers some reflection of and defensiveness about his own vice.

Other aspects of Huberd's summoner reflect his own character. The summoner's archdeacon, his immediate superior, knows not everything he wins in his various con games: this summoner skims off part of the take for himself. This relationship reflects that between Huberd and his brethren, for Chaucer told us in the *General Prologue* that "his purchas was wel bettre than his rente" (256), a reasonably clear indication that all he wins begging is not returned to his house, either in the form of licensing fee or free gifts. Moreover, his methods are more genial but really no less unprincipled than those of his summoner. The one threatens the archdeacon's curse and employs direct terror tactics; the other sings and smiles, but implicitly or explicitly his call to confession brings with it a threat of God's own curse. The summoner of the tale demands a twelve pence from his prey; Huberd is so clever and successful that "thogh a wydwe hadde noght a sho,/So pleasaunt was his '*In Principio*,'/Yet wolde he have a ferthyng, er he wente" (253-55). The *wydwe* recalls the *old rebekke* of his tale,

as the *twelf pens* and the *ferthyng* tie teller and tale together. And
we might further observe that just as the poor widow of the tale
turns in righteous anger on her predator and proves his ultimate
undoing, so the Summoner, Huberd's prey of the moment, turns
on him in anger and, despite his verbal poverty, does Huberd in.
Neither the summoner of the tale nor Huberd who tells it achieves
the goal on which he was intent.

Minor ironies abound. In the opening attack of summoner on
widow, Huberd unwittingly recalls the company he so often keeps:
" 'Com out,' quod he, 'thou olde virytrate!/I trowe thou hast som
frere or preest with thee' " (1581, 82). We can hardly read this
line, as Cawley would have us read it, as the willingness of a
self-confident Friar to laugh easily at himself in order to raise a
louder laugh at the Summoner's expense;20 it is, rather, a piece of
the Friar's and Summoner's consistent tendency to characterize
themselves as much as, even more than their opponents in their
own tales. The same thing must be said of the tale's crowning
irony: his characterization of the devil himself in terms that
suggest Huberd's own blence "of the genial with the corupt," as
Ruggiers puts it. Like the Friar, this devil is a sophisticated,
urbane gentleman of the world. "*Depardieux*...deere brother,"
he greets the summoner in the tale. And he even seems a trifle
apologetic about hauling the summoner off to damnation:

> "Now brother," quod the devel, "be nat wrooth;
> Thy body and this panne been myne by right.
> Thou shalt with me to helle yet to-nyght,
> Where thou shalt knowen of oure privetee
> Moore than a maister of dyvynytee."
>
> (1634-38)

We remember Harry's admiration of Huberd: "ye sholde be
hende/And curteys, as a man of youre estaat." Such is the
impression Huberd gives, although in all fairness to the devil, we
must admit that the fiend of his tale is in the end more just, even
more charitable than he. Certainly Chaucer perceives this irony,
and most probably the more perceptive pilgrims perceived it as
well. In spite of, or perhaps precisely because of his malicious
intent, Friar Huberd reveals himself to be a most unsavory
character.

Similar things might be said of the Summoner's performance.
Like the Friar before him, he enjoys at the beginning of his tale a
certain degree of sympathy from Host, pilgrims, even from
readers. We all sympathize with underdogs, particularly when
they are victims of unprincipled sharpies disguised as gentlemen

in a half-cope of double worsted. The shift of sympathies worked
by Huberd's unwitting self-revelation is measured by the Host's
reaction. Where he once addressed Huberd in the politest of terms
and urged him (believing the provocation just) to tell on his tale,
though that the Summoner rant and rave, Harry now urges *the
Summoner* to "Tel forth thy tale, and spare it nat at al" (1763). But
the Summoner begins to forfeit these sympathies almost as soon as
he opens his mouth: his tale, like the Friar's, is
self-characterization and self-damnation.

If the central vices of the *Friar's Tale* are greed and lechery, the
central concerns of the *Summoner's Tale* are greed and wrath, this
last the subject of a long sermon (Merrill calls it "the digression on
anger"[21]) by the Summoner's Friar John which, we are often told,
is inartistically long, generally inept, and largely irrelevant to the
action of his tale. Such may indeed be the case, but only if the tale
is viewed as a self-contained unit, unrelated to teller or other
pilgrims. To any other view of the tale, the sermon is crucial. Let
us recall that the Summoner, not Friar Huberd, rode quaking in his
stirrups for wrath at the beginning of this tale; ther sermon's
subject—indeed, the tale's emphasis on wrath—is a reflection of
the Summoner's self in his tale. And the tale's length does nothing
so much as show his ineptitude at preaching; far from a parody
"cunningly spun out by the Summoner to achieve the dramatic
effect and contrast afforded by Thomas' ultimate bequest,"[22] the
sermon is a clumsy attempt to imitate Friar Huberd's polished
rhetoric which, instead of undercutting Huberd by mocking his
exemplum preaching, satirizes the Summoner by showing his
thick-wittedness. As the sermon's subject ironically reflects his
most characteristic vice, its length reflects his own verbal
ineptitude.

Most important, however, the Summoner's exemplum reflects
its teller in the basic coarseness to which so many readers
object.[23] While the Summoner was described in the *General
Prologue* as lecherous as a sparrow, his sexuality is of a perverse
sort, as we have noted before. He knows the "yonge girles of the
diocise," and is their chief advisor. His harmonic accompaniment
to the Pardoner's love song and the terms in which Chaucer casts it
speak for themselves: "This Somonour bar to hym a stif burdoun"
(672). "It seems unlikely that we are doing the Summoner an
injustice," A. C. Cawley concludes, "if we suspect him of 'thilke
Abhomynable synne, of which that no man unnethe oghte speke ne
write; natheless it is openly rehersed in holy writ' (*Parson's Tale*,
910)." [24] He is not the sort to frequent the bawdy houses, as did
the summoner of Friar Huberd's tale; that was the character of

Huberd himself, who knew every *tappestere* better than any *beggestere*. Nor would he be the sort to kiss young wives the way Friar John kisses Thomas' wife in an obvious abuse of the kiss of peace: here the Summoner has accurately portrayed the moral defect of his antagonist. But the wife is only of passing interest, and the major sexual concerns of the tale are male and anal: the anecdote of the friars' nest below Satan's tail, the groping of Friar John down behind Thomas "aboute his tuwel...there and here" (2148). This is certainly a strange place to store gold, although Friar John shows no surprise in his reaction. In fact, he registers a certain amount of pleasurable anticipation: " 'A!' thoghte this frere, 'that shal go with me'!" We might expect reluctance or hesitation at the thought of such groping; there is none, and even after Thomas' gift proves nothing but gas, Friar John offers no evidence of revulsion. After a similar experience, Absolon in the *Miller's Tale* rubs his lips with dust, sand, straw, cloth, anything to cleanse himself. He is from that time "heeled of his maladie." But the only affront John sees is to his dignity: "this olde churl with lokkes hoore/Blasphemed hath oure hooly covent eke," he tells the franklin and his wife to whom he has repaired for comfort (2182, 83). Such would certainly not be the reaction of Huberd, who in his fastitious dress and affectation has much in common with Absolon. And while it in no way suggests that Friar John is homosexual, it does indicate the Summoner's inability to view the Friar from any perspective other than his own. The perversity of sexual relationships hinted at in the tale misses Huberd entirely; it reflects, rather, on the Summoner himself. Like the Friar before him, the Summoner hits himself as much as he hits his antagonist, and comes away very bloodied indeed.

Of course the tales are filled with other examples of failure of intent: both Friar and Summoner fail in the winning they intend, the friendships they count on, the images they attempt to project. Of course there is frustrated intent elsewhere in the frame—the Host, for example, fails singularly in his proclaimed desire for peace and an end to the quarrel (lines 1298, 1334, and 1762)—but the failure of these pilgrims' intentions is most crucial of all, for it involves the failure of art as a vehicle. The frustration of Friar John's desire for gold, or the Friar's summoner for twelve pence suggests merely that things don't work out the way nasty people plan them. The failure of Harry's attempts to impose peace is a failure in the social and political order, although it may be interpreted metaphysically as well. But the failure of pilgrims' attempts to make their tales do what they intend them to do—this is a failure of art, and an aesthetic matter. No matter how technically proficient one becomes, Chaucer implies, he will not produce great art without honest intentions. It is in this important dimension that the Friar-Summoner quarrel makes a statement beyond that of the Miller's and Reeve's tales, and that Chaucer proceeds on an aesthetic as well as a social and metaphysical plane in these two tales.

With the Friar's and Summoner's prologues and tales Chaucer reaches the metaphysical and aesthetic nadir of the *Canterbury Tales*.25 Put bluntly, everything is wrong, nothing is right: assertive human will has poisoned the church, wrought social chaos, reduced narrative to character defamation. The dislocation of social harmony begun at the pilgrimage's outset is complete: nothing but personal squabblings, pointed and vituperative attacks, and sullen wrath which threatens to silence all human discourse. Justice? A game played by squires. God's word? A gloss dreamt up by some ingenious friar. Art? Dirty stories. In touching bedrock, however, Chaucer reaches that point at which he can begin construction of an ordered cosmos, confronting first the problem of order and disorder being treated in the marriage metaphor, then the matter of human will, and finally the ultimate problem, the relationship of artist to Christian society, the function of art in effecting harmony and accomodating Christian metaphysics.

THE CLERK'S TALE

The Clerk's Tale, despite the fact that it is one of Chaucer's translations and may date to a period in Chaucer's career before the *Tales* had been fully conceptualized,26 is of all the tales one of the most carefully integrated into the pilgrimage dialectic. It is bound to the *Knight's Tale* and the *Man of Law's Tale* both structurally and thematically: like them it is a multipartite romance dealing with the laws that govern the universe and man's relationship to those laws. More comic than the *Knight's Tale*, more frankly allegorical than the *Man of Law's Tale*, it nevertheless calls both to mind. It shares with the Wife's prologue and tale a concern for marriage as an institution, it quarrels with the Wife on the matter of dominance and the efficacy of experience over theory.27 It begins with a pointed reference to Alison's remark to the effect that "it is an impossible/That any clerk wol speke good of wyves" (III 688-89), and it closes with a sarcastic and thoroughly uncharacteristic attack on the Wife and her ilk. It is tied to the tales of Friar and Summoner in its assessment of the role human will plays in the actual realization of human aspirations. It echoes concerns of Chaucer in the *General Prologue* and elsewhere in the *Tales* for time well spent:

> For thogh we slepe, or wake, or rome, or ryde,
> Ay fleeth the tyme; it nyl no man abyde.
>
> (118, 19)

It anticipates both Merchant's and Franklin's tales, in similar plot situations (both the Merchant's January and the Clerk's Walter, for example, first see their future brides in the market place, although they are obviously looking for and at different aspects of a woman; Griselda's behavior in her husband's absence is a marked contrast to the Dorigen's behavior in similar circumstances), and in verbal echoes (compare, for example, the Clerk's "that blisful yok/Of soverayntee, noght of servyse" [113, 14] with the Merchant's "Lyveth a lyf blisful and ordinaat,/Under this yok of mariage ybounde" [1284, 85]). One of Chaucer's additions to the tale even echoes the Miller's advice about meddling unnecessarily in wives' affairs:

> But as for me, I seye that yvele it sit
> To assaye a wyf whan that it is no nede,
> And putten hire in angwyssh and in drede.
>
> (460-62)

It is, then, an important part of the pilgrimage dialectic, not some afterthought or nearly irrelevant piece.

The *Clerk's Prologue* is particularly carefully constructed. It begins with a foreshadowing of the central topic of the tale, marriage, in Harry Bailey's remark about the Clerk riding "as coy and stille as dooth a mayde/Were newe spoused, sittynge at the bord" (2, 3). Of course the comment is intended to impugn the masculinity of this young Clerk, and it characterizes the Host as well. But it also functions as a natural imagistic bridge between the Wife's tale and the Clerk's. And insofar as marriage is emblematic of social order,28 the slur has a certain irony in the Host's mouth.

From here the *Prologue* moves quickly to a concern with time. "Every thyng hath tyme," Harry informs us, quoting Solomon, reasserting his authority, requesting of the Clerk a merry, unstudied tale, something appropriate to the game he has imposed upon the pilgrimage:

> Telle us som myrie tale, by youre fey!
> For what man that is entred in a pley,
> He nedes moot unto the pley assente.
> But precheth nat, as freres doon in Lente,
> To make us for oure olde synnes wepe,

Ne that thy tale make us nat to slepe.

                                              (9-14)

This insistence on game and play, and the concomitant denial of
religious seriousness is ironic in light of the penetential nature of
the pilgrimage and the Lenten season in which it is undertaken,
but it is characteristic of the Host and a measure of the point from
which the journey began. The distance this company has already
come is measured by the Clerk's qualification of Harry's rule:

> "Hooste," quod he, "I am under youre yerde;
> Ye han of us as now the governance,
> And therfore wol I do yow obeisance,
> As fer as resoun axeth, hardily."

                                              (22-25)

A submission, yes, but a qualified submission: "You have of us
now the governance; I will obey you *as far as reason requires.*"29
Very soon we will discover that reason does not demand too close
an adherence to Harry's request, for the tale is not merry in the
sense Harry intended (although like the *Man of Law's Tale* it
might just cause a man to weep for his sins). It has put some
students of Chaucer to sleep although more recent reactions
register moral outrage at Walter's insensitivity to Griselde's
humanity (or Griselde's insensitivity to her own children's lives),
and the need to defend Walter and Clerk and Chaucer from
charges of being grossly inhuman.30 But surely this is not the tale
Harry requests, a tale of studied and somber piety, and the Clerk
in telling it looks forward to a time beyond the present, a
goernance beyond the Host's:

> But deeth, that wol nat suffre us dwellen heer
> But as it were a twynklyng of an ye.
> Hem bothe hath slayne, and alle shul we dye.

                                              (36-38)

In view of the transitory nature of life, the poem with which
Petrarch prefaced his story becomes a thing irrelevant, and the
Clerk cuts it out. Here is a man intent on getting to the heart of the
matter, a serious fellow, one not given to game and trivia. And he
is a man who sees relatively clearly—more clearly, certainly, than
Knight or Wife or even Man of Law, although his vision, as we
shall see, has its limitations too.

It seems to me that the *Clerk's Tale* must be read as allegory.31
Not only is such an interpretation insisted upon by the Clerk
himself in his closing remarks, but the allegorical nature of the tale
is suggested at every turn of the plot. The kneeling subjects

thanking Walter "ful reverently" for agreeing to take a bride are clearly meant to suggest iconographically the company of saints reverencing Christ in medieval scenes of the Judgment (as in the *Knight's Tale,* 1175 ff.); the oxes' stall of 291 and 398 is an obvious figure for the stable at Bethlehem (lest we miss the point, the analogy is drawn explicitly by the Clerk in 207); the crown and new raiment given Griselda upon her return to Walter's favor are clearly emblematic of the crown of life and the new raiment attained by every faithful Christian in the New Jerusalem. The reaction of Griselda to Walter's initial proposal of marriage recalls the "Thy will be done" of Christ in Gethsemane and the Lord's Prayer:

> She seyde, "Lord, undigne and unworthy
> Am I to thilke honour that ye me beede,
> But as ye wole yourself, right so wol I.
>
> (359-61)

"I am not worthy to have you come under my roof," the Centurian told Christ (Matthew 8:8). The action of this tale is simply not realistic: people do not behave as either Walter or Griselda behave, unless the person happens to be Job (with whom Griselda invites constant comparison) — which brings us right back in allegory.

Once the allegorical nature of the tale is grasped, we cease to lament the irrational, callous, thoroughly reprehensible behavior of both Walter and Griselda, and come to grips with the tale's point.32 God calls man and, of his own accord, grants salvation and grace. Man, in a state of sin from birth, may suffer, but the suffering is always justified because man is man and God is God, and in the end suffering is finished and the reward is great. In fact, all that is required of man is patience and subjugation of his own will to divine will; unquestioned obedience, in other words, is the mark of the Christian. God may tempt man, but not beyond his capacity to endure, although from the human point of view such temptation may appear capricious and cruel. It is not. Always there is the crown and the robe waiting at the race's end:

> This storie is seyd, not for that wyves sholde
> Folwen Grisilde as in humylitee,
> For it were inportable, though they wolde;
> But for that every wight, in his degree,
> Sholde be constant in adversitee
> As was Grisilde; therefore Petrak writeth
> This storie, which with heigh stile he enditeth.

For, sith a womman was so pacient
Unto a mortal man, wel moore us oghte
Receyven al in gree that God us sent;
For greet skile is, he preeve that he wroghte.
But he tempteth no man that he boghte,
As seith Seint Jame, if ye his pistel rede;
He preeveth folk al day, it is no drede,

And suffreth us, as for oure exercise,
With sharpe scourges of adversitee
Ful ofte to be bete in sondry wise;
Nat for to knowe oure wyl, for certes he,
Er we were born, knew al oure freletee;
And for oure best is al his governaunce.
Lat us thanne lyve in vertuous suffraunce.
                                    (1142-62)

The modern reader will not appreciate those lines; they exceed his capacity to transcend his human insistence on human standards of justice. Of course the Christian mystery also transcends human understanding, and the loss of one jeopardizes the other; conversely, acceptance of one permits acceptance of the other. Both are brought together nicely by Chaucer and his Clerk in a key stanza which both exemplifies and explains that behavior moderns find so inexplicable and unappealing:

And thus she seyde in hire benigne voys,
"Fareweel my child! I shal thee nevere see.
But sith I thee have marked with the croys
Of thilke Fader—blessed moote he be!—
That for us deyde upon a croys of tree,
Thy soule, litel child, I hym bitake,
For this nyght shaltow dyen for my sake."
                                    (554-60)

pietism." But the Clerk insists that this is what it's all about.

In fact, our modern, temporal reactions are built into the *Clerk's Tale* in the corporate personage of Walter's people. Chaucer dwells some time on the narrator's reactions to what's going on and the various reactions of Walter's subjects to his alternate acts of benificence and cruelty. In these reactions we find articulated the human point of view:

The sclaundre of Walter ofte and wyde spradde,
That of a crueel herte he wikkedly,
For he a povre womman wedded hadde,
Hath mordred bothe his children prively.
Swich murmur was among hem comunly.
No wonder is, for to the peples ere
Ther cam no word, but that they mordred were.

> For which, where as his peple therbifore
> Hadde loved hym wel, the sclaundre of his diffame
> Made hem that they hym hatede therefore.
>   (722-31)

These, in turn, are very similar to comments made by the
Chaucerian narrator (or by the Clerk, although one does not think
of the Clerk as an ironist in this heavy-handed fashion) registering
his reservations about Walter's behavior:

> He hadde assayed hire ynoghe bifore,
> And foond hire evere good; what needed it
> Hire to tempte, and alwey moore and moore,
> Though som men preise it for a subtil wit?
>   (456-59)

> Among al this, after his wikke usage,
> This markys, yet his wyf to tempte moore...
>   (785-86)

Interestingly Fortune, which played such an important role in the
Knight's Tale, is here associated with human suspicions and
specious explanations of what's going on:

> "No man may alwey han prosperitee.
> With evene herte I rede yow t'endure
> The strook of Fortune or of aventure."
>   (810-12)

Walter's people curse Fortune as they accompany the deposed
Griselda back to her father's house. But such is not the nature of
the cosmos, Petrarch through this Clerk informs us: for those who
endure their trials in patience and submission, God's will is that
they shall inherit the kingdom. "Behold, my servant Job," says
the Lord. He tempts, but he also sustains and rewards.
   Metaphysically this position devlops that of the Man of Law,
reaffirming the benificence of well established and dependable
supernatural powers, but incorporating into his statement the role
of human will, a concern Chaucer has developed through the Wife
of Bath's prologue and tale, and the tales of the Friar and
Summoner.33 It denies, of course, the nominalism of the Miller
and Reeve, and the disorder of the Knight's cosmos. It also
responds to the Wife's assertion that experience, not authority of
abstract metaphysics, is the best grounds for developing social (or
marital) order. In fact, the Clerk asserts, order is to be discovered
in abstraction and metaphysics which appear absurd when cast in
concrete experiences, and in the subjugation of human will to that
of (the male) God. The Wife's assertion of her own will led her to a

distorted reality, a defective epistimology, and several inharmonious marriages. The Clerk shows her the proper station of will, true reality (a neo-Platonic insistence on the primacy of idea), the proper epistimology (authority, not experience), and a felitious marital relationship. He provides, in fact, the clue to a proper understanding of Chaucer's discussion of marriage so evident throughout the *Canterbury Tales:* what is at stake is not merely a human institution but the reflection in society of divine order and degree. It is to be expected that pilgrims like the Wife and Host, who assert constantly their own wills against the will of God, will have unfortunate marriages, just as it is to be expected that tales told with base motives will backfire. Art in one case, marriage in the other are but reflections in the microcosm of immutable laws of the macrocosm.

Artistically the tale also moves beyond the *Man of Law's Tale* in that it replaces example with allegory. The two are related, of course, but the one provides a realistic narrative (or what purports to be a realistic narrative) offering an example to which humans might aspire, whereas the other offers a narrative so un-naturalistic and unrealistic as to preclude serious attempts at emulation. We would not attempt to imitate Griselda; in fact, the Clerk makes a point of telling us not to emulate her. It can't be done, and there is no sense to insisting (as did the Man of Law) that it can. Women are not like this, and men should not be like Walter. The chaf of narrative is not to be taken as truth, but as a vehicle for truth; metaphysics comes through but not in, as it were, fiction. In this flirtation with allegory, of course, Chaucer moves close to a position which denies fiction entirely. He will ultimately deny fiction, all right, but not so much for allegory as for straight moral philosophy. But here he cannot rest: allegory itself has deficiencies, and this pilgrimage is not completed.

The defect of allegory is this: the chaf will not be denied, the narrative keeps intruding. As much as we would like to grasp this tale as an allegory of God's relationship with man, we keep seeing it as a marriage between man and woman. As much as we aspire to divine perspectives, as much as we are willing to admit our guilt and the justice of our suffering, we cannot. God keeps appearing a tyrant, submission to his will the most patent folly. We are not yet of the New Jerusalem, and the gulf between the two worlds still exists.

As much evidence as there is that Chaucer intended this tale to be read allegorically, there is certainly much evidence to suggest he knew it could not be read allegorically. If I see him correctly behind his work, I suspect that even he could not read—and therefore write—allegory. There is certainly precious little of it in the remainder of the *Canterbury Tales*, until we follow the pilgrims and the Parson and Chaucer himself right out of this world and into the next, right out of fiction and into grace. In one sense the tale's realism (and there are certainly elements of realism here, despite the absence of realistic cause and effect relationships) is a measure of Chaucer's denial of allegory.34 In another sense, the fact that Chaucer apparently goes out of his way to make the marquis more cruel than he is in Petrarch's tale, is an indication that Chaucer did not expect us to resist the temptation to humanize him and thereby demolish the allegory.35 But the clearest indication that Chaucer found this allegory, and by implication allegory in general, unsatisfactory is the abrupt return to reality in the Clerk's closing words and his (or is it the clerk's?) *envoy*. With line 1163 the aesthetics of the tale, and with them its metaphysics, collapse:

> But o word, lordynges, herkneth er I go:
> It were ful hard to fynde now-a-dayes
> In a toun Grisildis thre or two;
> For if that they were put to swiche assayes,
> The gold of hem hath now so badde alayes
> With bras, that thogh the coyne be fair at ye,
> It wolde rather breste a-two than plye.
>
> For which heere, for the Wyves love of Bathe,
> Whos lyf and al hire secte God mayntene
> In heigh maistrie, and elles were it scathe—
> I wol with lusty herte, fressh and grene,
> Seyn yow a song to glade yow, I wene;
> And lat us stynte of ernestful matere.
>
> (1163-75)

And we are off again into game, to realism, to frivolity. Harry's authority had been effectively denied in the Clerk's affirmation of a higher law; his game had been denied in favor of theological high seriousness; the chaos of the Wife and the Host had been resolved somewhat quickly into the order that comes from submissive will—all this is tossed aside.36 The Wife's sect is sarcastically elevated to a "heigh maistrie"; the Clerk sings us a song of the world with a lusty, green heart; we leave earnest material for more fun and games. The *envoy* returns us to the discord in which the tale began, as if nothing had happened. Ultimately, this time at least, realism triumphs over allegory and the tension of the tale is broken.

Patrick Morrow attributes this state of affairs to the condition of the Clerk himself; whether he is right or wrong, he correctly notes that the *Tales* are still in progress, that the pilgrimage has not yet

run its course, either metaphysically or aesthetically. All the
pilgrims are still en route, and Chaucer with them, and the failure
of the Clerk has been more than the failure of just a single pilgrim:

> Currently undergoing penance and having for the
> most part taken leave of the Pilgrims, he seems to
> be seeking some form of redemption. The Clerk
> may be "en wende Canterbury" in order to find a
> synthesis, a redemption from this world—*some*
> means for getting out of his predicament of
> ambivalence. How can ideal good regenerate real
> evil? Why must we have an opposing ideal and real
> morality? In his present state the Clerk has no
> chance of engaging in meaningful action that is
> both honest and assertive. He may be more right
> than the Wyf of Bath, but he is also projected as an
> embarassingly pale figure. Discretely, but
> painfully, he withdraws.37

Chaucer's pilgrimage, his dialectic, continues.

THE MERCHANT'S TALE

"Lat hym care, and wepe, and wrynge, and waille!" the Clerk
has advised, referring sarcastically to the unfortunate husbands of
the Wife's followers. And his advice, either the last of his *envoy* or
only a stanza away from the *Merchant's Prologue*, has struck a
responsive note, not only in Harry Bailey, but in another pilgrim as
well.38 "Wepyng and waylyng, care and oother sorwe," laments
the Merchant, "I knowe ynogh, on even and a-morwe" (1213, 14).
Largely ignoring the Clerk's metaphysics, the Merchant launches
into a dark diatribe on marriage, full of venom and all the heavy
irony two months of marriage can engender.

And the *Merchant's Tale* is dark: as dark as anything Chaucer
ever wrote, so goes the usual assessment, so dark as to be
uncharacteristic of Chaucer.39 January, "a worthy knight" of
some sixty years, decides to give over his lusty bachelorhood and
take a wife. "Were it for hoolynesse or for dotage,/I kan nat
seye," says the Merchant (1253-54); January thinks it's for
holiness, but we soon realize he's gone in the head. Despite
warnings from one of his brothers, the old January settles on
young May to be his bride. On their very wedding night January's
squire Damian is head over heels for the girl, and not four days
later he's made his confession of love to her. The tale culminates
with the young couple engaged in what Bernard Huppé calls
"arboreal sexual gymnastics"40 in a pear tree, with the

chagrinned January below on the ground. It's the old man-young
girl-handy lover triangle, someone says: the *Miller's Tale* retold by
the Merchant.

But this the *Merchant's Tale* is not, because it is not the simple
fabliau of the Miller, and because the Merchant's characters are
decidedly more unlovely than old John, vital Alison, and handy
Nicholas. The tale is morose in its irony, bitter in its
characterization. It begins, for example, with a one hundred
plus-line encomium on the virtues and pleasures of marriage from
a Merchant who has just complained bitterly about his own
unfortunate status as a preface to a tale of marital misfortune. The
sarcasm is indeed more bitter than anything else in Chaucer:

> And certeinly, as sooth as God is kyng,
> To take a wyf it is a glorious thyng,
> And namely whan a man is oold and hoor;
> Thanne is a wyf the fruyt of his tresor.
> Thanne sholde he take a yong wyf and a feir,
> On which he myghte engendren hym an heir,
> And lede his lyf in joye and in solas.
>
> (1267-73)

The irony in these lines is even more biting when we remember the
fruit of that pear tree in January's garden and May's pretense to
pregnancy (1. 2335) that caused him to allow her to climb up there
with Damian. Or consider these few lines:

> A wyf! a, Seint Marie, *benedicite!*
> How myghte a man han any adversitee
> That hath a wyf? Certes, I kan nat seye.
> The blisse which that is bitwixe hem tweye
> Ther may no tonge telle, or herte thynke.
>
> (1337-41)

This after the Merchant's remark about weeping and wailing and
care and sorrow: unrelieved, morose, even heavy-handed irony.

Even more unpleasant than this sustained irony is Chaucer's
portrayal of this tale's characters. We might have managed some
sympathy for John in the *Miller's Tale*, what with his generous
solicitiousness for Nicholas and his almost pathetic fear that Alison
may drown in this great flood; how much sympathy can we muster
for blind, foolish, self-deluded January as he considers in his mind
how he must offend poor May on their wedding night?

> But natheless yet hadde he greet pitee
> That thilke nyght offenden hire moste he,
> And thoughte, "Allas! O tendre creature,
> Now wolde God ye myghte wel endure

Al my corage, it is so sharp and keene!
I am agast ye shul it nat susteene.
But God forbede that I dide al my myght!
Now wolde God that it were woxen nyght,
And that the nyght wolde lasten evermo.
I wolde that al this peple were ago.''

                                    (1755-64)

Thinking this, January hustles his guests out the door as gracefully
as he can, packs himself full of aphrodesiacs and spices "Swiche
as the cursed monk, daun Constantyn,/Hath writen in his book *De
Coitu*'' (1810-11), then begins his attack on May, kissing her
roughly and rubbing her tender face "With thikke brustles of his
beard unsofte,/Lyk to the skyn of houndfyssh'' (1824-25). After a
long night's work, January downs a bit more wine and serenades
his love:

And upright in his bed thanne sitteth he,
And after that he sang ful loude and cleere,
And kiste his wyf, and made wantown cheere.
He was al coltissh, ful of ragerye,
And ful of jargon as a flekked pye.
The slakke skyn aboute his nekke shaketh,
Whil that he sang, so chaunteth he and craketh.

                                    (1844-50)

There can be no sympathy here. Nor can we admire May, who
reads Damian's love letter in the privy and engineers herself the
absurd consumation of their clandestine love up in that pear tree
by preying on January's desire for an heir or pride in his own
virility. Nor can we much admire the passive and cardboard
Damian, who is mostly just there to make the story go. More than
the tale's heavy irony and sarcasm, more than the remark about
"old beef" and "tendre veel" (1420) and the pun on *queynte*
(2061), more than the debasement of courtly love and the *Song of
Songs* (in January's speech of 2138 ff.), it is this grossness of
character which so repulses us in the *Merchant's Tale.*

Now there is no denying that the heavy ironies central to the
tale's point are more biting than we are accustomed to hearing
from Chaucer, and that the tale is obscene in the broadest sense.
But the situation is not quite as hopeless as it has been made out to
be, precisely because of material like the encomium on marriage
which create the strong ironies: they offer an alternative, an ideal,
a standard which wasn't present except by implication in the
Friar-Summoner interchange. This same quality distinguishes it
from the earlier fabliaux. J. A. Burrow has written,

> Unlike the other 'fabliau tales', but like the
> *Pardoner's Tale*, the story of January and May
> faces up to the moral issues it raises. This involves
> a radical modification of the fabliau method.41

This "facing up" comes in the form of ironic contrast between the
is and the *ought*, between delusion and reality, between an
explicitly stated ideal (and orthodox) view of marriage as a
sacrament and the debasement of that ideal in January's own
marriage. Following the Clerk, to whom his tale alludes at every
point, the Merchant views marriage as a metaphor; in fact, the
initial one hundred lines of his tale are an ironic delineation of the
marriage metaphor as it should be. Now the Merchant's phrasing
of this ideal is, as Bernard Huppé has noted, twisted in its
allusions and arguments,42 but there is no denying that his
depiction is of an ideal state of matrimony, and that it is cast in
strongly theological terms. Marriage is a holy bond (1261), a
paradise on earth (1265 and elsewhere in the tale), a blessing
ordained by God (1284), a great sacrament (1319) which mirrors as
an institution Christ's love of his Church and—thereby—the
principle of divine love which, according to Boethius, orders the
cosmos. This almost sounds like St. Paul lecturing us:

> I warne thee, if wisely thou wolt wirche,
> Love wel thy wyf, as Crist loved his chirche.
> If thou lovest thyself, thou lovest thy wyf;
> No man hateth his flessh, but in his lyf
> He fostreth it, and therfore bidde I thee,
> Cherisse thy wyf, or thou shalt nevere thee.
>
> (1383-88)

Clearly the emphasis on marriage as metaphor, as an emblem of
divine order and harmony, as a theological matter is a reflection of
the *Clerk's Tale* which preceded this. In fact, so heavy is the
theology here, so larded with references, oblique and direct, to
Church doctrine and ritual, that it appears the tale was intended
for some other pilgrim—perhaps the Monk—and switched to the
Merchant at some late date.43

A further reminder of the *ought* against which this *is* should be
measured is to be found in the tale's regular verbal and structural
allusions to the *Clerk's Tale*, for by reminding us constantly of the
Clerk's ideal the Merchant makes the moral norm (or the moral
ideal) very nearly explicit. The relationships between January in
this tale and Walter in the other are many, and they ought not to
be overlooked. Each is old and worthy when he decides to wed,
each searches for his bride in a market place setting, each involves

his counsellors in that search, each weds someone below him in age and social status, each tests his wife to the point where he is afraid she may not sustain it. The related contrasts are, of course, equally if not more important than the similarities, and we shall have to deal with them presently. For the moment, however, it is the similarities that draw Clerk's and Merchant's tales together and allow one to function as a very present, if ironic standard against which to measure the Merchant's perversion. This is something the Friar's and Summoner's tales did not do, at least explicitly; normative standards were absent entirely from the earlier fabliaux of the Miller and Reeve. Chaucer's dialectic does not pass over precisely the same ground twice.

The effect of the *Merchant's Tale*, then, is to heighten perversion and obscenity and, at the same time, to heighten the ideal against which this deformity is measured. The bitterness of the Merchant's irony derives precisely from this concurrent elevation and debasement. In the context of the *Canterbury Tales* the process serves to tie Merchant's and Clerk's tales closely together and allow the one to answer the other by continuing a process of "realistic debasement of an ideal" already begun in the Clerk's *envoy*. The Merchant develops more completely the attitude we sensed emerging at the close of the *Clerk's Tale*. "Yes," he says, "but..." The Clerk has posited an abstract, Neo-Platonic reality in the face of which human existence as normally experienced becomes meaningless illusion, then attempted to make that Neo-Platonic reality a pattern for behavior in the mundane, work-a-day world. The stance was dictated by the tale's theology, but it left the Clerk with a reality that was not reality: nobody behaves as Griselda. For the Clerk, we suspect, this ethereal world may have been sufficient (although see Morrow, as quoted above); his descent into realism in the *envoy* startles us. But for the rest of us, including both Chaucer and the Merchant, such idealism is intolerable and the descent into realism is but a measure of the tale's failure. From this point the Merchant picks up: yes, this is a fine ideal, perhaps the true nature of Neo-Platonic reality. But something happens when the real world—the world as I've been experiencing it these last few months—partakes of that universal. Your marriage metaphor has two legs, one in this world and one in another. If anything, the human institution of marriage is more real to me than God or his church, and you've largely ignored it. One end of your marriage metaphor isn't very much like the other.

What intrudes is, as we might expect, the human will. Walter

was a figure of God, imposing his will on Griselda, the patient
Christian. Metaphorically, then, January is a figure of God and
May a figure of the Church: "Wives, submit yourselves to your
husbands, as to the Lord," St. Paul has written (Ephesians 6.22).
And he has gone on to say "Husbands, love your wives, as Christ
loved the Church," an admonition the Merchant has introduced
directly into his tale (in lines 1382ff. quoted above). Loving a wife
as Christ loves his Church, as one loves his own flesh, one does his
wife no harm. A man may not hurt himself with his own knife,
January reasons (1840). True enough, but only insofar as figural
relations hold, only insofar as the Christian submits his own will to
that of the Lord. Assert human will, and both figural relationships
and the safety from one's own knife disappear.

January is no figure of Christ; he is rather a most self-willed
creature, debasing charity to sensuality and lust, indulging his
appetites, setting his own wit to legalistic games with religious
decrees:

> With face sad his tale he hath hem toold.
> He seyde, "Freendes, I am hoor and oold,
> And almoost, God woot, on my pittes brynke;
> Upon my soule somwhat most I thynke.
> I have my body folily despended;
> Blessed be God that it shal been amended!
> For I wol be, certeyn, a wedded man,
> And that anoon in al the haste I kan.
>
> (1399-1406)

Having had his paradise on earth, January will insure his soul with
a quick marriage, thereby evading the letter of God's law.
Justinus, an advisor asserting divine and natural justice as well as
common sense, is brushed aside; Placebo does, in fact, please.
High fantasy and curious business—the assertion of the mortal
will. To this end January devotes his waking moments, searching
for some tender veal which will satisfy his carnal appetite. When
Walter considered Griselda as a potential bride, he turned over in
his mind "hir wommanhede,/And eek hir vertu" (239-40); when
January considers May he ponders in his heart "Hir fresshe
beautee and hir age tendre,/Hir myddel smal, hire armes longe
and sklendre" (1601-2). His choice, obviously, is made on the
basis of physical attributes, and driven by a desire he can no
longer satisfy. Like the aged Reeve Oswald, January finds himself
propelled by a will too often indulged to be governed now,
although he's certainly warned again and again of his impending
undoing. Intention is blind, even to the fact that other mortals have
intent of their own (lines 2212, 2106, for example) which may work

at cross purposes to its self.

So January's intent, exercised so indulgently these sixty years, blinds him to truth; the separate intents of January, May, and Damian work that dark mischief so offensive in this tale. What the *Merchant's Tale* suggests is that human will operating in both the male and female of the species, manifesting itself in lust, prevents either male or female from becoming valid figures of Christ and his Church; the result is not the paradise of the *Clerk's Tale*, the heaven on earth anticipated by January, but the hell of the *Merchant's Tale*—not the blessed order of Paradise but the infernal (it is presided over by Pluto and his captive bride), disordered garden built by deluded January as a monument to concupiscence. The fruit of such a garden is the fruit of the pear tree: deceit, lust, delusion. Deliberately the Merchant parodies his moral norm, the Christ-Church marital relationship into which the Song of Songs had been allegorized:

> "Rys up, my wyf, my love, my lady free!
> The turtles voys is herd, my dowve sweete;
> The wynter is goon with alle his reynes weete.
> Com forth now, with thyne eyen columbyn!
> How fairer been thy brestes than is wyn!
> The gardyn is enclosed al aboute;
> Com forth, my white spouse!
> (2138-44)

Deliberately the Merchant allows May an ironic regard for her soul:

> But first and forward she bigan to wepe.
> "I have," quod she, "a soule for to kepe
> As wel as ye, and also myn honour,
> And of my wyfhod thilke tendre flour,
> Which that I have assured in youre hond,
> Whan that the preest to yow my body bond..."
> (2186-92)

Deliberately the Merchant consigns his garden to an old ravisher, the god of the underworld, old Pulto himself—here ironically beset by a very human and very shrewish wife with a strong will of her own. So all is disjointed: marriage, soul, religion, order. This, the Merchant suggests, is the way things look when you come at them from the other way around; man being a willful creature, it appears unlikely that he will figure divine order in any of his institutions or relationships.

Clearly the vehicle of this metaphor is at odds with its tenor, and just as the Clerk examined tenor and drew a misguided portrait of the vehicle, so the Merchant examines vehicle and draws a misguided conclusion about the tenor. Fortune (2057) assumes control of this tale, and with Fortune come all those uncertainties we saw so clearly in the *Knight's Tale* as resulting from destinal forces cut loose from Christian charity:

> Were it by destynee or aventure,
> Were it by influence or by nature,
> Or constellacioun, that in swich estaat
> The hevene stood, that tyme fortunaat
> Was for to putte a bille of Venus werkes—
> For alle thyng hath tyme, as seyn thise clerkes—
> To any woman, for to gete hire love,
> I kan nat seye; but grete God above,
> That knoweth that noon act is causelees,
> He deme of al, for I wole holde my pees.
>
> (1967-76)

Divine control in the *Merchant's Tale* assumes the same shape it found in the *Knight's Tale*: a squabble among the gods controls events among men. Interestingly, this is also a marital squabble, Pluto the hen-pecked husband, Proserpine the defender of married women. The Merchant arrives at this depiction of divine control from an examination of mortal marriage and an acceptance of marriage as a metaphor for divine order: given the metaphor and the vehicle, the Merchant could arrive at no other possible conclusion. And yet, as the explicit normative position developed throughout the tale demonstrates, the conclusion is dead wrong.

The *Epilogue* to this tale witnesses the continued development of several processes begun earlier in the Canterbury pilgrimage. The Host, whose view of reality has been flattered by this tale in much the way that Placebo's advice of 1491ff. suggested lords temporal be flattered, assents to the doctrine conveyed in the tale: his marriage is similar to that described by the Merchant, and his view of reality accords with that expressed by the pilgrim. The fictive is made real (as real as is the pilgrimage itself) and the distortions of the tale are connected with those of the "real" world of the pilgrimage:

> Lo, whiche sleightes and subtiltees
> In wommen been! for ay as bisy as bees
> Been they, us sely men for to deceyve,
> And from the soothe evere wol they weyve;
> By this Marchauntes tale it prevath weel."
>
> (2427-25)

Artistically Chaucer once again draws tale and teller together, so that one becomes the other and distinctions between levels of reality are difficult, if not impossible to draw. He has done this before in the Man of Law's references to Chaucer's poems, and he has done this in the *Merchant's Tale* proper in Justinus' reference to the Wife's sermon. The Chaucer cited by the Man of Law is not the Chaucer we see on this pilgrimage; Justinus could not have known the Wife of Bath; January, May, Pluto are no more real than Griselda and Walter, and thus no valid measure of real women's deceit. The net effect of this blurring of distinctions is to make metaphysical developments social developments, and to give social developents among the company of pilgrims a metaphysical significance. We may expect, then, resolution of metaphysical matters—if and when they come—to be reflected in the behavior of the pilgrims; we may also expect social developments in Chaucer's frame to be reflective of advances in metaphysics. Finally, we may assume Chaucer's discussion of marriage to be of far greater significance than back yard gossip on husbands and wives.

THE SQUIRE'S TALE

The Squire's aborted romance has proven one of the major enigmas of all the *Canterbury Tales,* for the last century at the very least. It has generated little comment in schoalrly journals (much of that concerning sources), and even book-length studies of the *Tales* often ignore it entirely.44 Recent years have witnessed more than one attempt to read it as a finished fragment, a tale deliberately interrupted in the style of *Sir Thopas* rather than a tale left incomplete,45 but such a reading, while useful and interesting, leaves us as far from the real problem posed by this tale as do most source studies. The real issue here is what, if anything, is going on in this tale?46

At first glance, the *Squire's Tale* appears both artistically inept and thematically out of place in the position it occupies among the other Canterbury tales. It spins its rhetorical wheels, spending considerable time not describing as assortment of banquets, arriving after some four hundred lines just about nowhere:

> The knotte why that every tale is toold,
> If it be taried til that lust be coold
> Of hem that han it after herkned yoore,
> The savour passeth ever lenger the moore,
> For fulsomnesse of his prolixitee;
> And by the same resoun, thynketh me,
> I sholde to the knotte condescende,
> And maken of hir walkyng soone an ende.
>   (401-8)

With these lines the Squire drops his narrative of Cambyuskan's gifts and turns to Canacee, her dream, and her conversation with the tercel. Neither half of the romance is particularly well related to the other, to other elements of the *Canterbury Tales*, or to the big finish promised by the Squire:

> First wol I telle yow of Cambyuskan,
> That in his tyme many a citee wan;
> And after wol I speke of Algarsif,
> How that he wan Theodora to his wif,
> For whom ful ofte in greet peril he was,
> Ne hadde he ben holpen by the steede of bras;
> And after wol I speke of Cambalo,
> That faught in lystes with the bretheren two
> For Canacee er that he myghte hire wynne.
>
> (661-69)

It is with considerable relief that we arrive finally at the Franklin's interruption of the romance (or Chaucer's abrupt farewell to an unfinished tale), and return to the matter at hand—marriage in its literal and metaphorical senses. What might Chaucer have in mind, we wonder. Is this but an interruption of the discussion of marriage, introduced for the sake of variety, as Kittredge would have it?47 Is it really only the rough draft of a tale to which Chaucer intended to return? An artistic lapse on the poet's part, perhaps? Or something of a characterization of the youthful Squire?48 Or something else entirely?

Let us note in beginning that the *Squire's Tale* is not utterly unrelated to other tales in the Canterbury collection, nor to other tales in its immediate proximity. Structurally and rhetorically it echoes the *Knight's Tale*, as has been noted on more than one occasion;49 in its concern for gentilesse it echoes the Wife of Bath and prepares us for the *Franklin's Tale*. In some respects it appears even to answer the Wife: in his contempt for commoners, the Squire denies the Wife's assertion that *gentilesse* comes from character, not birth, and strongly implies a distaste for the social implications of her courtly aspirations. Both developments prepare for the Franklin's assertion of *gentilesse* as a quality of birth *and* behavior ("You find more of it in the nobility," the Franklin seems to say, "although a clerk can manage occasional generosity. Things seep from the top down."), and his assertion of proper dominance in both marriage and society. It is possible the *Squire's Tale* exhibits some reaction to the Merchant's squire, Damian, or to the squire of the *Summoner's Tale*. In matters like the submission of pilgrim Squire to Host Harry Bailey, so evident in the *Squire's Prologue*, and the concern of this tale for illusion and reality (found before in the Merchant's tale of moral blindness, and after in the magic of the Franklin's French clerk, as well as in the tales of the Wife, the Friar, and even the Knight), the *Squire's Tale* is loosely tied to the whole of the *Canterbury Tales.*

These ties are, however, loose. Illusion and reality, *gentilesse,* marriage, rhetoric—it would be difficult to find any medieval narrative that dit not touch in some way on these themes. We are uncomfortable with mediocre art loosely associated with great art. And we are uncomfortable with the tale's departure from the subject at hand: marriage. Even given the metaphorical dimensions of this discussion of marriage, the Squire's awkward (and there is no use in denying the obvious) statement on will, order, and illusion does not fit easily into the metaphysical dialectic of the pilgrimage at this particular point. Now, suddenly, the marriage metaphor is dropped, marital and cosmic order is replaced by social order (itself a subdominant theme), and we examine once again the relationship between will and fruition. The Friar's and Summoner's tales reprsented an important, perhaps even a necessary, philosophical digression on a subargument soon to be incorporated into the *Tales'* primary dialectic. The *Squire's Tale* does not promise to be such a diversion. Why Chaucer should make such a shift at this point, is unlcear; I suspect he planned to devote more care to this tale later and develop the position at that time, or that he found the step in his dialectic unnecessary, a digression, and was prepared to drop the matter entirely. But two things are clear from the *Tales* as they presently stand: the *Squire's Tale* is something of a philosophical digression (although not entirely unrelated to the movement of Chaucer's mind), and—while digressive—the position is not precisely a return to one Chaucer had previously occupied.

Like the tales of the Friar and Summoner, the Wife, the Merchant—of so many pilgrims now—the *Squire's Tale* operates on two levels of fictional reality: that of the tale itself and that of the pilgrimage. Unlike most of the tales we've read thus far, the *Squire's Tale* moves beyond both, I believe, to comment on Chaucer and his role as artist. The confusion among realities, as well as deficiencies inherent in the tale itself, may well be one reason poet Chaucer despaired of bringing this tale to full fruition; or, since the tale concerns itself in a very real sense with will and fruition, and since, on at least one level of fictional reality, the obviously inadequate capabilities of the Squire frustrate his desire to tell a first rate romance, the tale collapses for this reason. In any event, a sorting out of realities and wills and orders becomes important.

The tale begins with an echo of the *Knight's Tale*: at Sarray there was once a noble king, Cambyuskan, "Which in his tyme was of so greet renoun/That ther was nowher in no regioun/So excellent a lord in alle thyng" (13-15). He is hardy, wise, and powerful. To Cambyuskan are brought gifts which are at the same time tributes to his power and devices through which he might exercise his will: a steed of brass which "Kan in the space of o day natureel—That is to seyn, in foure and twenty houres—/Wher-so yow lyst, in droghte or elles shoures,/Beren youre body into every place/To which youre herte wilneth for to pace" (116-20), a mirror in which he may discover friends and foes to his reign, a ring which will allow its wearer to talk with birds, and a naked sword which will cut with its blade and heal with its flat side, as Cambyuskan pleases. The gifts are tucked away, not for the most part to be used again in the tale, but the Squire's point is clear: the king may use them at his will and his will alone.

One gift is used: on a whim Canacee rouses herself early in the morning, wanders off into the park, and—aided by her ring—overhears the complaint of a gentle falcon lamenting her lost love. The perverse fellow has thrown her over for an itinerant kite, with whom he is quite taken up despite differences of social rank. He's willed himself to the kite; the falcon willed herself to him, and now to death. Canacee nurses her and, we are informed, will induce Cambalus, her brother, to win back the bird's true love. Now obviously will does not play a prominent role in all this; at least the importance of will to the bird's plight is not emphasized as it might have been. We may, however, say that the fowl's plight suggests the disaster of submitting one's self unthinkingly to the wrong sort of lover (governor), just as the first segment of this romance suggested, however obliquely, that the proper sort of ruler is he who is born to the post and deserves the position. The common folk are stupidly suspicious of the horse; the falcon is grieved by an unwise submission, even though it proceeded from the purest of motives.

On the second level of fiction, that of Chaucer's pilgrimage to Canterbury, the matter of will and fruition is more in the forefront. It is, in fact, the Squire's ready submission of his own will to that of the Host, ("for I wol nat rebelle/Agayn youre lust" he tells Harry), proceeding again from the purest of motives, which precipitates this disastrous performance. Purity of will and purpose is not always enough, Chaucer seems to say, developing the position of the Friar-Summoner exchange (in which he discovered that base purposes invariably frustrated anticipated fruition). Human capability and the choice of lord have much to do with the realization of one's dreams. "My wil is good," the Squire informs us, "and lo, my tale is this" (8). The tale, however, is a disaster for a couple of reasons: incapacity on the part of the Squire, and unwise submission to the Host. What we discover in this tale is that subjugation to Harry breeds artistic as well as social and moral disorder. It leads to a squandering of time which the Squire seems so ironically intent on avoiding and so helpless to prevent:

> I wol nat taryen yow, for it is pryme,
> And for it is no fruyt, but los of tyme;
> Unto my firste I wole have my recours.
>
> (73-75)

Precious small fruit, this. If the falcon's experience demonstrated the danger of unwise submission inside the tale ("my wyl was his willes instrument;/That is to seyn, my wyl obeyed his wyl/In alle thyng," she tells us in lines 568-70), then the Squire's experience demonstrates the disaster of unwise submission in the fiction of the pilgrimage. Once again the realities of tale and pilgrimage merge to demonstrate Chaucer's point: it is not enough to subject one's self and one's will to another, even with the most innocent of motives, if one is careless about a master.50

Inasmuch as the failure of the Squire is an artistic failure rather than a social or metaphysical failure, the tale has particular importance to Chaucer the poet. Unwise submission may produce social dislocations (as it has); it may produce a distorted world view (as it has). In either case the artist's *art* remains untouched. But if unwise submission produces defective art—defective not in the sense that it fails to fulfil the artist's bad intention, but in that it proves ineffective in bringing to fruition his best intentions—then Chaucer as an artist is in trouble. The wonders brought from Arabia and India are in one sense like Chaucer's art; both, in their own way, are marvelous. The brass horse and Chaucer's pilgrimage will, in point of fact, take the rider or author anywhere he wishes to go within the space of one day natural. Like the mirror, Chaucer's art enables him to see where he is not, to examine a possibility without actually committing himself to it (and thereby foresee whether or not he may fall into any adversity). Like the ring, Chaucer's art enables him to converse freely with birds (the *Parliament of Fowles*, the *Nun's Priest's Tale*, the *Manciple's Tale*), and—most significantly—to understand persons outside of himself. Like the naked sword, Chaucer's art can cut and it can heal. This is remarkable power, not to be used by the wrong sort of will committed, however purely, to the wrong sort of authority.

Through these symbols and the Squire's comments on them (and the people's reactions to them), Chaucer is able to comment upon the function and possibilities of art, and see for himself the potentiality inherent in his own role as artist. He may explore the furthest reaches of metaphysical speculation, examine positions other than those he might wish to adopt himself, dissect and then rebuild society. And his construct takes him were he alone choses to go: against the will of the owner, the horse of brass cannot be moved by other people. "And cause why? for they kan nat the craft." The reaction of common folk to this art is amazement and suspicion; they wonder, Chaucer tells us, as do people when they speculate about thunder, the tide, mist. And the common folk do not understand art any more than they trust it. But their experience, as demonstrated in the music and dance (emblematic of festive harmony and order) which follow the arrival of these gifts, suggests that art works its magic even on them, much as Stevens' wilderness found itself reordered by the alien jar atop that hill in Tennessee.

It is at this point that teller meets tale and poet, that Chaucer's Squire intrudes upon what he has been saying about art. For as much as the Squire is indeed the teller of this tale, he is nevertheless distrustful of art, inexperienced as an artist, inadequate to making the brass steed move. "Ye gete namoore of me," he informs us (343) after several pleas of artistic inadequacy which—unfortunately for his tale in the fictive reality of the pilgrimage—are not the standard medieval modesty formulae. But Chaucer is not his Squire, and what Chaucer has suggested to us in this bit of speculation is that we watch him make his own brass steed run, that we be aware of the potential adversity and treason he's busy examining in the mirror of art, that we recognize the fact that it is fiction which has cut in this pilgrimage and that fiction may heal—beginning with the resolution of the marriage disorder in the *Franklin's Tale*.

Insofar as it comments on will, the *Squire's Tale* is not entirely out of place here between the Shipman and the Franklin, but insofar as it moves on to comment on art and the role of art, it might better have awaited the completion of the marriage discussion and, perhaps, some social developments which take place during the *Pardoner's Tale*. It would appear to fit more into the discussion of fragment VII, which focuses more on the aims and methods of art, than into this discussion of order. Perhaps Chaucer found the matter of intentional subjugation of the will to be as much related to marriage as a metaphor as it is related to art;

I think the two strands will ultimately merge: as the submission of woman is figural of man's submission to a benevolent deity, so the artist as Christian ultimately must submit his will to a benevolent God. The full fruition of this line of development, however, will not come until the *Parson's Tale*, indeed until after the *Parson's Tale*, and there is no hint of it in the Squire's discursive romance.

THE FRANKLIN'S TALE

When Kittredge proposed his marriage group some sixty years ago, he viewed the *Franklin's Tale* as the culmination of the pilgrims' debate, a subsumption of the chivalric code into the marital relationship which produced harmony:

> The soundness of the Franklin's theory, he [the Franklin] declares, is proved by his tale. For the marriage of Averagus and Dorigen was a brilliant success...Thus the whole debate has been brought to a satisfactory conclusion, and the Marriage Act of the Human Comedy ends with the conclusion of the *Franklin's Tale*.51

Subsequent critical statements have revised the constituency of the so-called marriage group or denied it altogether,52 developed the tale as a characterization of its teller,53 or examined at length the Franklin's concept of *gentilesse*.54 Amid all this, Kittredge's view of the tale as culmination of a conscious debate on marriage, combining the best elements of courtly behavior and Christian doctrine, has remained—until recently—surprisingly durable.55 Probably Kittredge is correct in his assertion that the tale marks an end of explicit examination of marriage-as-metaphor, for although the subject of marriage comes up again in later tales (the Nun's Priest's for example), and although marriage functions elsewhere as a metaphor for social and metaphysical order (indeed, this use ranges from the *Knight's Tale* at one end of the *Tales* to the *Parson's Tale* at the other56), the focus of later tales shifts to other subjects. And again, there can be little doubt that at the conclusion of the *Franklin's Tale* harmony and charity prevail, both in the marriage itself and, radiating outward in every direction from the marriage, in the social, metaphysical, even the commercial spheres as well.

But the harmonies which mark marriage, nature, society at tale's end have not been present from its inception; those harmonies have been restored in the process of the Franklin's narrative. In fact, there is a point in which everything in this tale is quite out of joint: the marriage seems to be (pardon the pun) on the rocks as Averagus leaves his bride "two yeer" to "seke in armes worshippe and honour"; the bride, caught in idle jest and unthinking promises, is searching for the courage to kill herself; squire Aurelius vibrates between despair and joy; the rocks which form part of God's providential plan are tampered with by a clerk using "magic natural" in response to a hot young lover's prayers not to a Christian god, but to pagan deities. Kittredge and his followers would have it that the restoration of harmony which follows this discord is Chaucer's (or the Franklin's) vindication of the relationship established at the tale's beginning between Averagus and Dorigen in that mutual reunuciation of sovereignty and will: despite the assorted visicitudes of absence, carelessness, deception, and even black magic, true love and *gentilesse* come shining through. "The contact of mutual fidelity, put to a test by a tempter, is finally vindicated through the agency of a liberating love extending out of a domestic situation into other spheres of the social world."57 This is not quite what happens in the tale, however, for it is precisely the relationship delineated in the tale's opening lines which precipitates this near tragedy. That relationship changes considerably before the situation resolves itself and tragedy turns to comedy.

In his remarks interrupting (or following, as your preference may be) the unfinished *Squire's Tale*, the Franklin evidences both a concern for *gentilesse* and a willingness to submit himself to the rule of the Host:

> "In feith, Squier, thow hast the wel yquit
> And gentilly. I preise wel thy wit,"
> Quod the Frankeleyn, "considerynge thy yowthe,
> So feelyngly thou spekest, sire, I allow the!
>   (673-76)

We may assume from remarks like these either that the Franklin is pretentious, stupid, and unfit for his business,58 or that he is being kind. Certainly he attributes to the Squire a sophistication patently absent from his tale, and if he is serious, he is very misguided. He must also appear naive and misguided in his submission to Harry Bailey:

> "Gladly, sire Hoost," quod he, "I wole obeye
> Unto your wyl; now herkneth what I seye.
> I wol yow nat contrarien in no wyse
> As fer as that my wittes wol suffyse.
> I prey to God that it may plesen yow;
> Thanne woot I wel that it is good ynow."
>   (703-8)

The *Squire's Tale* has clearly demonstrated the misfortune attendant on such an easy submission to governors of the Host's ilk; other tales and Harry's reaction to them have made it manifestly clear that to please Harry is not necessarily to tell "good ynow." The Franklin's easy subjugation to Harry and his promise to please him in a tale invite disaster. If he is serious.

Which, I am convinced, he is not. Just as the compliment on the Squire's gentility and character was meant to sooth a bruised ego and smooth over a potentially embarrassing situation (and I am not above suspecting the Franklin invented all that business about his son just to bolster the poor Squire's ego), so the obsequious submission to the Host's desires is meant as nothing more than the sort of politeness which comprises a substantial part of true *gentilesse*. It is a nominal submission, just as the Franklin's purported ignorance of rhetoric is nominal only, just as the lordship of Averagus is, in his tale's initial phases, a nominal lordship, "the name of soveraynetee." With considerable tact, the Franklin sees the pilgrims through a difficult situation, and everyone saves face. We will see the Knight working in a similar manner shortly; we will see the pilgrims working in harmonious consort before the pilgrimage is out. It is a mark of the pilgrimage's progress, both social and metaphysical, that potentially acrimonious situation is so easily resolved. And it is a mark of the Franklin's own charitable self-effacement that he is the agent of this social harmony. His action here in the link between Squire's and Franklin's tales is a measure of the metaphysics of his tale, and a good indication that he knows what he's talking about: harmony is the result of charitable behavior.

The Franklin's self effacement, however, is deceptive: behind the appearance is a man in full control of himself and ready to assert *gentilesse* with all the powers of rhetoric while agreeing to forget the subject and disclaiming verbal proficiency. He is a marked contrast to say, the Wife of Bath and the Host himself, both of whom demand dominance and appear to exert strong control over themselves and others, both of whom can control neither themselves nor others. And the Franklin is a marked contrast to the Squire, who has neither the appearance nor the reality of control. The tale shows us the necessity for control by one whose lordship appears only nominal (indeed, I would argue, *is* nominal as the tale opens; the Franklin shows us just how such an one operates in the "real world" of the pilgrimage.

The tale proper opens with a description of the marital relationship established between Averagus and Dorigen and an assertion of the harmony which grew from it:

Ther was a knyght that loved and dide his payne
To serve a lady in his beste wise;
And many a labour, many a greet emprise
He for his lady wroghte, er she were wonne,
For she was oon the faireste under sonne,
And eek therto comen of so heigh kynrede
That wel unnethes dorste this knyght, for drede,
Telle hire his wo, his peyne, and his distresse.
But atte laste she, for his worthynesse,
And namely for his meke obeysaunce,
Hath swich a pitee caught of his penaunce
That preyvely she fil of his accord
To take hym for hir housbonde and hir lord,
Of swich lordshipe as men han over hir wyves.
And for to lede the moore in blisse hir lyves,
Of his free wyl he swoor hire as a knyght
That nevere in al his lyf he, day ne nyght,
Ne sholde upon hym take no maistrie
Agayn hir wyl, ne kithe hire jalousie,
But hire obeye, and folwe hir wyl in al,
As any lovere to his lady shal,
Save that the name of soveraynetee,
That wolde he have for shame of his degree.
                                                    (730-52)

Several elements in this relationship are significant, not the least
of which is what amounts to the complete submission of Averagus
to the will of Dorigen. His pain is to serve her, both before and
after their marriage—in fact, all his great labors and mighty
enterprises are wrought with but one end in mind: to please
Dorigen. He swears of his free will to take no mastery against her
will, he promises to obey her and follow her will in all things "as
any lovere to his lady shal." In fact, it is this "meke obeysaunce"
that Dorigen finds most attractive in Averagus, that causes her
finally to take him for her lord, or such lordship as men have over
their wives—which proves in this case to be precious little indeed.
The retention of the name of sovereignty by Averagus is but a sop
which will not conceal the very real sell out on Averagus' part.
Chaucer underlines the circumstances to which Averagus reduces
himself in that final line: "for shame of his degree." In short,
Averagus is dominated, as hen-pecked in his way as Chauntecleer
or Harry Bailey or the Wife's husbands. Dorigen's promise to be
his "humble trewe wyf" is small recompense indeed: he has the
name of sovereign and the roll of vassal, she the nominal
submission and the actual authority. His promise is "suffraunce"
(788); hers is "That nevere sholde ther be defaute in here" (790).
The one suffers; the other is merely "not defective." In fact there
is little of the reciprocity described by the Franklin later in his

introduction:

> For o thyng, sires, saufly dar I seye,
> That freendes everych other moot obeye,
> If they wol longe holden compaignye.
> Love wol nat been constreyned by maistrye.
>
> (761-64)

Such reciprocal obedience would amount in effect to mutual independence, a fact the Franklin himself implies within ten lines of his ironic comment about "friends" obeying each other:

> Wommen, of kynde, desiren libertee,
> And nat to been constreyned as a thral;
> And so doon men, if I sooth seyen shal.
>
> (768-70)

This may look good enough on paper, but such mutual independence has nothing much to do with marriage. The position is self-contradictory: men and women both desire liberty, but he who has most patience, gives in most easily, and suffers the most will prove most successful in love. Liberty and suffering are mutually exclusive, as are both halves of the arrangement described in lines 791-93:

> Heere may men seem an humble, wys accord;
> Thus hath she take hir servant and hir lord,—
> Servant in love, and lord in marriage.

Marriage does not work this way; neither does true *gentilesse*. Chaucer has wrestled with the problem before in his artistic career,59 and found a strictly courtly definition of *gentilesse* incompatible with the natural state of things. To Chaucer, true *gentilesse* is, in Sledd's words, "a complex of interdependent virtues, which are the same virtues, though they may appear in different relationships, and which, for Christians, are anchored in the nature of God and His creation."60 Or, as Lindsay Mann has put it more recently, "true nobility, opposed to false, bodily, inherited nobility, is identical with moral virute."61 This virtue, this *gentilesse*, makes its first appearance in the *Canterbury Tales* in the *Franklin's Tale*; it will reappear in the *Parson's Tale*:

> Now been ther generale signes of gentillesse, as
> eschewynge of vice and ribaudye and servage of
> synne, in word, in werk, and contenaunce;/and
> usynge vertu, curteisye, and clennesse, and to be
> liberal, that is to seyn, large by mesure; for thilke
> that passeth mesure is folie and synne./Another is
> to remembre hym of bountee, that he of oother folk

> hath receyved./Another is to be benigne to his
> goode subgetis; wherefore seith Senek, "Ther is
> no thing moore convenable to a man of heigh
> estaat than debonairetee and pitee.../Another is,
> a man to have a noble herte and a diligent, to
> attayne to heighe virtuous thynges.
>
> (464-69)

This is the *Gentilesse* of the action of the *Franklin's Tale*, but not necessarily of the relationship between Averagus and Dorigen as the tale begins.

That initial relationship, the Franklin shows us almost immediately, is built on sand, and thus vulnerable to the first waves that splash upon it. Not a hundred lines after the "prosperity" and "blisse and solas" of this union are described, Averagus has left his bride for the shores of Britain, leaving her ennervated and helpless in her desire for him. Averagus, no doubt, is off to work more of those many labors and great undertakings which endear him to Dorigen; she would prefer her cake (the great undertakings) and eating it as well (keeping Averagus home). Dorigen fails to realize that "al his [Averagus'] lust he sette in swich labour" (812) primarily because it pleases her, and that she herself is thereby the cause of her own distress. Instead, she laments her plight self-pityingly:

> Desir of his presence hire so destreyneth
> That al this wyde world she sette at noght.
> Hire freendes, which that knewe hir hevy thoght,
> Conforten hire in al that ever they may.
> They prechen hire, they telle hire nyght and day
> That causelees she sleeth hirself, allas!
>
> (820-25)

This provides, incidentally, an interesting and ironic foreshadowing of this tale's near disaster! In any event, Averagus is gone, and frail Dorigen is left to her own devices. She proves inadequate indeed, unworthy of Averagus' complete submission, and unable to fulfill her promise never to be found at fault. At first, as we have noted, she is ennervated entirely; she needs him more than he needs her, as the saying goes, although she would not admit the fact. Like the Wife of Bath, who thinks she loved most those she easily dominated but in reality loved most the man who boxed her ears, Dorigen is pleased with a man obedient to her every whim, although in reality she needs somebody to lean on. The woman is, as others have pointed out, confused about the real and the illusory.

In no place is her confusion more apparent than in her complaint against God and His Providence for creating those "grisly feendly rokkes blake" which seem to her a foul confusion of work:

> "Eterne God, that thurgh thy purveiaunce
> Ledest the world by certein governaunce
> In ydel, as men seyn, ye no thyng make.
> But, Lord, thise grisly feendly rokkes blake,
> That semen rather a foul confusion
> Of werk than any fair creacion
> Of swich a parfit wys God and a stable,
> Why han ye wroght this werk unresonable?
> For by this werk, south, north, ne west, ne eest,
> Ther nys yfostred man, ne bryd, ne beest;
> It dooth no good, to my wit, but anoyeth.
> Se ye nat, Lord, how mankynde it destroyeth?
> An hundred thousand bodyes of mankynde
> Han rokkes slayn, al be they nat in mynde,
> Which mankynde is so fair part of thy werk
> That thou madest lyk to thyn owene merk.
> Thanne semed it ye hadde a greet chiertee
> Toward mankynde; but how thanne may it bee
> That ye swiche meenes make it to destroyen,
> Which meenes do no good, but evere anoyen?
> (865-84)

These lines must constitute a puzzling digression unless we view Dorigen's character as seriously flawed and the tale itself as dealing with true and false perceptions of order and hierarchy. Charles A. Owen, Jr. reads them as "a sign of weakness, of unwillingness to accept the real world";62 Gerhard Joseph reads them as "a brief, but nevertheless dramatically crucial, metaphysical revolt";63 Edwin Benjamin sees them as the sign of pride.64 All of this the complaint is. It denies God's Providence, His wisdom, even His goodness. It asserts Dorigen's view of things in the face of divine wisdom, and suggests a usurpation of divine prerogatives as Dorigen would like to assume the role of Creator and rearrange reality to suit her, just as she has rearranged marital hierarchies into what she, no doubt, finds a very comfortable arrangement. The blindness of Dorigen's position will be found ultimately in the outcome of her little adventure "on her own," and in line 1354, where Fortune, not herself, is blamed for the disaster which threatens to engulf her.

Immediately after her denial of God's Providence, Dorigen wanders into one of those gardens so common to medieval literature, the significances of which have been described before by D. W. Robertson, Jr.65 Aurelius, lusty servant to Venus, requests "her company"; she is shocked:

> But now, Aurelie, I knowe youre entente,
> By thilke God that yaf me soule and lyf,
> Ne shal I nevere been untrewe wyf
> In word ne werk, as fer as I have wit;
> I wol been his to whom that I am knyt.
>
> (982-86)

The key line here, of course, is "as fer as I have wit." Frail Dorigen: no sooner does she give Aurelius this "fynal answere" than she turns around and qualifies it: she will be his when all the rocks are gone from the coast. "Thanne wol I love yow best of any man,/Have heer my trouthe," she promises. Now obviously this promise is a direct outgrowth of Dorigen's mistrust of God's Providence evidenced in her complaint about those rocks; just as obviously it proves an unintentional invitation to disaster. Aurelius, after some hesitation and a prayer to Apollo and Diana, is off to Orleans to enlist the aid of a dabbler in "magyk natureel" who will make the rocks appear to disappear. The pagan gods and magic, given opportunity by Dorigen's assertion of her own will and denial of God's primacy and beneficence as Creator, prove effective...for a while at least. They would probably not work nowadays, the Franklin informs us, because "hooly chirches feith in oure bileve/Ne suffreth noon illusioun us to greve" (1133, 34). An interesting comment: apparently the efficacy of illusion depends on a denial of faith and the erection of disbelief (and human will) in its place. But the deed is done, and Aurelius rushes off to inform Dorigen. Again she is shocked:

> In al hir face nas a drope of blood.
> She wende nevere han come in swich a trappe.
> "Allas," quod she, "that evere this sholde happe!
> For wende I nevere by possibilitee
> That swich a monstre or merveille myghte be!
> It is agayns the proces of nature."
> And hoom she goth a sorweful creature.
>
> (1340-46)

That Dorigen should *wish* reality altered seems natural enough to her; that she should assert herself over husband and God seems natural enough; that nature should in fact change, that she should be caught in her games—this is against the process of nature.

Dorigen's response to these developments is suicide—or an attempt at suicide, since her will proves insufficient even to this. In a rather long recitation of sundry exempla culled from—of all places—Jankyn's book of wicked wives,66 Dorigen reviews precedents for suicide, places the blame squarely on Fortune, and settles on a solution not sanctioned by the Christian Church:

"Allas," quod she, "on thee, Fortune, I pleyne,
That unwar wrapped hast me in thy cheyne,
Fro which t'escape wool I no socour,
Save oonly deeth or elles dishonour;
Oon of thise two bihoveth me to chese.
But nathelees, yet have I levere to lese
My life than of my body to have a shame,
Or knowe myselven fals, or lese my name;
And with my deth I may be quit, ywis."

(1355-63)

This list is, significantly, primarily pagan, as if to point up the metaphysics of Dorigen's position. And it is disorganized, a reflection of her own general disorganization and confusion.67 And it is, finally, a company which Dorigen will never join: she complains a day or so without mustering the courage to act, and on the third night Avergus is home.

With the arrival of Averagus, the Franklin's plot begins to mend, not because he assumes the role he and his lady had settled on previously, but because he asserts both the name and the power of authority in a manner which directly violates their earliest agreement. It is difficult to agree with Sledd that Averagus does not assert mastery;68 rather, we are more tempted to agree with the assessment of Alan T. Gaylord:

> In making the grand moment of the Tale the impassioned statement of principle issuing from Averagus' mouth, the Franklin has forgotten that in allowing him to play such a role he is, in effect, making him break his first marriage promise, in spirit if not in letter. In the crisis of the Tale Averagus plays a most lordly role. He has all the answers, and all the commands, and the "soveraynetee" that he exercises is considerably more than just in name.69

Whether we agree with Gaylord's assessment of the Franklin's awareness or not, we must recognize that the marital harmony of this tale is reestablished on a basis quite different from that presented at the tale's outset.70 Averagus' will, even his arrogance put him in the position of Walter in the *Clerk's Tale*, a fact Chaucer (and the Franklin?) recognizes, as evidenced by an appeal, similar to that made in the *Clerk's Tale*, that the reader not judge Averagus too harshly or too hastily:

> Paraventure an heep of yow, ywis,
> Wol holden hym a lewed man in this
> That he wol putte his wyf in jupartie.

> Herkneth the tale er ye upon hire crie.
> She may have bettre fortune than yow semeth:
> And whan that ye han herd the tale, demeth.
>
> (1493-98)

Averagus lays down the law: Dorigen shall hold her truth, and her husband charges further, with a most uncourtly threat, "I yow forbede, up peyne of deeth,/That nevere, whil thee lasteth lyf ne breeth,/To no wight telle thou of this aventure" (1481-83). With this assertion of male dominance, the marriage and surrounding social relationships evidence a marked return to health. Aurelius releases Dorigen from her oath; the clerk of Orleans releases Aurelius of his debt.

> Averagus and Dorigen his wyf
> In sovereyn blisse leden forth hir lyf.
> Nevere eft ne was ther angre hem bitwene.
> He cherisseth hire as though she were a queene,
> And she was to hym trewe for everemoore.
>
> (1551-55)

The tale is at an end.

The *Franklin's Tale* has been an assertion of harmony in marriage, and thus in the social and metaphysical realms for which marriage functions as a metaphor; the harmonies of this tale's conclusion are not, however, predicated on the specious terms described by the Franklin at his beginning. They derive from a dominance of man over woman, however gentle and however underplayed, a dominance which is in accord with nature and God, a dominance similar to that of the *Clerk's Tale*. The difference—and it is an important difference—between the Franklin's position and the Clerk's is this: while the Clerk was, until his *envoy*, content to ignore the literal leg of his metaphor, and whereas the Merchant argued the incompatibility of physical and metaphysical legs, the Franklin asserts the harmony of tenor and vehicle. In living a harmonious, ordered, natural life man does indeed subject his will to God's, accept for truth a reality he cannot always comprehend, act out of charitable *gentilesse* which is a Christian as well as a chivalric viture; in living a harmonious, ordered, natural marital life, the woman does subject her will to her husband's. The Clerk ignored human problems; the Merchant argues that in most marriages each partner asserts his own will; the Franklin demonstrates that a harmonious marriage must figure celestial hierarchies. This is not the way a modern mind would have wished Chaucer's discussion of marriage to end, but it is a typically medieval attitude and philosophically crucial to

Chaucer's and the pilgrims' developing metaphysics. In the *Franklin's Tale* poet and pilgrims arrive at an affirmation of Divine Providence, an affirmation of God's good order. Moreover, the Franklin asserts, this **Providence** operates in everyday life quite unspectacularly; to assume, as did the Man of Law, that Providence works only in wonders and miracles is nearly as wide of the mark as to assume it never touches mortal man at all. The resolution of the marriage-as-metaphor issue amounts to an affirmation of divine order operative in the day-to-day affairs of man. The tale is thus pivotal in the pilgrimages of the Canterbury company, of the pilgrim poet, and of artist Chaucer. Having affirmed the existence of a benevolent Providence *and* its impingement upon the affairs of men, Chaucer is free to deal at further lengths with two other questions which naturally arise from such a metaphysical position, questions he has broached earlier but never resolved entirely: what does a man do to attune himself to this cosmic order, and what is the artist's role in a cosmos so governed?

FOOTNOTES TO CHAPTER III

1 *A Reading of the Canterbury Tales,* p. 107: "If there is much that outraged the Miller in the *Knight's Tale,* there is even more in the *Man of Law's Tale* to outrage the wife. . . She must expose such foolishness, and she doesn't need authorities like Innocent III to support her understanding."

2 See especially the work of D. W. Robertson, Jr. in *A Preface to Chaucer,* pp. 317-22.

3 The cataloguing of such readings seems almost an exercise in pedantry. See especially Norman Holland, "Meaning as Transformation: *The Wife of Bath's Tale,*" *College English,* 28 (1966), 279-90; Theodore Silverstein, "The Wife of Bath and the Rhetoric of Enchantment; or, How to Make a Hero See In the Dark," *Modern Philology,* 58 (1961), 153-73; and Aaron Steinberg, "*The Wife of Bath's Tale* and Her Fantasy of Fulfillment," *College English,* 26 (1964), 187-91.

4 Paul Ruggiers (*The Art of the Canterbury Tales*) has this to say: "The beliefs that the generative process is sacred, that chastity may be offensive to God, that the organs of generation may be honestly defended even at the risk of being offensive to fastitious audiences, have the respectable authority of writers of the School of Chartres to support them. . . To put it another way, as one aspect of the rationale which seeks through the amatory instincts the clue to the higher love of God [the point of view may be familiar to moderns]" (p. 199). Trevor Whittock is also impressed by the Wife and affirms the validity of her position: "Hers is a rejection of transcendental religion. She is, to refer to a Yeats poem again, the self as opposed to the soul." *A Reading of the Canterbury Tales* (Cambridge: the University Press, 1968), p. 123.

5 The Wife and the narrators of fabliaux are closely related. In her prologue, for example, Alisoun echoes verbally the *Miller's Prologue:* "By this proverbe thou shalt understone,/Have thou ynogh, what that thee recche or care/How myrily that othere folkes fare?" (328-30). Moreover, while the Miller frets about what wives *might* do and shows what clerks are busy doing, the Wife reveals what wives actually do in demonstrating from experience the contrivance of women against both husbands and clerks. Both the Wife and the Reeve, on the other hand, reminisce on the pleasures of green youth while revealing that, despite their age, they have lost little desire. All three pilgrims, I suspect, come off as physical and spiritual

grotesques.

6 Especially useful on this point is Daniel S. Silvia, Jr., "Glosses to the *Canterbury Tales* from St. Jerome's *Epistola Adversus Jovinianum,*" *Studies in Philology,* 42 (1965), 28-39.

7 "*The Wife of Bath's Tale* and Mediaeval Exempla," *English Literary History,* 32 (1965), 442.

8 p. 445.

9 D. W. Robertson, Jr., *A Preface to Chaucer,* p. 323. The majority of Robertson's fifteen-page discussion of the Wife's prologue is devoted to demonstrating Alison's misuse of authority and the way in which those very authorities she cites, when fully understood, ironically undercut the position she uses them to support.

10 The passage is mentioned by Jerome in *Adversus Jovinianum,* where he asserts that it is better to marry and eat barley bread than to be a fornicator and *stercus bubulum,* but it is better yet to be a virgin and eat wheat bread. See *Patrologia Latinum* 23, col. 229 and Robertson, p. 328.

11 See F. M. Salter, "The Tragic Figure of the Wyf of Bath," *Transactions of the Royal Society of Canada,* 48 (1954), 1-13. Whittock finds her comic, Ruggiers finds her pathetic; both agree that what she really wants is to be accepted, in the old cliché, for what she really is.

12 See Robert Pratt, "Jankyn's Book of Wikked Wyves: Medieval Anti-Matrimonial Propaganda in the Universities," *Annuale Medievale,* 3 (1962), 5-27.

13 Jerome writes, quoting a book *On Marriage,* worth its weight in gold which passes under the name of Theofrastus, "A wise man therefore must not take a wife. For in the first place his study of philosophy will be hindered, and it is impossible for anyone to attend to his books and his wife." "Against Jovinianus, book I" in Phillip Schaff and Henry Wace, eds., *A Select Library of Nicene and Post Nicene Fathers,* VI (Grand Rapids, Michigan: Wm. B. Eerdmans Publishing Company, 1961 p. 383).

14 As Huppé observes (p. 108), "The Wife of Bath confronts dogmatic truth and, with her dangerous little learning, denies it. The vigor of her apology and argument is in direct ratio to their fallacy. Her self-defense is inadvertent confession."

15 *A Preface to Chaucer,* p. 321.

16 Vance Ramsey, "Modes of Irony in the *Canterbury Tales*" in *Companion to Chaucer Studies,* ed. Beryl Rowland (New York: Oxford, 1968), pp. 291-312.

17 The list of commentators on irony in these two tales is long

indeed: John F. Adams, "The Structure of Irony in *The Summoner's Tale*," *Essays in Criticism*, 12 (1962), 126-32; Paul E. Beichner, "Baiting the Summoner," *Modern Language Quarterly*, 22 (1961), 367-76; Earle Birney, " 'After His Ymage'—The Central Ironies of the *Friar's Tale*," *Medieval Studies*, 21 (1959), 17-35, and "Structural Irony Within the *Summoner's Tale*," *Anglia*, 78 (1960), 204-18; Adrien Bonjour, "Aspects of Chaucer's Irony in *The Friar's Tale*," *Essays in Criticism*, 11 (1961), 121-27; Paul Ruggiers, *The Art of the Canterbury Tales*, pp. 90-108.

18 "Exemplary Figures as Characterizing Devices in the *Friar's Tale* and the *Summoner's Tale*," *University of Mississippi Studies in English*, 3 (1962), 37.

19 " 'Entente' in Chaucer's *Friar's Tale*," *Chaucer Review*, 2 (1968), 171.

20 A. C. Cawley, "Chaucer's Summoner, the Friar's Summoner, and the *Friar's Tale*," *Proceedings of the Leeds Philosophical and Literary Society*, 8 (1957), 176.

21 Thomas F. Merrill, "Wrath and Rhetoric in *The Summoner's Tale*," *Texas Studies in Literature and Language*, 4 (1962), 342.

22 Baker, "Exemplary Figures as Characterizing Devices," 39.

23 One such reader was Theodore Roosevelt, who registered his opinion in a letter to Thomas Lounsbury: "But having just reread Chaucer in consequence of your book, I must protest a little against some of his tales, on the score of cleanliness. It seems to me that the prologue to the Sompnour's tale, and the tale itself, for instance, are very nearly indefensible...I don't think they have a redeeming feature." *Letters of Theodore Roosevelt*, ed. E.E. Morison (Cambridge, Mass., 1951), 275-76.

24 "Chaucer's Sommoner, the Friar's Summoner, and the *Friar's Tale*," 174.

25 By "artistic nadir" I do not wish to imply that these tales reflect less talent or work on Chaucer's part; they do not. I mean merely that within the confines of Chaucer's frame, art is being perverted to very base use.

26 Kock, ten Brink and Mather regard the tale as dating to the period of the *Canterbury Tales*, while Pollard and Skeat date it to immediately after Chaucer's first Italian journey. Tatlock equivocates, but dates it ":after 1387." See *The Development and Chronology of Chaucer's Works*, pp. 156-64.

27 Cf. Donald C. Baker, "Chaucer's Clerk and the Wife of Bath on

the Subject of *Gentilesse*," PMLA, 67 (1952), 631-40.

28 See Bernard Huppé, *A Reading of the Canterbury Tales*, p. 145.

29 On the matter of obedience, see Donald H. Reiman, "The Real *Clerk's Tale*; or Patient Griselda Exposed," *Texas Studies in Literature and Language*, 5 (1963), 359. He and I agree on this minor point, although I could hardly agree with him or J. Mitchell ("The Philosophy of the Clerk of Oxford," *Modern Language Quarterly*, 19, 3-20) in their contention that the tale is satirical.

30 See Reiman (above) and, of course, James Sledd, "The *Clerk's Tale*: The Monsters and the Critics," *Modern Philology*, 51 (1953), 73-82. And see Baker (above), "It [the *Clerk's Tale*] is not, of course, one of the great poems of the *Canterbury Tales*, and no amount of closer reading will make it so." Delightfully honest!

31 Cf. Paul Ruggiers, *The Art of the Canterbury Tales*, p. 219: "The level of meaning towards which we are irresistably impelled is the highest level of allegorical interpretation."

32 As two different critics thinking independently have come to realize, we are not expected to condemn Abraham for being careless of Isaac's life. See Trevor Whittock, *A Reading of the Canterbury Tales*, p. 145, and Charles Muscatine, *Chaucer and the French Tradition*, p. 193.

33 In "The Concept of Order in Chaucer's *Clerk's Tale*," *Journal of English and Germanic Philology*, 56 (1957), S. K. Heninger Jr. argues that what is most important in the *Clerk's Tale* is "the repeated allusions to the scholastic concept of a divinely-ordained universal order. A comparison of the tale with its sources reveals that the most overt statements of order are additions by Chaucer, a fact which gives these allusions added significance" (p. 382). Later Heninger states, "the Clerk's purpose in telling the tale (naturally a religious purpose) is to illustrate the beneficial results of upholding the natural order in all phases of human experience, of which marriage is only the example under present discussion." (p. 383).

34 On realism in the tale, see Whittock ("The successful interplay of parable and 'realism' in the *Tale* can above all be seen in the character of Griselda" [p. 150]) and Patrick Morrow, "The Ambivalence of Truth in Chaucer's 'Clerk's Tale'," *Bucknell Review*, 34 (1974): "Underneath the surface of a standard ideal world where the action is heart-rending, Chaucer inlays a 'real' world. This actual world is juxtaposed against the ideal world in order to create value conflicts" (p. 74), and again, "Thus the

Clerk forces us to read his tale on two levels—the real and the ideal—and than makes each continually undercut the other" (p. 83). Bernard Huppé reads this realism as irony (*A Reading of the Canterbury Tales*, p. 138).

35 Donald Reiman, "The Real Clerk's Tale," 363.

36 It might, of course, be argued that the tale has had some effect, to judge from the Host's reaction: "By Goddes bones,/Me were levere than a barel ale/My wyf at hoom had herd this legende ones!/This is a gentil tale for the nones..." (1213a-16a). But in this reaction Harry takes the literal, not the allegorical meaning, misses the Clerk's point about submission and will, and goes on to find the performance in perfect accord with his own purpose, his own will.

37 "The Ambivalence of Truth," 90.

38 The seven-line stanza which may separate Clerk's statement from Merchant's echoing is preserved in only a minority of manuscripts, and is printed by Robinson as "probably part of a cancelled link" (892). It may just as well have followed line 1162 or 1169 as 1212, which would have brought Clerk's statement and Merchant's echo into immediate proximity. This borrowing in the *Merchant's Prologue* of the last line of the Clerk's envoy is, incidentally, very strong evidence for a Clerk-Merchant order of the tales, although one group of manuscripts places it between the tales of Squire and Wife of Bath. See Albert C. Baugh, "The Original Teller of the Merchant's Tale," *Modern Philology*, 35 (1937-38), 15.

39 Opinion here is very nearly unanimous. "The perfect expresion of the Merchant's angry disgust at his own evil fate," wrote Kittredge, who went on to speak of the tale's "savagery of the whole, which has revolted so many readers." This in "Chaucer's Discussion of Marriage," *Modern Philology*, 9 (1912), 435-67. Tatlock spoke of its unrelieved acidity and found it without a trace of Chaucer's usual warm-hearted tolerance and genial humor, in "Chaucer's *Merchant's Tale*," *Modern Philolgy*, 33 (1936), 367-81. Hugh Holman called it "one of the most savagely obscene, angrily embittered, pessimistic, and unsmiling tales in our language," in "Courtly Love in the Merchant's and Franklin's Tales," *English Literary History*, 18 (1951), 243. "Negation, perversion, are characteristic of the narrative tone," wrote Muscatine in *Chaucer and the French Tradition* (p. 231). A "carefully savage treatment of blindness of heart and the biting commentary upon old age usurping the privileges of the

young'' was Ruggiers' judgment (*The Art of the Canterbury Tales*, p. 108). A couple of minority voices stand out. Bertrand Bronson found in the tale a bit of good-natured humor: ''Afterthoughts on the *Merchant's Tale*,'' *Studies in Philology*, 58 (1961), 583-96. And Trevor Whittock believes ''the effect is clearly comic, and probably intentionally so on the Merchant's part (as well as on Chaucer's). His outburst against his wife is not the outburst of a bitterly disappointed husband, but a piece of humorous rhetoric (amusingly taken seriously by the simple Host) which forms a prelude to his ribald, down-to-earth tale'' (*A Reading of the Canterbury Tales*, p. 153).

40 *A Reading of the Canterbury Tales*, p. 149.

41 ''Irony in the *Merchant's Tale*,'' *Anglia*, 75 (1957), 200.

42 *A Reading of the Canterbury Tales*, pp. 151ff.

53 Relevant to this point are the curious lines 1251 (''As doon thise fooles that been seculeer''), 1322 (''I speke of folk in seculer estaat''), and 1383ff., which sound more like a sermon than anything we might expect from the Merchant. Also significant are the emphasis on marriage as sacrament, and the familiarity with clerks and their writing (''And yet somme clerkes seyn it nys nat so,/Of which he Theofraste is oon of tho'' 1294, 95) which suggest an ecclesiastical narrator. Like a cleric, the Merchant frequently and easily cites authority. The matter was first broached in writing by A. C. Baugh, ''The Original Teller of the Merchant's Tale,'' although both Manly and Robinson speculate on alternate tellers in the notes to their respective editions of the *Canterbury Tales*. Manly favors the Monk, Robinson registers no choice from among the pilgrimage's clergy, and Baugh favors the Friar. Baugh's speculation has been answered, unconvincingly I believe, by John Elliott, Jr., ''The Two Tellers of *The Merchant's Tale*,'' *Tennessee Studies in Literature*, and Germaine Dempster, ''The Original Teller of the *Merchant's Tale*,'' *MP*, 36 (1938-39), 1-8.

44 For example, Paul Ruggier's *The Art of the Canterbury Tales*, Bernard Huppé's *A Reading of the Canterbury Tales*, and D. W. Robertson, Jr.'s *A Preface to Chaucer*. Helen Corsa dismisses the tale in a couple of pages in *Chaucer: Poet of Mirth and Morality*.

45 See Nevill Coghill, *The Poet Chaucer* (Oxford: The University Press, 1961), p. 167; G. E. Hadow, *Chaucer and His Times* (New York: Holt, 1914), p. 80; D. A. Pearsall, ''The Squire as Story-Teller,'' *University of Toronto Quarterly*, 34 (1964), 90; Joyce E. Peterson, ''The Finished Fragment: A Reassessment

of the *Squire's Tale,*" *Chaucer Review,* 5 (1970), 62-74; and Trevor Whittock, *A Reading of the Canterbury Tales,* p. 163.

46 Nothing at all, argue many people. The better part of a century ago, G. L. Kittredge wrote, "nothing has been farther from the thoughts of every reader than that Chaucer meant his Squire's Tale for anything more—or less—than a romance. Nowhere does he seem freer from any hint of a hidden meaning." "Supposed Historical Allusions in the Squire's Tale," *Englische Studien,* 13 (1889), 4. More recently Pearsall has observed, "the 'fruyt' of the *Squire's Tale* turns out to be precious small" (above, p. 86), and Ruggiers has commented, "what we might have had from the *Squire's Tale,* were it finished, we cannot say" (*The Art of the Canterbury Tales,* p. 239). Corsa finds the tale "as close to a first draft as any tale in the Canterbury collection" (*Chaucer: Poet of Mirth and Morality,* p. 166).

47 "Chaucer's Discussion of Marriage," *Modern Philology,* 9 (1912), 435-67.

48 See especially Pearsall and Whittock (above), but note also the objection of Corsa: "But the embarrassed awkwardness with which the tale is told, the absence of a sense of order or form, the moments of dullness, do not fit the young man who 'koude songes make and wel endite./Juste and eek daunce, and weel purtreye and write'." (*Chaucer: Poet of Mirth and Morality,* p. 168.) Joyce Peterson has suggested that the tale is really about story-telling, that the efforts of the Squire at creating a narrative of sustained interest repeatedly recoil against him because of his youthful inexperience and defects of vision, evidenced by a comparison of his "worthiness" with that of his father in the descriptions of the *General Prologue* (see "The Finished Fragment," above).

49 See especially Marie Neville, "The Function of the *Squire's Tale* in the Canterbury Scheme," *Journal of English and Germanic Philology,* 50 (1951) 167-79.

50 Trevor Whittock sees this the *Squire's Tale* as "an indulgence in illusion—the illusions of romance" cherished for its own sake. Part of the Illusion is the Squire's—that he can, in his affectation and youthfulness, manage the tale he attempts; part of the illusion stems from simple infatuation with prettiness and romance. Whittock underplays the importance of volition, emphasizes Chaucerian satire of "art for art's sake." See *A Reading of the Canterbury Tales,* pp. 163-69.

51 "Chaucer's Discussion of Marriage," *Modern Philology,* 9 (1911-12), 66.

52 Kittredge's views were challenged early by H. B. Hinckley, "The Debate on Marriage in the *Canterbury Tales*," *PMLA*, 32 (1917), 292-305, and C. P. Lyons, "The Marriage Debate in the *Canterbury Tales*," *English Literary History*, 2 (1935), 252-62; the group has been extended to cover other tales by John S. Kenyon, "FurtherNoteson the Marriage Group in the *Canterbury Tales*," *Journal of English and Germanic Philology*, 15 (1916), 282-88, by W. W. Lawrence, "The Marriage Group in the *Canterbury Tales*," *Modern Philology*, 11 (1912-13), 247-58, and by Albert Silverman, "Sex and Money in Chaucer's *Shipman's Tale*," *Philological Quarterly*, 32 (1935), 329-36.

53 Particularly important in this respect is R. M. Lumiansky, *Of Sondry Folk* (Austin: University of Texas Press, 1955), pp. 180-93.

54 Most significant here is Lindsay A. Mann, " 'Gentilesse' and the Franklin's Tale," *Studies in Philology*, 63 (1966), 10-29, but see also Charles A. Owen, "Crucial Passages in Five of *The Canterbury Tales:* A Study in Irony and Symbol," *Journal of English and Germanic Philology*, 52 (1953), 294-311.

55 Cf. D. S. Brewer, *Chaucer* (London: Longmans, 1953), pp. 170-72, Neville Coghill, *The Poet Chaucer* (London: Oxford, 1949), pp. 170-72, H.S. Corsa, *Chaucer: Poet of Mirth and Morality* (Notre Dame, Indiana: University of Notre Dame Press, 1964), C. Hugh Holman, "Courtly Love in the Merchant's and the Franklin's Tale," *English Literary History*, 18 (1951), 241-52, and Trevor Whittock, *A Reading of the Canterbury Tales*, 170-84.

56 For a succinct but exceptionally useful survey of marriage-as-metaphor in the *Canterbury Tales*, see Robertson, *A Preface to Chaucer*, pp. 374-77.

57 Paul Ruggiers, *The Art of the Canterbury Tales*, p. 226.

58 R. M. Lumiansky, in "The Character and Performance of Chaucer's Franklin," *University of Toronto Quarterly*, 20 (1951), 344-56, has argued that the Host's rude interruption and the Franklin's meek acceptance of the rebuke reflect an impatience on Harry's part and a Franklin struggling with matters above his social status, and attempting as best he can not to appear presumptuous.

59 *The Parliament of Fowles*, for example, would appear to be an unsuccessful attempt to synthesize courtly values and behavior and "natural love" as personified in lady Nature, the vicar of the Lord. Nature works for the common good (social harmony)

and the all-essential procreation of species; the courtly birds, so intent on gentle games, find themselves unmated at the poem's end. A similar case might be made for *Troilus and Criseyde* as chaucer's attempt to fit the courtly code into a scheme of cosmic love articulated in, for example, the proem to book III. The synthesis never works there either. What Dante managed, Chaucer could not.

60 James D. Sledd, "Dorigen's Complaint," *Modern Philology*, 45, (1947), 40.

61 " 'Gentilesse' and the *Franklin's Tale*," *Studies in Philology*, 63 (1966), 15.

62 "The Crucial Passages in Five of the Canterbury Tales."

63 "The Franklin's Tale: Chaucer's Theodicy," *Chaucer Review* 1 (1966), 23.

64 "The Concept of Order in the *Franklin's Tale*," *Philological Quarterly* 38 (1959), 23.

65 "The Doctrine of Charity in Medieval Literary Gardens," *Speculum*, 26 (1951), 24-49.

66 See Robert A. Pratt, "Saint Jerome in Jankyn's Book of Wikked Wyves," *Annuale Mediaevale*, 3 (1962), 5-27.

67 See Donald C. Baker, "A Crux in Chaucer's *Franklin's Tale:* Dorigen's Complaint," *Journal of English and Germanic Philology*, 60 (1961), 62.

68 "Dorigen's Complaint," 39.

69 "The Promises in 'The Franklin's Tale'," *English Literary History*, 31 (1964) 343-44.

70 See Edwin Benjamin, 119. This view is supported by A. M. Kearney, "Truth and Illusion in *The Franklin's Tale*," *Essays in Criticism*, 19 (1969), 246-53, and to a considerable degree by Gerhard Joseph ("Chaucer's Theodicy"), although Joseph sees the reordering of values as more the natural unfolding of Providence than Averagus' determined reassertion of the dominance without which any marriage must come to grief.

CHAPTER IV

FRAGMENTS VI AND VII: THE MATTER OF ART

There is no link between the *Franklin's Tale* and Fragment VI, nor is there any real link between the Pardoner's and Shipman's tales; Fragment VI floats free in the Canterbury scheme, appearing in the Ellesmere group of manuscripts after the *Franklin's Tale*, in most of the other manuscripts after the *Canon's Yeoman's Tale*, and in the Chaucer Society order after the repositioned *Nun's Priest's Tale*.1 In its artistic astringency it is more reminiscent of the *Legend of Good Women* than the *Canterbury Tales;* in its overt moralizing, in its general strangeness, the *Physician's Tale* has much in common with the *Manciple's Tale* and the *Parson's Prologue*, and it might fit well between the confession of the Canon's Yeoman and the Manciple's strange examplum. On the other hand, the *Pardoner's Tale*, to which the Physician's is connected by Harry's comments in the Pardoner's introduction, is one of the most artistically dense performances in the *Canterbury Tales*, and in its naturalism closer to the art of the first half of the pilgrimage than to that of the second. The *Pardoner's Prologue* and *Tale* argue for placement of fragment VI earlier in the pilgrimage than fragment VIII. On the third hand, the closing lines of the *Pardoner's Tale* evidence a social harmony clearly established by the end of IX but conspicuous in its absence in VII, so a position somewhere after the *Nun's Priest's Tale* might best suit the fragment. Thematically, it seems to me, the fragment should come later than it does in the Ellesmere order, and much later than it would in the Chaucer Society order; I would be most comfortable with a position after VII but before IX, although in the last analysis the two tales of this fragment may be profitably treated right where they stand in the Ellesmere order.2

THE PHYSICIAN'S TALE

In fact, it is not difficult to find connections between the Franklin's and Physician's tales. Dorigen, for example, has considered suicide at great length in the *Franklin's Tale* as a method of preserving her honor:

> "Hath ther nat many a noble wyf er this,
> And many a mayde, yslayn hirself, allas!
> Rather than with hir body doon trespas?"
> (V, 1364-66)

In language that recalls Dorigen's predicament and her solution, the Physician recounts Virginia's conversation with her father:

> "O mercy, deere fader!" quod this mayde,
> And with that word she bothe hir armes layde
> Aboute his nekke, as she was wont to do,
> The teeris bruste out of hir eyen two,
> And seyde, "Goode fader, shal I dye?"
> Is there no grace, is ther no remedye?"
> "No, certes, deere doghter myn," quod he.
> (231-37)

In both tales women find themselves confronted by two ways: either death or shame; in the *Physician's Tale* Virginia, in contrast to Dorigen, takes the road less traveled. It is not fanciful to suppose that Dorigen's decision provoked the response embodied in the Physician's exemplum. Nor is it entirely fanciful to see in the Physician's own avoidance of rhetorical elaboration a reflection of the Franklin's disavowal of "colours of rethoryk." And we might read the Physician's Virginius, "fulfilled of honour and of worthynesse" (2), as his answer to the Franklin's worthy knight, Averagus.

In the final analysis, however, it seems to me that the *Physician's Tale* is a significant departure from the *Franklin's Tale*, indeed, from the style and thematic concern of most of the tales we've seen thus far. Earlier work focused on the problem of order in the Creation, and on the possibilities of knowing that order. Intent and will were ancillary concerns related, when considered, to the larger issue of order. The *Physician's Tale* accepts the order arrived at in the *Franklin's Tale* and moves on to other topics. God's in his heaven and all is right with the world; how does one behave himself, and—more particularly—how does the artist behave himself? The nature and function of art, a minor topic heretofore, becomes the major concern of Chaucer in the reamining tales. With it are considered such adjuncts as will, governance, and an increasingly strong concern for one's soul. Through all this, Chaucer progressively personalizes his pilgrimage, moves through a wide variety of artistic styles and techniques, and finally escapes the world of art entirely. The artist, it might be observed, arrives ultimately at a point not far distant from that of Virginius in this tale: he kills his child to save it. But that is to move ahead of ourselves.

The *Physician's Tale* lacks introduction; it opens with a long, apparently digressive piece on the art lavished by Nature, God's "vicaire general" (20) on Virginia, and admonitions to governors and parents who have such youngsters under their authority. These preliminaries take up fully one third of the tale, although they are a long way from its thematic center which, according to Trevor Whittock, is the unpleasant but self-evident truth that "The innocent shall suffer and the wicked shall be punished."3 I suspect, however, that in this case preliminaries are more important than tale; at the very least they explain an otherwise unpalatable narrative by providing a key to our understanding of the Physician's rigid, Puritan moralism.4 At the most they provide an entirely new focus for the tale by subsuming the matter of suffering and punishment into aesthetic considerations.

To begin with, the Physician delineates a relationship between diety, nature, and creation which allows creation to reflect divine wishes:

> For Nature hath with sovereyn diligence
> Yformed hire [Virginia] in so greet excellence,
> As though she wolde seyn, "Lo! I, Nature,
> Thus kan I forme and peynte a creature,
> Whan that me list; who kan me countrefete?
> Pigmalion noght, though he ay forge and bete,
> Or grave, or peynte; for I dar wel seyn,
> Apelles, Zanzis, sholde werche in veyn
> Outher to grave, or peynte, or forge, or bete,
> If they presumed me to countrefete.
> For He that is the formere principal
> Hath maked me his vicaire general,
> To forme and peynten erthely creaturis
> Right as me list, and ech thyng in my cure is
> Under the moone, that may wane and waxe;
> And for my werk right no thyng wol I axe;
> My lord and I been ful of oon accord.
> I made hire to the worshipe of my lord;
> So do I alle myne othere creatures,
> What colour that they han, or what figures."
> Thus semeth me that Nature wolde seye.

                                        (9-29)

Nature creates to the glory of her Lord, Virginia and all other earthly creatures. Implicit in this speech of Nature's is both a defense of Virginius' concern for his daughter's moral well-being (she is not her own self, nor even his, but God's, and must be protected as a trust) and a warning to other artists: the artist and the Lord of Creation (the first artist, of whom he is type and descendant) must be of one accord; artist creates to the glory of God. That this directive is more than polite explanation by Nature of her own role is made evident by the mention of artists Pygmalion, Appelles, and Zanaiz (Zeuxis?). The inclusion of Pygmalion, moreover, contains a further caution to mortal artists: in his person we may be expected to recognize a man whose assertion of personal whim against natural (and thus divine) law resulted in a most unfortunate state of affairs.5 Let your will conform to divine will, Chaucer through Nature tells artists, himself included.

Thus created, Virginia is a paragon of virtue: she embodies "as wel in goost as body" (43) all the Christian virtues: humility, abstinence, temperance, patience. More significantly, "after hir degree/She spak, and alle hire wordes, moore and lesse,/Sownynge in virtue and in gentilesse" (52-54). She is eager to put off idleness and sloth and will have none of wine and drink, which encourages lechery. She flees the company of fools: festivals, revels, dances...and, most likely, pilgrimages the likes of which this one has, under Harry Bailey's governance, become. The stringent morality of Virginia anticipates the *Parson's Tale* as the Physician's high seriousness about morality in art anticipates Chaucer's own retraction, which is one reason this tale would prove more appropriate in a position late in the pilgrimage. For the moment, however, the position appears deficient, for while Virginia may flee the fool, the fool will not be avoided. Sooner or later a confrontation becomes inevitable: Apius' designs on Virginia's chastity manifest themselves in a particularly unpleasant scheme which perverts justice and morality, and threatens for a moment to prevail. The children of this world are wiser in their generation, as the Good Book says.

We do not like to see virtue suffer, in this world or in the next, and our initial response is to object, as some critics have, to "Virginia's inhuman resignation before her fate." We might even draw the conclusion that "the Physician's god, like Jepthah's, is a harsh and cruel deity."6 Such simply is not the case, however, as we have had occasion to note before: just as well reproach the Lord for allowing Job to suffer, the Prioress' young saint to die, Walter for testing Griselda, God for testing Abraham. What we witness in the *Physician's Tale* is that carelessness of mortal existence so characteristically medieval and so thoroughly Christian:

> And after, whan hir swowning is agon,
> She riseth up, and to hir fader sayde,

"Blissed by God, that I shal dye a mayde!
Yif me my deeth, er that I have a shame;
Dooth with youre child youre wyl, a Goddes
        name!"

                                    (246-50)

Such rigid moralism we moderns cannot deal with, just as we
cannot deal with Chaucer's decapitation (or castration) of his art in
the retraction to the *Canterbury Tales.* For medieval Chaucer, I
suspect, matters were much less difficult.

It is entirely a matter of governance, the Physician implies.
Nature creates in accord with God's will; man must govern himself
and his children in strict accord with that will. This is the second
major thrust of the Physician's digressions, of his advice on
governance. Touching on the Host's role as lord and governor of
this pilgrimage, and on the artist's responsibility for his art, the
Physician's advice is in complete accord with Nature's statement
of her role:

And ye maistresses, in youre olde lyf,
That lordes doghtres han in governaunce,
Ne taketh of my wordes no displesaunce.
Thenketh that ye been set in governynges
Of lordes doghtres, oonly for two thynges:
Outher for ye han kept youre honestee,
Or elles ye han falle in freletee,
And knowen wel ynough the olde daunce,
And han forsaken fully swich meschaunce
For everemo; therfore, for Christes sake,
To teche hem vertu looke that ye ne slake.
A theef of venysoun, that hath forlaft
His likerousness and al his olde craft,
Kan kepe a forest best of any man.
Now kepeth wel, for if ye wole, ye kan.
Looke wel that ye unto no vice assente,
Lest ye be dampned for youre wikke entente;
For whoso dooth, a traitour is, certeyn.
And taketh kep of that that I shal seyn:
Of alle tresons sovereyn pestilence
Is whan a wight bitrayseth innocence.
Ye fadres and ye moodres eek also,
Though ye han children, be it oon or mo,
Youre is the charge of al hir surveiaunce,
Whil that they been under youre governaunce.
Beth war, that by ensample of youre lyvynge,
Or by youre necligence in chastisynge,
That they ne perisse; for I dar wel seye,
If that they doon, ye shal it deere abeye.

                                    (72-100)

The passage is fraught with echoes of Chaucer's art and life: a warning to the Wife of Bath in line 79, reflections of Chaucer's life as a forester in his later years, a nod to Harry as governor, a foreshadowing of the Parson's insistent moralism. The governor is responsible: parent for child, ruler for people, artist for art. And he had best take care lest those under his governance be lost for his negligence.

Within the confines of the *Physician's Tale* (and they are, by in large, the confines Chaucer ultimately imposes on his own work of art), Virginius' governance is responsible: Virginia dies to live, and in the process restores to the world of this tale justice and morality: evil is punished, good triumphs. "Heere may men seen how synne hath his merite," the Physician admonishes his listeners (277). "Therfore I rede yow this counseil take:/Forsaketh synne, er synne yow forsake." "Wherfore I biseke yow mekely, for the mercy of God, that ye preye for me that Crist have mercy on me and foryeve me my giltes;/and namely of my translacions and endytinges of worldly vanitees, the whiche I revoke in my retracciouns," Chaucer the poet wrote later (X, 1084, 85). Now the position of the *Physician's Tale*, demanding proper governance and moral responsibility, need not lead directly to the retraction of most of Chaucer's art; it is possible, as we have seen in the twentieth century, for satire, farce, even "pornography" to be moral in the broadest sense, to have "redemptive social value." In the tales which follow the Physician's we will see Chaucer examining art from every conceivable perspective, testing the responsibility of various aesthetics, wrestling with the inter-related wills of artist, audience, and deity, and arriving unavoidably if reluctantly at the decision that being responsible does indeed involve retracting much of what has been written (and ceasing to write more), of beheading his own child. This movement is the movement of the remainder of Chaucer's pilgrimage.

THE PARDONER'S PROLOGUE AND TALE

The immediate measure of the failure of the *Physician's Tale* is Harry Bailey's reaction, just as the more remote measure of that failure will be the Pardoner's willful perversion of his virtue-inducing art. Together the two form a double answer to the Physician: art which is intended to elicit virtuous behavior may fail because of its audience's inability to comprehend it fully; art which might lead to virtue may be perverted by an insincere artist and thereby rendered ineffective.7 Such objections prevent the

Physician's Tale from being Chaucer's final statement on art, and insure the continuance of his dialectic; in fact, they propel us headlong into a lengthy and profound examination of art, its motives, its methods.

Certainly the Host has been impressed by the *Physician's Tale*: he inveighs mightily against the false justice of Apius. To this extent the Physician's narrative has proven instructive. But certainly the Host's oath is not virtue (as the Parson had made abundantly clear on an earlier occasion), and his misinterpretation of the exemplum evident in subsequent remarks indicates that he has missed its point entirely. Virginia is pitiable because she bought too dearly her beauty; the moral is that one should beware the gifts of Fortune and Nature (as far as Harry is concerned, both are alike), that beauty is as often a curse as a blessing. Clearly the Host has learned nothing about divine order and Providence, or even about the necessity for drastic action in the face of evil.8 The Host's reaction is blind and emotional, and demonstrates nothing so much as the tale's failure to teach him anything. Such a response was scarcely what the Physician had in mind when he argued the harmony of wills between artist and God, and an ennobling didacticism as a justifiable aesthetic. Perhaps it is Harry himself who best describes the effect of this narrative: "But natheless, passe over, is no fors." Still untutored, the governor turns to his drink and with an insulting insinuation requests a ribald tale from the Pardoner:

> Thou beel amy, thou Pardoner," he sayde,
> "Telle us som myrthe or japes right anon."
> "It shal be doon," quod he, "by Seint Ronyon!"
> (318-20)

The gentles, however, rebel as one: more attentive to the Physician's advice and obviously discomforted at the prospect of a ribald tale from the likes of the Pardoner, whose physical defect has set him apart from the center of the human community, the good folk request a moral thing, something to teach them virtue, "and thanne wol we gladly heere." And the Pardoner, agreeable to anything which promises to win him acceptance in the fellowship of the pilgrims, assents: "I graunte, ywis," he says. He will follow the aesthetic of the Physician and give them art leading to virtue. But his intent is base, his motives reprehensible, and the moral force of his narrative will be lost, undermined by his own bad example.

Early in his prologue, the Pardoner asserts, "For certes, many a predicacioun/Comth ofte tyme of yvel entencioun" (407, 8). This is his *apologia pro vita sua*, the justification of his own immoral behavior. The assertion is, in a sense, an echo of the Physician's dictum that those who know best "the olde daunce" make the best governors; the best thieves make the best game wardens. The Pardoner clings to the notion, and reasserts it in lines 429ff:

> But though myself be gilty in that synne,
> Yet kan I maken oother folk to twynee
> From avariace, and soore repent.

To the Pardoner, however, this justification becomes a license to steal, a blanket absolution for his own malice:

> Thus quyte I folk that doon us displesances;
> Thus spitte I out my venym under hewe
> Of hoolynesse, to semen hooly and trewe.
>   (420-22)

The fact that good may often come of evil intention does not, however, excuse one who preaches against that same vice which characterizes his own action, because such marginal good does not excuse the enormity of his immorality. It would not excuse it in normal circumstances, and it certainly does not excuse it on this pilgrimage. For we discover at the tale's conclusion that no good comes from the Pardoner's preaching. When he attempts to hawk his wares, we find he has brought the company not to true religion but to chaos and dissention, because his intent is bad, because his own immorality, emblemized in his physical sterility, shines through his preaching.9 As the Squire put it, one can speak only as he is able: the Pardoner is incapable of art which engenders virtue.

The precise motivation behind the Pardoner's extraordinary confesssion has been the subject of considerable critical discussion; indeed, explanations of the Pardoner's behavior probably account for a volume of printed matter greater than that of a full edition of the entire *Canterbury Tales*.10 In fact, the mere review of such explanations makes for a rather hefty essay. At issue is this: why should the Pardoner bare his soul to these pilgrims in the first place, and then, having confessed to the basest of behavior with the basest of motivations, reverse himself and attempt to con the company with the very game he has just exposed? Is he merely being compulsive? Does he repent his moments of honesty at the tale's conclusion? Does he sincerely believe the pilgrims are so mesmerized by his sermon as to be ripe for picking? Is the initial confession all part of a con game designed to throw pilgrims off their guard, ingratiate the Pardoner with the

pilgrims, prior to the big sell? Or does the Pardoner have no real
intention of selling anything, being "on vacation" rather than on
business? Or is he up to something else entirely?

The Pardoner's performance begins with his interruption of the
Wife of Bath's prologue[11] an interruption which, as Sedgewick
has shown, must have preceded his tale.[12] It is a curious
interruption in many respects, not the least of which is his
insistence on taking a wife:

> Up stirte the Pardoner, and that anon:
> "Now, dame," quod he, "by God and by Seint
>   John!
> Ye been a noble prechour in this cas.
> I was aboute to wedde a wyf; allas!
> What sholde I bye it on my flessh so deere?
> Yet hadde I levere wedde no wyf to-yeere!"
>
>   (III, 163-68)

Now even the obtuse narrator of the *General Prologue* has
observed that the Pardoner can have no possible use for a wife; the
musical interchange between himself and the Summoner suggests
that, if anything, he would prefer male companionship. The
pilgrims are very much aware of this fact, and it is probably this
more than anything else which casts him outside the pale of
normal, healthy society. They will accept ribaldry from the Miller
and the Reeve, unpleasant a chap as he may be, because they are
whole men. But they will not accept such lewd ribaldry from the
Pardoner because of his peculiar deficiency.[13] In light of his
sexual predilections and the virtually universal recognition of his
perversion, the Pardoner's "I was aboute to wedde a wyf" is an
especially peculiar remark. "This is jocosity, of course," writes
Segewick,[14] although it would seem to call for an explanation
more sophisticated than that. More likely that the Pardoner,
sensitive to his rejection and the reason for it, does his best to
conceal the obvious with joking remarks designed to buy his way
into the fellowship's good humor, and at the same time glancingly
suggest that he is not as he appears. In fact I would suggest that
the need to belong, to be a part of the Canterbury community,
explains the Pardoner's performance far more satisfactorily than
any explanation based on his avarice and deceit. True, the
Pardoner is avaricious; true he is deceitful. But avarice is not his
primary motivation on this pilgrimage, and his deceit is but an
adjunct to concealing that peculiar physical defect which
emblemizes his spiritual deficiency. Since the beginning of the
Canterbury pilgrimage, when he found himself tucked off in a

corner with the Summoner and relegated to the very end of
Chaucer's descriptions of the pilgrims, the Pardoner has felt
himself estranged. His interruption of the Wife is an initial
attempt to join the group; his prologue and tale, told after some
thought following a rather sharp rejection by the gentils, are
another such attempt. *are his prologue + tale.*

"I moot thynke/Upon som honest thyng while that I drynke,"
the Pardoner informs us at the end of his *Introduction*. The
thought has, no doubt, been prompted by the gentils' clamor and
by the Host's own suggestive address: "Thou beel amy, thou
Pardoner" (318). The Host suspects! They all suspect! The
remarks to the Wife have not been enough! The Pardoner laughs
Harry's pun off with one of his own ("It shal be doon, by Seint
Ronyon!"), sets his mind to working, and begins his
counter-attack with a drink. The Pardoner will show us what a
regular fellow he is: drinking, swearing, confessing to all manner
of vice, but jealously guarding that one truth which separates him
from the other pilgrims. And why not? Confession worked for the
Wife of Bath, for the Reeve, for the Merchant. There was little
objection after the Miller's bawdy tale, no objection preceding the
Cook's response in kind. If he can show himself a regular (read
"sinful") fellow, "just one of the boys," the Pardoner reasons, he
may yet achieve the acceptance he seeks. And so the confession
begins: *If he reasons by maby showing himself a Regular fellow "just ____"*

> What, trowe ye, that whiles I may preche,
> That I wol lyve in poverte wilfully?
> Nay, nay, I thoghte it nevere, trewely!
> For I wol preche and begge in sondry landes;
> I wol nat do no labour with myne handes,
> Ne make baskettes, and lyve thereby,
> By cause I wol nat beggen ydelly.
> I wol noon of the apostles countrefete;
> I wol have moneie, wolle, chese, and whete,
> Al were it yeven of the povereste page,
> Or of the povereste wydwe in a village,
> Al sholde hir children sterve for famyne.
> Nay, I wol drynke licour of the vyne,
> And have a joly wenche in every toun.
> But herkneth, lordynges, in conclusioun:
> Youre likyng is that I shal telle a tale.
> Now have I dronke a draughte of corny ale,
> By God, I hope I shal yow telle a thyng
> That shal by reson been at youre likyng.
>   (439-58)

"I hope to tell you something to your liking," the Pardoner
concludes after his remarkable confession to extortion, greed,

drunkenness, and yes, there it is, lechery: "And have a joly wenche in every toun." Perhaps this will be swallowed with the rest, the Pardoner will appear a rogue (like the rest) but normal, and this isolation will be ended. Especially, the Pardoner reasons, if the tale is as verbally polished, as smooth, as professional as he knows it will be.

The Pardoner's intent is frustrated, however: his performance does not win him a place among the rest of the pilgrims. Instead he suffers the acute embarrassment of having that which he wished to conceal pointed out in the coarsest of terms by Harry Bailey. His art proves in the last analysis insufficient to its intended ends, for Chaucer has moved beyond the position of the *Miller's Tale* and Reeve's requiting: the didactic tale which, unlike those of the Friar and Summoner, might in other circumstances cause folk "to twynne/From avarice, and soore repente" is subverted by the intentions of its teller.

We can see the failure of intent on several levels as prologue and tale progress. The decision of the tale's three revelers to go out, find death, and put an end to him once and for all is most manifestly frustrated by their own corruption. Similarly, the tale's injunction that we avoid homicide, gluttony, luxury, and gambling is similarly ineffective. So too the exhortations against drunkenness and swearing. Indeed, the initial two hundred lines of this tale are a curiously digressive series of highly rhetorical homilies against drunkenness, gambling, and great swearing, which is "a thyng abhominable," to use the Pardoner's exact words. But the tavern (or alestake) setting in which the tale is told, insisted upon by Chaucer on three separate occasions, clearly indicates that the drunkenness and gluttony reviled by the Pardoner are both a part of his own behavior and that of his audience. The Host's angry reaction to the Pardoner's appended invitation that he come up and receive pardon may, in fact, stem from the corny ale he himself has drunk; certainly his outraged "by the croys which that Seint Eleyne fond" (951) is a clear indication that the Pardoner's injunction against swearing has fallen on deaf ears—or, more precisely, that something has blinded the eyes and deafened the ears of his audience to the tale's moral sentence. Of course, if it be assumed that the Pardoner's intent is in truth to win money or power over the Host, the tale fails in that as well: the Pardoner has none of Harry's money, and wins the respect of no one.

The tale fails in other respects. The Pardoner has argued that from evil intention some good may flow; being evil himself, he might inspire good in others. But it is clear from the *Prologue* that the sort of preaching this Pardoner manages will not elicit goodness or religiosity or salvation of generosity in any of his audience. He sugars his tongue, we are informed, "to stir hem [the lewd folk] to devocioun" (346), but the sort of devotion which might result from his performance is the superstition fostered by those preposterous claims about the pseudo-relics he vends: this bone, washed in water, will cure cattle of worms and sores, cause sheep to multiply, cure jealousy (and the gout?). Here is a glove you can wear when planting your crops to insure a rich harvest. And so on. The crass materialism of such a speech is obvious, as is the attitude it must have fostered in the parishioners who heard it. Religion is something one does to make the crops grow, to cure the cattle, to cuckold one's husband. The net effect is the impoverishment of the parishioners (and the parish) materially and spiritually, since religion is perverted to superstition, spirituality to materialism, and the means of grace to a means of income. So perverse is this Pardoner that he has the good folk creating sins to confess to him, lest they appear a terrible and unrepentant sinner or a wanton wench. It is this perversion of his role as a means of grace, this abrogation of the divine will and purpose, which renders the Pardoner's ministry sterile.

The major failure of the Pardoner's art, however, is in its inability to win for him the acceptance he seeks within the human community. We spoke earlier of the Pardoner's need to belong and of his willingness to confess virtually anything to conceal the defect which isolates him. One suspects that by the end of his tale, the man has succeeded: the apparent conclusion elicits no response from Host or pilgrims, who ride spell-bound and impressed:

> —And lo, sires, thus I preche.
> And Jhesu Crist, that is oure soules leche
> So graunte yow his pardoun to receyve,
> For that is best; I wol yow nat deceyve.
>
> (915-18)

This much is clear: the Pardoner believes he has succeeded, for it is his sense of acceptance which leads him to offer jokingly his pardon to the pilgrims and suggest that the Host, "moost envoluped in sinne," come forth and kiss his relics. "I am in youre felawshipe yfalle," the Pardoner tells the pilgrims happily (938), and he believes it. Now he can joke and laugh with the Host as did the others, and receive Harry's coarse but sincere approbation.

What the Pardoner receives is quite different from what he expects, however, for he has managed to deceive only himself. He is not fallen into the pilgrims' fellowship, and he has not concealed his deformity:

> I wolde I hadde thy coillons in myn hond
> In stide of relikes or of seintuarie.
> Let kutte hem of, I wol thee helpe hem carie;
> They shul be shryned in an hogges toord!
>
> (952-55)

The Pardoner is reduced to sullen, wrathful silence. His magnificent performance has not done its work after all.

All does not end unhappily, however. At the insistence of the Knight, Pardoner and Host kiss and ride forth their way...together, with the pilgrims, laughing and playing. In one sense this is mere social convention, courtesy initiated by the courteous Knight to smooth over an embarrassing moment. In another sense it may be Chaucer's practical joke on Harry Bailey, whose own masculinity is tenuous enough. But I think we must see it in another light as well: the kiss emblemizes harmony after disruption and—even more important—acceptance at least of the Pardoner into the fellowship of the pilgrimage, in spite of or perhaps because of this latest embarrassment. Ultimately the eunuch does find his way into the human community, but only after he has confessed (although under obvious duress) and done due penance for his sins. The sterility he sought to conceal was, metaphorically, his own spiritual enormity which, concealed, rendered all other confession meaningless. If Sir Gawain fails to confess the belt, all else proves empty. The implications of those concluding lines of the *Pardoner's Tale*, then, are considerable: despite the most dazzling show of technical proficiency, art may fail if the will of the artist is not one with the will of the Lord; but on the other hand, art may function, despite the will of the artist, as a form of confession which may purify the artist unaware. In retrospect we may view many of the earlier tales as confession: the Wife's, the Friar's, the Summoner's, the Merchant's, the Reeve's. But grace has not followed them as it follows the Pardoner's confession, perhaps because artist Chaucer was not then considering art as confession, perhaps because his pilgrimage had not yet progressed metaphysically and aesthetically to this stage. At present, however, a new note has been injected into the fiction: art is confession, on which hangs the fate of the artist. And with that realization yet another consideration: *respice finem*. Look to death, both spiritual and physical. Time grows tight. The pilgrimage hastens inexorably toward its conclusion.

THE SHIPMAN'S TALE

For all the artistic thinness of, say, the *Second Nun's Tale* or the
prosy tedium of Chaucer's own *Tale of Melibee*, for all the flatness
of the Squire's romance or strangeness of the *Physician's Tale*, the
Shipman's Tale is virtually unmatched in the Canterbury collection
as an accident which is really not quite certain just what it's all
about. It seems loosely related to the marriage theme, although it
floats free from other tales devoted to the subject and offers no
fresh perspective or unique view of the institution. It does not
appear to deal with metaphysical or aesthetic matters so crucial to
other tales. It is not absurd enough to be a parody, nor is it rich
enough to generate the excitement attendant on the Pardoner's or
Wife's or Nun's Priest's tales. We are, in the last analysis, neither
attracted to its characters (as in the *Miller's Tale*) nor repulsed by
them (as in the *Merchant's Tale*). The story is competent enough,
but we keep feeling as though we've been through all this before:
the Miller, the Reeve, the Wife, the Merchant. The tale has
generated little significant criticism;15 in fact, one study of the
fragment it introduces all but ignores it entirely.16

We moderns, I rather suspect, are not alone in our uncertainty;
indications are strong that Chaucer himself was not sure just what
he wanted to do with this tale. It has no proper prologue, although
the *Epilogue* to the *Man of Law's Tale*, if authentic (and I suspect
it is), might function as the briefest of introductions. Moreover,
the tale proper contains those enigmatic lines which have caused
most, but not all, critics to read the tale as originally intended for
the Wife of Bath:17

> But wo is hym that payen moot for al!
> The sely housebonde, algate he moot paye,
> He moot us clothe, and he moot us arraye,
> Al for his owene worshippe richely,
> In which array we daunce jolily.
> And if that he noght may, par aventure,
> Or ellis list no swich dispence endure,
> But thynketh it is wasted and ylost,
> Thanne moot another payen for oure cost,
> Or lene us gold, and that is perilous.
>
>   (10-19)

One suspects, finally, that the tale was indeed intended for the
Wife: some lines recall her very words, her very philosophy:

> And wel ye woot that wommen naturelly
> Desiren thynges sixe as wel as I:

They wolde that hir housebondes sholde be
Hardy, and wise, and riche, and thereto free,
And buxom unto his wyf, and fressh abedde.
(173-77)

But this tale does not develop the Wife's personality as does the
romance Chaucer ultimately produced for her, and a shift was
made well into the *Canterbury Tales'* development. I suspect that
Chaucer wrote the tale for the Wife, for a position following the
Man of Law's Tale; then replaced it with the Wife's present tale,
intending to leave the tale where it was and move the Wife and her
new tale to another position (this fabliau of a merchant, his wife,
and a monk, Chaucer may have thought, would make a smoother
introduction to the other tales on marriage already written and in
place, while the Wife might be used to cap a discussion); then
wrote the *Man of Law's Epilogue* designed to introduce the
Wife's-become-Shipman's tale; then changed his mind and
allowed the Wife and her new tale to follow the Man of Law (a wise
choice), and found himself with a leftover epilogue and tale for
which he had little use but with which he was unwilling to part.
Unwilling to lavish time on a mediocre piece, he left the tale as we
have it today: set in the mouth of a pilgrim most unsuited to
telling it, complete with references to "us women." An anomaly.
An unclaimed tale of minimal importance.

In these circumstances, Chaucer has managed admirably in
positioning the *Shipman's Tale* after the Pardoner's and
Physician's tales, for in a subtle manner the tale picks up the
Pardoner's motif of gold and the Physician's concern for
governance. Here, as in the *Pardoner's Tale*, gold emblemizes a
worldliness which cannot lead elsewhere but trouble, to a physical
or spiritual death. By standards which have gained increasingly
universal acceptance, the merchant of this tale is a most successful
man: he has much gold in counting house, the hundred franks
requested by Dan John is but a pittance. He is not even visibly
upset when he discovers his wife has taken these hundred franks
and spent them on clothes. A fine house and a well dressed wife
are, in fact, measures of his success and insurance of a reputation
which will allow him to borrow more gold when and where he
pleases. And the merchant is wealthy precisely because the
borrowing and lending of gold has been the main preoccupation of
his life. As he patiently explains to his spouse,

"Wyf," quod this man, "litel kanstow devyne
The curious bisynesse that we have.
For of us chapmen, also God me save,

And by that lord that clepid is Seint Yve,
Scarsly amonges twelve tweye shul thryve
Continuelly, lastynge unto oure age.
We may wel make chiere and good visage,
And dryve forth the world as it may be,
And kepen oure estaat in pryvetee,
Til we be deed, or elles that we pleye
A pilgrymage, or goon out of the weye.
And therfore have I greet necessitee
Upon this queynte world t'avyse me;
For everemoore we moote stonde in drede
Of hap and fortune in oure chapmanhede.

(224-38)

While this chapman is busying himself about "this queynte world," wary of accident and fortune, his friend the monk is busying himself about another "queynte world", taking advantage of the merchant's preoccupation with cash flow. It is not irrelevant that while his wife is renting herself to his "cousin," the merchant is arranging deals which net him at least a thousand franks over cost: his narrow focus on the goods of this world sets up his abuse by John. It also sets up his wife's cover-up, as she reifies her self into a commodity and urges her husband to "score it upon my taille" if he finds any debt outstanding. The marital relationship, made symbolic of God's good order in the earlier tales on marriage, is cast here in terms of dollars and cents, of a debt to be scored on the wife's tail (this word "debt," incidentally, is yet another indication that the *Shipman's Tale* belonged once to the Wife of Bath). Not only has the commercial superceded the spiritual, it has engulfed the spiritual—at least for the duration of this fabliau.18

The *Shipman's Tale* debases more than marriage, however; the merchant's mention of pilgrimage in those lines quoted above suggests an awareness on his part of the life-as-pilgrimage motif which underlies the structure of the *Canterbury Tales*. But the line is curious in its connection of concentrating on worldly affairs and the pilgrimage motif: he must concentrate lest he be forced to "go out of the way" or "play a pilgrimage." Game here has become earnest, and earnest game: Chaucer suggests through the Shipman that this manner of life is precisely the opposite of the pilgrimage on which he and his pilgrims find themselves, a "play pilgrimage" of commerce and mamon. The remark would be particularly appropriate in a tale told by the Wife of Bath, whose fondness for pilgrimages and for wandering by the wayside had been noted in the *General Prologue*; but the remark will fit a context which places it after the *Pardoner's Tale*, with its allegorical crooked way at the end of which the three revelers find their pot of gold. In either context our attention is directed immediately to the spiritual nature of pilgrimage, and we draw a mental contrast between the merchant's play pilgrimage (and the Wife's pilgrimages, or the revelers' journey) and this Canterbury pilgrimage.

One further consideration ties this tale to a position after the *Physician's Tale*: its comment on parental governance, a matter so lightly treated as to be almost but not quite imperceptible. The merchant's concern for gold devlops from a concern for governance of worldly affairs: one must take care, and taking care means piling up specie. He is also concerned that his wife display similar diligence, and he admonishes her upon his depature for Flanders that she "honestly governe wel" his house. Of course her governance, like his, is in reality a mismanagement, a parody of good governance found so necessary in the *Physician's Tale* and, by inference, in the Pardoner's performance. The wife's governance amounts to slandering her husband ("the worste man/That evere was sith that the world bigan," she tells Dan John, cheap and short and no good in bed), backing herself into a financial corner, and then hopping into bed with her husband's best friend to raise the cash she needs to bail herself out. Relevant to all this is some curious business early in the tale:

> This goode wyf cam walkynge pryvely
> Into the garden, there he walketh softe,
> And hym saleweth, as she hath doon ofte.
> A mayde child cam in hire compaignye,
> Which as hir list she may governe and gye,
> For yet under the yerde was the mayde.

(92-97)

The maid child does not leave Dan John and the good wife through their ensuing conversation, in which she offers to do him "what plesance and service/That I may doon, right as yow list devise." The Shipman does not tell us the age of this young lass, but such considerations are irrelevant: whether she understands this conversation or not, there will be others like it, rest assured, and the education this youngster receives under the wife's governance will not be one of which the Physician would have approved. The girl is not vital to the fabliau's plot, as are virtually all elements of any fabliau, unless we consider the matter of governance. On the other hand, governance is not a major theme of this tale; it is touched lightly upon in this scene with wife, child, and monk, and in the merchant's admonition to his spouse mentioned earlier. Chaucer does not choose to make governance a major issue of the tale, although it certainly is an important part of both fragment VI and the rest of fragment VII.

In fine, the *Shipman's Tale* relates loosely to a couple of thematic motifs developed elsewhere in the *Canterbury Tales:* pilgrimage, governance, the goods of the spirit and the goods of mamon. But it fails to make a significant statement about either metaphysics or aesthetics, and it fails to develop social relationships among the pilgrims. It does not fit into the Canterbury pilgrimage, either at the point indicated by fragment VII or at the point indicated by fragment B2. Structurally and thematically, it floats, one of the least significant of all the Canterbury tales.

THE PRIORESS'S TALE

Like the *Physician's Tale*, the *Shipman's Tale* is passed over lightly by Harry as he looks around for someone in the company to tell the next tale: "But now passe over, and lat us seke aboute,/Who shal now telle first of al this route/Another tale" (443-45). His choice is the Prioress, who is politely requested in uncharacteristic subjunctives,

> I wolde demen that ye tellen sholde
> A tale next, if so were that ye wolde.
> Now wol ye vouche sauf, my lady deere?
>   (449-51)

"Gladly," she responds, then begins with a pietistic modesty formula protesting her utter inadequacy, and follows that with a brief saint's life. Echoing the admonition of the Squire, she reminds us of her own painfully obvious inadequacies and requests the aid of God and Mary; following the moral precept of the Physician, she presents a narrative which will engender in its listeners true Christian virtue. The two together are important, for the one delineates the tale's aesthetic while the other explains the inadequacy of that aesthetic to artist Chaucer and its subsequent rejection in the Canterbury dialectic.

By both position and maternal instinct, Madame Eglantine is an instructor, both to her own wards and the human community to which she is now an example. Quite naturally she has been moved by the Physician's advice on education and governance of the young, just as she has been upset by Harry's comments about monks following the *Shipman's Tale*. She briefly says her piece on the one ("As monkes been—or elles oghte be") and moves on to a tale designed to promote piety and reverence of Mary in her

immediate audience, the Canterbury pilgrims. If we are to judge
from their reaction to this miracle, the tale succeeds: "Whan seyd
was al this miracle, every man/As sobre was that wonder was to
se." For a minute even the Host is silent. The tale teaches.

And the tale is about teaching, about an education which
promotes religion and virtue. Madame Eglantine's seven-year old
school fellow daily attends a Christian school in which he is taught
"Swich manere doctrine as men used there,/This is to seyn, to
syngen and to rede,/As smale children doon in hir childhede." A
far cry this from modern schools, but—as the tale makes
abundantly clear—a very excellent education insofar as the lad's
soul is concerned. The youth is especially impressed with the
Virgin Mary; he has a simple, genuine reverence which leads him
to resolve above all else to learn "Alma Redemptoris" in the
Virgin's praise. One gets the impression this lad may be
something of a sluggard in other lessons: hearing song, he
wanders dreamily off to investigate:

> This litel child, his litel book lernynge,
> As he sat in the scole at his prymer,
> He *Alma redemptoris* herde synge
> As children lerned hire antiphoner;
> And as he dorste, he drough hym ner and ner,
> And herkned ay the wordes and the noote,
> Til he the firste vers koude al by rote.
>
> (516-22)

The primer is set aside; the boy stands listening to music. A friend
informs him that the song is made in praise of Mary and the primer
is forgotten entirely. It does not matter that his primer is a lesson
far more difficult than the memorization of a simple song, or that
the matter contained in that primer would, from a practical point of
view, be far more useful than "Alma Redemptoris." Religious
awe, not worldly knowledge, is the proper end of the child's
education, implies the Prioress, and his decision is commendable.
In fact, it turns him into a saint. Given the tale's conclusion, there
can be no condemnation of the schoolboy's decision, no
accusations of laziness or simplicity. His attention is on Christ's
mother ("On Cristes mooder set was his entente") and he loves
her "alwey, as after my konnynge" (657). This is the cause of his
reward, and within the context of the story his behavior and
education are inviolable.

So too is the education offered to the pilgrims by the Prioress in
this simple tale and in the example of her life. Reactions to both
the Prioress and her tale are invariably mixed: on the one hand the
tale is demonstrably Christian and thoroughly religious; on the

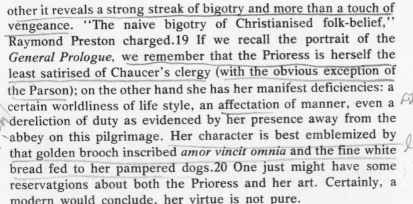

other it reveals a strong streak of bigotry and more than a touch of vengeance. "The naive bigotry of Christianised folk-belief," Raymond Preston charged.19 If we recall the portrait of the *General Prologue*, we remember that the Prioress is herself the least satirised of Chaucer's clergy (with the obvious exception of the Parson); on the other hand she has her manifest deficiencies: a certain worldliness of life style, an affectation of manner, even a dereliction of duty as evidenced by her presence away from the abbey on this pilgrimage. Her character is best emblemized by that golden brooch inscribed *amor vincit omnia* and the fine white bread fed to her pampered dogs.20 One just might have some reservatgions about both the Prioress and her art. Certainly, a modern would conclude, her virtue is not pure.

But Chaucer will not allow us to draw such a conclusion: he himself seems to smile benignly on his creation, especially in the *General Prologue*, even after all allowances have been made for the personna he assumes in reporting the pilgrimage. The true key, however, to understanding and evaluating both the Prioress and her art is to be found in the close ties Chaucer allows Madame Eglantine to draw between herself and her schoolboy.21 They begin in her prologue and continue throughout the tale:

> But as a child of twelf month oold, or lesse,
> That kan unnethes any word expresse,
> Right so fare I, and therfore I yow preye,
> Gydeth my song that I shal of yow seye."
> (484-87)

Like her schoolboy, the Prioress is devout. Like her schoolboy, her talent is insuficient to a sophisticated expression of her faith. Like her schoolboy, the Prioress is prone to wander away from what more worldly and more sophisticated people might consider pressing matters to simple things like going on pilgrimages and listening to songs. Like her schoolboy, the Prioress offends us at times (indeed, one wonders just who is more insensitive: the Prioress ranting about "these cursed Jews" or the schoolfellow singing *"Alma Redemptoris"* as he strolls through the town's Jewry). But like her schoolboy, Madame Eglantine loves God always after her own ability, and that is all that matters. As her surrogate in her tale is saved, so the Prioress is saved. She may be naive, she may be derelict, she may be affected, but she is pure of intent, and this is reason enough for grace.22

Didactic art, embodying orthodox theology, told with good intent: this would seem to be a resting point, Chaucer's last word on the matter of aesthetics and will. Instead, the *Prioress's Tale* proves to be only the beginning of a discussion of stories and story-telling that extends through fragment VII and on almost to the very end of the *Tales*. Reviewing the tales of fragment VII, Alan Gaylord writes:

> The shape of the whole of Fragment VII, or more accurately, the shape of the ideas which hold it together, seems to me controlled by a single, though admittedly very broad subject: *the art of story telling*. To read the fragment as a whole is to be drawn to consider the art as more than that which is demonstrated as the characters recite; it is to come to sense that a topic is being developed, even if implicitly and by non-expository means, and to see that it touches upon three things: the artist's responsibility to his audience, the audience's responsibility to the artist; and the nature of the best kind of story he may tell.23

A "Literature Group," Gaylord terms the fragment. And, as we have seen and will see, he is correct: with the exception of the *Shipman's Tale*, which fits nothing at all, every tale in this fragment, as well as some before it and after it, focus on the matter of aesthetics: how best to tell a tale, given the metaphysics developed over earlier fragments. But the *Prioress's Tale*, it would seem, ends a discussion before it begins, by positing a kind of instruction and demonstrating the validity of that instruction. One cannot quarrel with God and argue that no, after all, this isn't worthy art even though the Prioress and her surrogate are saved. Nor can one argue with any degree of theological legitimacy that the tale is doctrinally unsound. But one can (and Chaucer does) argue this: the Prioress's art is valid only given the Prioress's self and her audience. It will engender piety in simple folk, just as it is a sincere manifestation of faith only from a simple person. It is unlikely, however, that Chaucer the artist, so much more sophisticated than Madame Eglantine, will achieve the same grace she managed with the same sort of tale, because such an art is not peculiar to his talent. His art would not look anything like hers, nor would the art of several other pilgrims on this journey (the Nun's Priest comes immediately to mind). Chaucer, the sophisticated artist of *Troilus and Criseyde*, cannot rest with simplistic saints' lives and false modesty formulae. He seeks something further, something which can accomodate his personal sophistication and at the same time reflect honest intentions and harmony with divine Providence.

CHAUCER'S TALES OF THOPAS AND MELIBEE

The *Prioress's Tale* has brought artist Chaucer to a moral dilemma: should he as artist eschew his own sophistication and write simple devotional materials for simple, devout minds, thereby winning for himself a place in heaven at the expense of his own artistic development? Or are other artistic possibilities open to him, possibilities for a more subtle engendering of moral virtue? Is, for example, everything he has written thus far in the *Canterbury Tales* without merit because it fails to induce morality in a manner described by the Physician and exemplified by the Prioress? Certainly this matter touches Chaucer deeply, and it is time for him to enter the Canterbury discussion personally as a spokesman for his art. First, not surprisingly, Chaucer examines the potentialities of satire, then he asserts the value of direct homiletic narrative of a type more complex and more intellectual than that envisioned and exemplified by Madame Eglantine. In this sense the tales of Thopas and Melibee are a matching set: each represents the artist's defense of a mode of artistic instruction more sophisticated than the art of the Prioress, the one indirect and amusing, the other direct and grave. In the process yet another unknown is drawn into Chaucer's consideration of art: audience. If audience does not understand, the poet discovers, then art fails. Yes, it would seem that brighter people might be permitted to produce complex art; but even if the artist is sound of mind and will, if his audience cannot comprehend that art, his rhyming "is nat worth a toord!"

Sir Thopas, we have come to agree after much discussion early in the century, is a parody. Whether it parodies all romances or merely tenth-rate tail-rhyme romances popular in the fourteenth-century low countries is quite academic:24 the tale is a brilliant burlesque, as anyone who has spent time rummaging through mediaeval romance well knows. It is, of course, pointless, to belabor the finer points of Chaucer's humor: nothing is deader than humor analysed blow by blow, inch by inch, point by point. But it is not pointless to observe that Chaucer was not simply playing games in all this, that the tale represents more than "Chaucer at play, having no end of fun with the romances and his readers and himself."25 The tale is amusing, but it has a point which would be dear to Chaucer's heart as an artist and romancer: the brand of art we've been getting from our minstrels lately is pretty terrible stuff, and here's what's wrong with it. Like all parody, the *Tale of Sir Thopas* has a good deal of critical judgment buried in its stanzas, if we are alert to what's going on.

Of course all good satire works this way, positing norms outside itself against which the deformity of an author's satiric presentation is measured. Certainly a satire may have aesthetic or moral value even though it does not present directly aesthetically satisfying art and morally edifying behavior; that was, in fact, the crux of Ben Jonson's defense of satire as a mode to those who complained he never "punished vice or folly" directly on stage. It is the crux of many a pornography case, the loop-hole through which many a blue film escapes the censor's dictum that it behave morally. Good satire, in addition to being humorous, is also moral, and thereby has the better part of both worlds. Moreover, its subtlety and indirection commend it to an author of talent and sophistication, to an artist like Chaucer. And Chaucer, in examining satire, is in effect examining his own art as we find it in the *General Prologue* and throughout many of the *Canterbury Tales*. The *Tale of Sir Thopas* is by no means the only tale Chaucer knows—in this he allows persona to stand in front of poet—but there can be no doubt that the real subject of *Sir Thopas* is of primary improtance to Chaucer the artist.

To be moral, however, satire must be properly understood. A satiric pornographic movie is not satire if its audience does not perceive it as such; then it is merely pornographic. And when the audience to which a parody is read fails to recognize the poem as parody, then it is nothing more than "drasty rhymyng." This much Chaucer recognizes with the Host's interruption of his tale. Harry had requested a tale of mirth, breaking the silence which followed the Prioress's performance and looking to re-establish his own brand of humor. And he had done so with a characteristic insult to pilgrim Chaucer:

> And sayde thus "What man artow?" quod he;
> Thou lookest as thou woldest fynde an hare,
> For ever upon the ground I se thee stare...
> He semeth elvyssh by his contenaunce,
> For unto no wight dooth he daliaunce."
>   (695-98, 703-4)

We might guess from these remarks and what we know of Harry's character already that he is in no position to appreciate the subtle art of satire, Chaucer's tale "of myrthe and of solaas." If we did not know pilgrim Chaucer better, we might suspect he had Harry in mind when he entreats his audience "Now holde youre mouth, *par charitee,*/Bothe knyght and lady free,/And herkneth to my spelle" (891-93). The Host *does* miss the "solaas" of this tale, and therewith Chaucer's aesthetic point is made: if audience misses the satiric thrust of satire, then it is lost as an art form. It will not lead to virtue, not to a moral or social or artistic reformation of those deformities being satirized. With the Host's charge that he does nothing but waste time, artist and pilgrim Chaucer reject satire as a sophisticated mode of engendering virtue and attempt something more direct.

In introducing his second tale, Chaucer offers some observations, soon to be echoed in the *Nun's Priest's Tale*, which reveal him to be particularly conscious of the aesthetic question now under discussion:

> It is a moral tale vertuous,
> Al be it told somtyme in sondry wyse
> Of sondry folk, as I shal yow devyse.
> And thus: ye woot that every Evaungelist,
> That telleth us the peyne of Jhesu Crist,
> Ne seith nat alle thyng as his felawe dooth;
> But nathelees hir sentence is al sooth,
> And alle acorden as in hire sentence,
> Al be ther in hir tellyng difference.
> For somme of hem seyn moore, and somme seyn
>   lesse,
> Whan they his pitous passioun expresse—
> I meene of Mark, Mathew, Luc, and John—
> But doutelees hir sentence is al oon.
>
> (940-52)

The telling may vary, Chaucer informs us, but the truth is all one; there are many modes of artistic truth, many vehicles for the conveyance of morality. The implication is that *Melibee* is no more or less a valid vehicle for virtue than *Sir Thopas*, if both are properly understood, and that tales like the Knight's and Miller's and Man of Law's each offer in their turn valid forms of art. The issue is, of course, which best communicates author's (presumably virtuous) intent to his audience.

The *Tale of Melibee*, then, is a different artistic possibility for Chaucer. Whether it be direct moral instruction or moral allegory,26 it is something quite different from the satire of *Sir Thopas*. And for all the moaning and groaning of twentieth century critics,27 it seems to me that Chaucer finds this aesthetic far more satisfactory than the satire he attempted earlier: it is closer in theme and content to the central concerns of the Canterbury pilgrimage than was *Thopas*, and the Host's reaction, while far from total comprehension, evidences a greater understanding of this tale than of its predecessor. The *Tale of Melibee* plays a significant role in both the discussion of aesthetics under way in fragment VII, and the movement of Chaucer's human community from disunity to harmony along the pilgrimage route. On the one hand it offers an artistically responsible, if relatively humorless, alternative to the Prioress's simplistic saint's life. Here too is morality and virtue, but it is morality which lacks the sentimentalism and simplicity of Madame Eglantine's tale. Yes, the opportunity is there for emotionalism in the brutal assault on Melibee's wife and daughter which opens the narrative, but the artist prefers to condense his description to a very few unemotional lines:

> Upon a day bifel that he for his desport is went into the feeldes hym to pleye./His wyf and eek his doghter hath he left inwith his hous, of which the dores weren faste yshette./Thre of his olde foes han it espyed, and setten laddres to the walles of his hous, and by wyndowes been entred,/and betten his wyf, and wounded his doghter with fyve mortal woundes in fyve sondry places,—/this is to seyn, in hir feet, in hire handes, in hir erys, in hir nose, and in hire mouth,—and leften hire for deed, and wenten away.
>
> (968-72)

Instead Chaucer concentrates his attention on Melibee's unreasoned reaction, and Dame Prudence's wise and tempering advice. By example and by explicit statement, then, the tale disavows emotionalism. And by example and content the tale demands a higher intellectual response than that elicited by the *Prioress's Tale:* the freight of authorities cited, quotations repeated, examples recounted all suggests a learning far in excess of the mind of the simple but redeemed Madame Eglantine. While this sort of art may not be as fun as that of *Sir Thopas*, it is not contemptuous of the artist's skill as are the tales of Prioress and Physician. In fact, in its ascension to moral allegory, it offers a mode of art well beyond either.

The measure of this tale, like that of *Thopas*, is to be found in the Host's reaction, not so much in his approbation as in his altered behavior and attitudes: neither silence nor interruption, but a recognition of the tale's content (here is the way women ought to act!) and a genuine appreciation of the character of pilgrim Chaucer. Certainly the morality of this tale has been much more easily grasped by Harry than that implicit in the satire which preceded it:

> Oure Hooste seyde, "As I am feithful man,
> And by that precious corpus Madrian,
> I hadde levere than a barel ale

That Goodeleif, my wyf, hadde herd this tale!
For she nys no thyng of swich pacience
As was this Melibeus wyf Prudence.

                                              (1891-96)

The content of this tale is also of some significance to the
Canterbury dialectic. It is, first and foremost, a tale about proper
governance, an object lesson to the Host, inter alia, on the duties
and obligations of power. It is a tale about reason and charity.
Melibee refuses initially to be governed by either, rejects his
wife's advice, acts precipitously and unreasonably, mistakenly
ascribes his station in life to Fortune ("Fortune hath norissed me
fro my childhede, and hath holpen me to passe many a stroong
paas"), and prepares for a war of vengeance. Sounding very much
like certain twentieth century politicans, he argues, "If I ne venge
me nat of the vileynye that men han doon to me,/ I sompne or
warne hem that han doon me that vileynye, and alle othere, to do
me another vileynye." In all of this he is corrected by the
arguments and the sententious examples of his wife. The
correction, one suspects, is directed more to the Canterbury
pilgrims themselves than to an angry husband. The entire human
community—Chaucer included—is urged to eschew violence and
live in reason and charity. Again levels of fictional reality begin to
disintegrate. The tale corrects Alisoun, Wife of Bath, and
Goodeleif, Harry's better half. Upon completion it is immediately
applied to a real life situation by the Host when he drops his
patronizing attitude toward Chaucer and indicates a preference in
his own life for peace and harmony:

I woot wel she wol do me slee som day
Som neighebor, and thanne go my way;
For I am perilous with knyf in honde,
Al be it that I dar nat hire withstonde,
For she is byg in armes, by my feith:
That shal he fynde that hire mysdooth or seith,—

                                              (1917-22)

It is not that Harry wishes to fight; it's merely that he's pushed to
it. Actually, he'd rather sit quietly and live in peace with God and
neighbor. Well—he is not wholly repentant, of course, but we
sense a continuance of the transformation of character begun after
the *Pardoner's Tale* and emblematic of the spiritual regeneration
taking place as the pilgrimage works its way toward Canterbury.
Actually metaphysical, social, and aesthetic developments all
come together at the conclusion of this tale in those closing lines,
"For douteless, if we be sory and repentant of the synnes and

giltes which we han trespassed in the sight of oure Lord God,/he is
so free and so merciable/that he wole foryeven us oure giltes,/and
bryngen us to the blisse that nevere hath ende." Again, and more
clearly than earlier, we see an explicit concern with the
pilgrimage's spiritual dimension and a foreshadowing of *Parson's
Prologue* and Chaucer's own retraction. Dull though it may be, the
Tale of Melibee represents a significant development in the
pilgrimage's social, metaphysical, and aesthetic movement to a
position not far distant from that Chaucer will ultimately take as
the *Tales* reach their conclusion.

THE MONK'S TALE

At the beginning of the *Monk's Tale*, as we noted earlier, Harry
Bailey finds himself in the unusual state of approving pilgrim
Chaucer's performance and retreating from the sarcastic
condescension with which he had previously treated the pilgrim.
For a second time the host has been instructed. This reversal of
attitude, coupled with Harry's confessions of marital strife which
accompany it, suggest that Harry is undergoing a transformation
of character at the same time he is losing his grip over the
pilgrimage. First the Knight's enforced peace between Host and
Pardoner, now this. Finally, in an effort to reassert his former self
and the governance he thought was his, Harry turns to the Monk
and requests more mirth:

> "My Lord, the Monk," quod he, "be myrie of
>   cheere,
> For ye shul telle a tale trewely.
> Loo, Rouchestre stant heer faste by!
> Ryde forth, myn owene lord, brek nat oure game.
>   (1924-27)

Two attitudes war against each other in the lines recording Harry's
request: the awareness of time implicit in "Loo, Rouchestre stant
heer faste by!" and the assertion of the Host's will implicit in his
many oaths: "by my trouthe," "Upon my feith," "by my fader
soule." On the one hand we are conscious of the fact that time is
tight and not to be wasted; on the other hand we are reminded that
human will, in the personage of the Host, intrudes ever anon. Here
is an interesting tension, for it is not resolved with the Host's
submission to the Monk, who exhibits similar dualities.

Harry is impressed with the Monk—not for his spiritual
commitment but because of his obvious virility—and considers
him as a worthy pilgrim indeed, a counter tò his own hen-pecked
self. He is not above admiring openly the man's strength and

virility and potentiality (not all of which, we understand from the *General Prologue*, has remained potentiality). "A man deserving to be an officer, even a governor," Harry concedes. But these remarks comment not only on the Host's inadequacies and distorted sense of values, but on the Monk's image as well. He comes off as a strong, masculine figure—such is the gist of Harry's remarks here, Chaucer's observations of the *General Prologue*, the Prioress's remark about monks as holy men, and—by implication—the Shipman's depiction of monk as seducer in his tale. It may in fact be for precisely this fact that the Monk chooses moral tragedies instead of the mirth Harry requested.28 In any event, the Monk is clearly not pleased with his own image (we can imagine the look he has given Harry to elicit the Host's remark "But be nat wrooth, my lord, though that I pleye") and sets out to correct it as best he can. He does so by assuming temporarily the dominance Harry has so easily yielded him, and telling his tragedies rather than furthering the Host's game. Confused himself and alternately worldly and religious, the Monk is no ideal governor; his own moral ambivalence is reflected in his tale, which attempts solid instruction and takes the form of a sermon,29 but posits Fortune as a deity presiding over human affairs and asserts the essential tragedy of human experience. While Harry is now apparently unsure of himself and cognizant of the fact that events may range out of his control, he is manifestly ill-advised in his choice of a successor. For his part, the Monk has learned patience, but he has not managed submission to divine Providence or, in the finaly analysis, even a recognition of that Providence.

The *Monk's Tale* is, in reality, a collection of short tales *"De casibus virorum illustrium."* Like Chaucer's *Tale of Melibee*, this collection is often viewed by Chaucerian critics as dull and artless;30 one, in fact, has gone so far as to argue that the Monk is punishing the Host for "his vulgar familiarity by subjecting him to a dull, learned sermon."31 Other critics, allowing their ingenuity to do for the Monk's lack of perception, have argued somewhat unconvincinly that the stories represent a variety of perspectives on Fortune, a dialectic analagous to the dialectic of the *Canterbury Tales*, in which "the Monk veers from one to the other and back again for a multiplicity of reasons until the two [sides of his debate] collide in this one last tale, and the Monk reaches to the striking image of Fortune covering her bright face with a could just when men seem to know and to trust her (3955-56)."32 Now it seems to me that the tale is neither dull in the sense that *Sir Thopas* or the *Squire's Tale* are made to be dull, nor is it a clever dialectic which arrives ultimately nowhere. It is an oversimplification of a complex

issue treated elsewhere in the *Canterbury Tales* by the Knight,33
an examination by Chaucer of morality conveyed through exampla.
If *Sir Thopas* was too subtle, the *Tale of Melibee* too complex,
perhaps the simplicity of the Monk's sermon will instruct an
audience:

> I wol biwaille, in manere of tragedie,
> The harm of hem that stoode in heigh degree,
> And fillen so that ther nas no remedie
> To bringe hem out of hir adversitee.
> For certein, whan that Fortune list to flee,
> Ther may no man the cours of hire withholde.
> Lat no man truste on blynd prosperitee;
> Be war by thise ensamples trewe and olde.
>
> (1991-98)

What we have here is the advice of Dame Prudence without her
faith in God's goodness positioned behind Fortune. Earlier in his
literary career, Chaucer wrestled with the tragedy of human
experience, as must every true artist, and the technical language
here is ample evidence of his theoretical knowledge of tragedy as a
genre. But these tales, no matter how popular they might have
been in Chaucer's own age and later under a different title, are
rejected by both pilgrims and artist because they do not accord
with previously accepted conclusions about divine governance,
and because they assert an artistic tragic meaninglessness. The
measure of this denial is the Knight's intrusion into the *Monk's
Tale* and the evidence of the prologue to the *Nun's Priest's Tale*
that Harry Bailey wasn't even listening. Once again defective art
proves to be ineffective art.

"That ye han seyd is right ynough, ywis," explains the Knight
probably because the Monk's position accords well with his own;
the objection is not that the Monk has spoken falsely, but that
"litel hevynesse/Is right ynough to muche folk, I gesse"
(2769-70). But the Knight's position was the starting point of this
pilgrimage, and a return to it on the part of the Monk would
amount to unfortunate circularity. And, furthermore, there is no
reason—except the Monk's obvious streak of secularity—to
renege on the cosmology agreed to earlier in the pilgrimage. Harry
Bailey's objection, unlike that of the Knight, is to the veracity of
the tales and to aesthetics: "Youre tale anoyeth al this
compaignye," the Host complains, "Swich talkyng is nat worth a
boterflye/For therinne is ther no desport ne game" (2789-91). As
is frequently the case, the Host speaks better than he knows: the
tales have lacked truth, but not because they lack game; and they
have proven inadequate art, not so much because they were

serious as because people didn't listen. Certainly Harry was not
paying much attention: he has caught only the final line or two of
the last tale:

> He spak how Fortune covered with a clowde
> I noot nevere what; and als of a tragedie
> Right now ye herde.

(2782-84)

The Host requests another sort of tale. The Monk, his vision
imperfect and his talents inadequate, declines the invitation.
"Nay..., I have no lust to pleye," he tells the Host. And Harry
turns to the Nun's Priest.

THE NUN'S PRIEST'S TALE

R. M. Lumiansky would have us believe that Harry, bested by
the Monk, turns to a "scrawny, humble, and timid" Nun's Priest
as to someone he can dominate and thereby reassert his authority
over the other pilgrims.34 Others have seen the Nun's Priest as a
more substantial bodyguard for the Prioress and her charges.35
All critics agree on one point, however: the Priest is one of the
shrewdest, most subtle pilgrims in the company and tells one of
the most subtle, sophisticated, significant of the *Canterbury Tales*.
"A high-water mark of complex thematic statement in the
Canterbury Tales," writes Paul Ruggiers.36 A summary of "all
the themes central to the fragment," claims Helen Corsa.37 "No
other work he [Chaucer] wrote is so rich in juxtaposition of styles
and rhetorical devices," states Trevor Whittock.38 From the
modern point of view at least, the *Nun's Priest's Tale* marks the
apogee of the second half of the Canterbury pilgrimage.

Thematically the tale returns to concerns and motifs which
Chaucer has dealt with throughout the *Canterbury Tales*: Fortune,
free will and predestination, order and disorder in the cosmos, art
and aesthetics. Lines radiate from the *Nun's Priest's Tale* to
virtually every other tale told on the pilgrimage. Of course the
Priest's remark "Lo, how Fortune turneth sodeynly" (3403) recalls
the *Monk's Tale*, and the Boethian pilosophising of the cock recalls
the Knight's. But that series of learned exempla, offered by
Chauntecleer in support of his argument that dreams do indeed
have meaning, recalls the pilgrimage's other exempla: the Friar's
and Summoner's tales, the *Prioress's Tale*, the *Man of Law's Tale*
(in the second exemplum's reference to shipwreck), the *Monk's
Tale* again. Chauntecleer and Pertelote's debate brings to mind

the entire marriage group, as well as the *Tale of Melibee* in which Prudence offered her husband such sage advice. Chauntecleer's line, "My gold caused my mordre, sooth to sayn" reminds us vaguely of the Pardoner's sermon; the Priest's defensive "Thise been the cokkes wordes, and nat myne;/I kan noon harm of no womman divyne" (3265-66) sound like an open apology to the overbearing Wife of Bath. And the Priest's closing admonition to his audience: "Taketh the moralite, goode men"—how many of the Canterbury tales does that line bring to mind? Surely the *Nun's Priest's Tale*, no less than the *Parson's Tale*, points outward to all the other tales of Chaucer's pilgrimage and is a significant summing up of the artist's position prior to the last few developments of the pilgrimage and the company's entrance into Canterbury.

The specific occasion of the Priest's tale, however, is the debate on aesthetics which has been taking place throughout fragment VII. His contribution to the discussion is a simple tale "of a cok.../That took his conseil of his wyf, with sorwe" (3252-53). It is followed by a frank assertion that the tale has moral meaning and an invitation to those who disagree to "take the moral":

> But ye that holden this tale a folye,
> As of a fox, or of a cok and hen,
> Taketh the moralite, goode men.
> For seint Paul seith that al that writen is,
> To oure doctrine it is ywrite, ywis;
> Taketh the fruyt, and lat the chaf be stille.
> (3438-43)

We shall hear these lines again in Chaucer's *Retraction:* "For oure book seith, 'Al that is writen is writen for oure doctrine,' and that is myn entente." The concept is important to Chaucer, especially at this stage of the pilgrimage, and it was important to mediaeval exemplum preaching, in which context the *Nun's Priest's Tale* is most profitably considered. Art constructs a narrative (or draws a narrative from natural, human, or biblical history) upon which grammar constructs a gloss from which listeners draw moral sentence. We have seen such exempla earlier in the *Canterbury Tales* in the tales of the Man of Law and the Clerk, although the Clerk's narrative was so allegorical as to lack any pretense to reality. Certainly this aesthetic is not original to Chaucer's Nun's Priest; it was the dominant aesthetic of the late middle ages,39 having gained currency among friars of the twelfth century and set the model for subsequent homiletic and visual art.40 Narrative, gloss, moral sentence: the backbone of fourtheenth-century homiletic aesthetic theory.

Not insignificantly, this aesthetic is imposed by the Priest upon a fable drawn from the popular *Roman de Renart*41 at a time when fables from the *Roman* and elsewhere had achieved considerable popularity with preachers,42 circulating widely in the collections of such noted mediaeval preachers as Nicole Bozon, Odo of Cheriton, Jacques de Vitry, and John Bromyard.43 The allegorized fable had, by the fifteenth century become such a commonplace as to inspire a collection by that schoolmaster of Dunfermline, Robert Henryson.41 And the fable had, by Chaucer's day, become a staple of visual art, carved into misericords and pillars, painted into manuscripts, adorning door jambs in churches all across England.45 Certainly Chaucer the poet would have been more than familiar with the story of the cock and hen from any number of sources, and the use to which it was being put in fourteenth-century homiletics.46 The Nun's Priest's tale of Chauntecleer and Pertelote, then, would have seemed as natural in the mouth of a priest as the Miller's fabliau seems in the mouth of a drunken wrestler.

What is surprising, or more properly perplexing, is the wealth of moral sentence which has been derived from the tale. Chauntecleer himself offers one moral:

> For he that wynketh, whan he sholde see,
> Al wilfully, God lat him nevere thee!
>
> (3431, 32)

It is, incidentally, the same moral appended to the tale by the anonymous scribe who attached the tale to the eighth century *Romulus* manuscript at Rheims. The fox answers with a moral of his own:

> "Nay," quod the fox, "But God yeve hym meschaunce,
> That jangleth when he sholde holde his pees."
>
> (3433, 34)

For his part, the Nun's Priest offers a lesson of his own:

> Lo, swich it is for to be recchelees
> And necligent, and trust on flaterye.
>
> (3435, 36)

But this is not the same moral he has suggested earlier: "Wommennes conseils been ofte colde" (3256). Obviously, as Walter Scheps and many others before him have observed, any fable which can produce as many different morals as the *Nun's*

Priest's Tale does cannot be considered typical. Furthermore, the various morals contradict, rather than complement each other.47 Speaking when one should be silent is irrelevant to sleeping when one should see; in fact, it is by inducing speech that the sleeper redeems himself. And vice versa. Either moral invalidates the contention that woman's counsel was responsible for the whole unfortunate episode, and in doing so relegates approximately two thirds of the tale to irrelevance. In fact, as most modern critics agree, not one of the four explicitly stated morals adequately explains a tale which Chaucer has clearly taken great pains to work into a real literary masterpiece. We might settle for this kind of a moral with the Prioress's or Manciple's tales, but here it is completely insufficient.

Dissatified with Chaucer's (or the Nun's Priest's) aphorisms, critics have moved on to morals of their own. John Spiers believes that the tale's theme is simply that pride goes before a fall, and what we read is a variety of forms of pride before a variety of falls.48 J. Leslie Hotson reads the tale as historical allegory.49 R. Leneghan reads it as rhetorical parody.50 A host of recent critics reads it as religious allegory.51 Each, of course, finds the other's reading inadequate; and each *is* inadequate. Possibly the true moral, as poet Chaucer and pilgrim Priest see it, is the ambiguity of human experience, or the inconstancy of Fortune, or the inscrutability of God. Or just possibly Chaucer intends none of these at all, although he certainly invites each in its turn. In following the Nun's Priest's invitation, we are following an invitation to engage in a practice which Chaucer finds insufficient justification for art: we are asked to moralize fiction into instruction which art will not support. We commit the error to which many of Chaucer's contemporaries as well as the Parson will object,52 and Chaucer has prepared certain pitfalls for us. The aesthetic of the *Nun's Priest's Tale,* in the final analysis, is an anti-aesthetic, a denial of fable (in both its broadest and narrowest sense) as a vehicle for the conveyance of morality. As each moral collapses upon itself, we are drawn ever closer to the inevitable conclusion: moral sentence cannot be carried in the vehicle of narrative art, for the art keeps getting in the way, obstructing and undercutting morality at every turn.

Take, for example, the purported historical allegory in this tale. Now Chaucer is not generally conceded to have been a politically oriented writer in the sense we know Shakespeare of Yeats or Byron to have been. Only the *Book of the Duchess* is universally conceded to relate to the poet's lengthy life of public service and his close affiliation with the courtly elite of fourteenth century

England, and it is not really a poem on the political situation per
se. But the attitude strikes one as more than a bit unusual, since
our experience in English literature has been that great writers,
especially writers as close to politics as Chaucer, have reflected a
great deal of the political goings on of their age in their art. J.
Leslie Hotson, predictably, has made a start in interpreting the
Nun's Priest's Tale along political lines,5 although his views have
found a chilly reception among other readers of the poem. Hotson
observes that the fox of this poem is a typically named Russell,
notes further that he has inexplicably turned from a red fox to a
"col-fox, ful of sly iniquitee," observes the mock heroic nature of
the tale itself and the inadequacy of standard morals, and looks in
the direction of history. Nicholas Colfax, we are told, was a minion
of Mowbray involved in the murder of the Duke of Gloucester at
Calais in 1397 upon the order of Richard II, by whom he was later
pardoned. Sir John Russell turns out to have been another of
Mowbray's underlings. Indirectly, then, the fox of the *Nun's
Priest's Tale* is associated with Richard II via Mowbray.
Chauntecleer's colors identify him as Bolingbroke, and the events
of the tale become an historical allegory describing the initial fall
(banishment) of Henry Bolingbroke after the celebrated duel at
Coventry in 1398, and his subsequent return to England and
political grace. The tumult attending the departure of
Chauntecleer from the widow's yard reflects the tumultuous
send-off given Henry when he left England for exile; the undoing
of Russell represents the return of Henry IV and the discomfiture
of his enemies.

Now all of this is not as absurd as it may sound; Hotson's
argument is more thorough and more convincing than my brief
summary. What is significant is his own admission that "much is
left unexplained; that some of the passages which I have not dealt
with appear to deny the probability of my suggestions."54 He is
correct; the fact is that it remains largely improbable. But the hints
of historical allegory, rooted in Chaucerian alterations of his
source, seem to invite while at the same time denying such a
moral, and the whole historical business comes off very
ambivalently. *J. Leslie Horton*

While the historical allegory has found little support among
critics, another equally inadequate allegory has generated
considerable enthusiasm, especially in recent years. The details of
a Christian allegory will virtually sketch themselves once the
proposition is presented: into Chauntecleer's garden sneaks the
devil-fox, flattering him and—as poor Chauntecleer heeds the
advice of his wife—carrying him off to his damnation. The

Neville
Coghill

barnyard groans with the fall of Chauntecleer, as did Cration with
the Fall of Adam. But, in the words of one such allegorization,
"since Christian hope extends to the last, the once uxorious
Chauntecleer now turns for divine aid against an adversary as
powerful as Daun Russell, and with all the alertness of his
celebrated nature, he begs for help."55 Divine intervention in the
personage of the Holy Spirit (who else could inspire so silly a fowl
to such heroic endeavor?) rescues Chauntecleer, who flies to a tree
(type of the cross, anti-type of the tree in Eden), where he is saved.
The allegory is given textual support not only by the frequent
appearance of this cock and fox fable in medieval homiletic
collections, but by a passage in the tale itself ("Wommennes
conseil broghte us first to wo,/And made Adam fro Paradys to
go,/Ther as he was ful myrie and wel at ese") and by other usages
of the cock and fox story in medieval art and literature.56

Like the historical allegory, however, this spiritual allegory is
denied by the fable itself. Chauntecleer saves himself—there is no
divine intervention, either from the forces of Holy Church
ineffectually pursuing the demon-fox out of the garden, or from
divine Providence. Russell, having entered the garden, addresses
himself not to Pertelote-Eve, but to Chauntecleer-Adam.
Biblically, of course, Adam is seduced through his spouse; in the
Nun's Priest's Tale, Pertelote is off-stage long before the fox
makes his appearance. There is, in addition, no biblical analogue
for Chauntecleer's dream and the ensuing discussion. The tale
does indeed throw out "a light allegorical hint," as Neville Coghill
and J.R.R. Tolkien put it,57 and the Christian allegorical
interpretation might explain those otherwise puzzling lines on
predestination and free will (3229-50), but in the finaly analysis
such an allegory proves no more useful or adequate than Hotson's
historical allegory or the simple morals offered by fox, cock, and
Priest.58

Again and again the *Nun's Priest's Tale* invites critical
explanation only to deny meaning in contradiction and absurdity.
The ultimate measure of such ambivalence must be the nature of
Chauntecleer and lady Pertelote themselves. On the one hand they
are so very human, spouting high pilosophy and tricked out in the
plumage of noble lord and lady. "Have ye no mannes herte, and
han a berd!" Pertelote rants in 2920. But on the other hand they
are so very animal, fluttering into trees, pecking up worms and
corn, complaining that the perch is too narrow to allow for
Chauntecleer to ride his wife properly. The human and the animal
coexist in this tale, sometimes within a line or two of each other:

> Thus roial, as a prince is in his halle,
> Leve I this Chauntecleer in his pasture,
> And after wol I telle his aventure.
>
> (3184-85)

At the very moment when we begin to take Chauntecleer seriously, there he is pecking up laxatives, fluttering up into trees, acting his old silly self. Such ambivalence undercuts any serious attempt to heed the Priest's admonition and take a moral from the tale. We cannot. Every time we try, we are reminded that this *is*, after all, only a couple of very chickeny chickens in the back yard of some poor widow. And this is precisely the reaction Chaucer anticipates, because it is the position at which he himself has finally arrived in the dialectic of fragment VII. Fable is, finally, fable—nothing more, nothing less. It will not serve to convey high sentence or even simple morals. "Take the fruit, leave the chaf," the Priest enjoins us, knowing full well we cannot.59 "Why sholde I sowen draf out of my fest,/Whan I may sowen whete, if that me lest?" questions the Parson (X 35, 36) when asked for a fable. "Thou getest fable noon ytoold for me;/For Paul, that writeth unto Tymothee,/Repreveth hem that weyven soothfastnesse,/And tellen fables and seich wrecchednesse" (X 31-34). The connection between the *Parson's Prologue* and the *Nun's Priest's Tale* is as clear as it is obvious: fable—in both the broader and narrower meaning of the word—is being rejected as a vehicle for metaphysics. Chaucer has arrived at an aesthetic which denies art entirely. The pilgrimage is very nearly complete.

FOOTNOTES TO CHAPTER IV

1 For a more detailed treatment of the position of fragment VI, see Robinson, p. 726.

2 Most commonly, however, the *Physician's Tale* is not considered at all. Cf. Corsa, Huppé, Muscatine, Robertson, and Ruggiers. Whittock devotes a chapter of some six pages to the *Physician's Tale*. There is virtually no significant criticism in journals.

3 *A Reading of the Canterbury Tales*, 180. Corsa (p. 122) would have the tale's theme be "the preservation of 'holy chastity' at the cost of life."

4 Both Corsa ("given to flatly dogmatic statements", "has neither zest nor joy in the world he sees with humorless and impoverished eyes") and Whittock ("Chaucer is dramatising his pilgrim's spiritual vision, and asking the reader to recognise its defects") object to the rigid morality of the Physician's position.

5 For discussion of the medieval position on this story, see Robertson, *A Preface to Chaucer*, pp. 99-103.

6 Both remarks are Whittock's, p. 183.

7 "There is a strong flavor of the didactic in the tale," writes Ruggiers of the *Pardoner's Tale* (p. 122), "Yet the didacticism must be seen in the light of the speaker's intention, an intention which undermines its ostensible morality."

8 This, Ruggiers assumes (p. 122) is the theme of the *Physician's Tale*.

9 Central to any understanding of the moral implications of this Pardoner's physical deficiency is Robert P. Miller's essay, "Chaucer's Pardoner, the Scriptural Eunuch, and *The Pardoner's Tale*," *Speculum*, 30 (1955), 180-99.

10 Interpretations of the Pardoner's behavior antedating 1940 have been admirably summarized by G. G. Sedgewick in his essay "The Progress of Chaucer's Pardoner," *Modern Language Quarterly*, 1 (1940), 431-58. Since then Paul F. Baum has produced a useful bibliography of criticism in his *Chaucer: A Critical Appreciation* (Durham: Duke University Press, 1958), pp. 44-59. A list of the most crucial studies of the Pardoner would include, but not restrict itself to the following: George L. Kittredge, *Chaucer and his Poetry* (Cambridge, Mass.: Harvard University Press, 1915), pp. 211-18; Sedgewick (above); R. M. Lumiansky, "A Conjecture Concerning Chaucer's Pardoner," *Tulane Studies in English*, 1 (1949),

1-29; Alfred L. Kellogg, "An Augustinian Interpretation of Chaucer's Pardoner," *Speculum,* 26 (1951), 465-81; Robert P. Miller (above); James L. Calderwood, "Parody in *The Pardoner's Tale*," English Studies 45 (1964), 302-9; David Harrington, "Narrative Speed in the *Pardoner's Tale*," Chaucer Review, 3 (1968), 50-59; Ruggier's essay in *The Art of the Canterbury Tales,* pp. 121-30; and Whittock's essay in *A Reading of the Canterbury Tales,* pp. 185-94. My own view of the Pardoner's performance derives in the main from E. Talbot Donaldson's notes in *Chaucer's Poetry* (New York: Ronald Press, 1958).

11 On this interruption, see Arthur K. Moore, "The Pardoner's Interruption of the *Wife of Bath's Prologue*," *Modern Language Quarterly,* 10 (1949), 49-57.

12 "The Progress of Chaucer's Pardoner," p. 446.

13 The assertion of Tupper that "he—and not the Friar, who 'knew the tavernes wel in every toun' (Prologue, A 240)—was deemed the typical tavern-reveler of the company, fond of both his glass and his lass" would seem, in light of the narrator's comments of the *General Prologue,* the gentles' reactions of the *Pardoner's Introduction,* and the Host's behavior in both *Introduction* and *Tale,* to be untenable. See "The Pardoner's Tavern," *Journal of English and Germanic Philology,* 13 (1914), 563.

14 "The Progress of Chaucer's Pardoner," p. 445.

15 Most recent criticism focuses on puns and word-play, or the problem of teller. Ruggiers' essay (*The Art of the Canterbury Tales,* pp. 80-89) is probably the most useful entry to the tale.

16 Alan T. Gaylord, "*Sentence* and *Solaas* in Fragment VII of the Canterbury Tales: Harry Bailey as Horseback Editor," *PMLA* 82 (1967), 226-35.

17 The conjecture was first offered by J.S.P. Tatlock in *The Development and Chronology of Chaucer's Works,* Chaucer Society, Second Series, No. 37 (London, 1907). Frederick Tupper objected in "The Bearings of the Shipman's Prologue," *Journal of English and Germanic Philology,* 33 (1934), pp. 352-72; he was seconded by Robert L. Chapman, "The *Shipman's Tale* Was Meant for the Shipman," *Modern Language Notes,* 71 (1956), 4-5. But virtually all contemporary critics agree with Tatlock: William W. Lawrence, in "Chaucer's *Shipman's Tale*," *Speculum,* 33 (1958), 56-68; and Lumiansky (*Of Sondry Folk,* p. 74), Ruggiers (*The Art of the Canterbury Tales,* p. 80), and Whittock (*A Reading of the Canterbury Tales,* p. 195).

18 The term *fabliau* is used here very loosely. In "The Facade of Bawdry: Image Patterns in Chaucer's *Shipman's Tale*," Janette Richardson argued with some degree of cogency that the tale is not a true fabliau in that it carries a norm absent in the genre (and in Chaucer's "pure fabliaux," the Miller's, Reeve's, and Cook's tales).

19 *Chaucer* (New York: Sheed and Ward, 1952), p. 207.

20 The character of Madame Eglantine has been scrutinized on more than one occasion. Most significant are the studies of Eileen E. Power, "Madame Eglantyne, Chaucer's Prioress in Real Life," *Medieval People* (Boston: Methuen, 1924), chap. 3; and Sister Madeleva, *Chaucer's Nuns and Other Essays* (New York: Appleton, 1925).

21 Whittock also notes the significance of these parallels, but sees them as designed to "give added authenticity and relevance to the *Tale*" (*A Reading of the Canterbury Tales*, p. 205). Kittredge was also aware of them, which caused him to read the *Tale* as a case of thwarted motherhood. See *Chaucer and His Poetry* (Cambridge, Mas.: Harvard University Press, 1915), p. 155.

22 Maurice Cohen, ignoring this fact, has been lead to read the Prioress as "an anal-erotic type. Condemned to genital renunciation and the guilt atending her unsuccessful repressions, she seeks to overcome her ambivalence toward the father and religious personages who have imposed an impossible sacrifice on her." Cohen argues that therefore "it should be realized that Chaucer's characterization of the Prioress is not an 'affectionate...portrait' of a 'perfect lady'," but a vicious satirization. This is nonsense. See "Chaucer's Prioress and her Tale: A Study of Anal Character and Anti-semitism," *Psychoanalytic Quarterly*, (1962), 232-49.

23 "*Sentence and Solaas* in Fragment VII of the *Canterbury Tales*," 226.

24 The notion of *Thopas* as satire can be traced to Thomas Tyrwhitt's edition of the *Tales*, re-edited by C. C. Clarke (Edinburgh, 1868). "Sir Thopas was clearly intended to ridicule the 'palpable, gross' fictions of the common rhymers of that age" (I, cxxxii). This has proven a majority view: see A. Wigfall Green, "Chaucer's 'Sir Thopas'," *University of Mississippi Studies in English*, 1 (1960), 1-11 and Charles A. Owen, Jr., " 'Thy Drasty Rhymyng...'," *Studies in Philology*, 63 (1966), 533-64. However, John M. Manly believed the satire directed more against Flemish imitations of English romances than at the English originals; see "Sir Thopas, a Satire," in

Essays and Studies by Members of the English Association
(Oxford: Clarendon Press, 1928), 13, 52-73. Miss Lilian
Winstanley thought the piece a satire against Philip van
Artevelde; see *The Tale of Sir Thopas*, ed. Lilian Winstanley
(Cambridge, Eng.: Cambridge University Press, 1922). Both
Manly and Winstanley are rebutted by William W. Lawrence,
"Satire in *Sir Thopas*," *PMLA*, 50 (1935), 81-91. Arthur K.
Moore, "*Sir Thopas* as Criticism of Fourteenth-Century
Minstrelsy," *Journal of English and Germanic Philology*, 53
(1954), 532-45 argues that Chaucer's parody is of "the minstrel
equally with the poorer romances and the Flemings."

25 John M. Manly, "The Stanza-forms of *Sir Thopas*," *Modern Philology*, 8 (1910), 1-4.

26 See Paul Strohm, "The Allegory of *The Tale of Melibee*," *Chaucer Review*, 2 (1967), 32-42. The tale has also been interpreted as having political significance, although those interpretations are currently out of favor. See J. Leslie Hotson, "The *Tale of Melibeus* and John of Gaunt," *Studies in Philology*, 18 (1921), 429-52; William W. Lawrence, "The Tale of Melibeus," *Essays and Studies in Honor of Carleton Brown* (New York, 1940), pp. 100-10; and Gardiner Stillwell, "The Political Meaning of Chaucer's *Tale of Melibee*," *Speculum*, 19 (1944), 433-44.

27 W. P. Ker has written, "The *Tale of Melibeus* is perhaps the worst example that could be found of all the intellectual and literary vices of the Middle Ages—bathos, forced allegory, spiritless and interminable moralising." See "Chaucer" in *English Prose*, vol. 1, Fourteenth to Sixteenth Centuries, ed. Henry Craik (Macmillan, 1893), p. 40. Trevor Whittock writes, "The *Tale of Melibeus* is an enormous bore, and the bane of commentators," and moves on to speculate that it was a commissioned translation, requested of Chaucer by a friend "who had a low regard for poetry, art or genuine thought, but who wished at times to be informed on matters of fashionable interest," then included by Chaucer in the *Tales* as a mischievous afterthought (*A Reading of the Canterbury Tales*, pp. 210-13). Such a notion in itself preposterous: Chaucer was certainly not about to waste time or parchment on so lengthy a bad joke if he had found it necessary to interrupt the infinitely funnier joke of *Sir Thopas* after a couple of hundred lines. The most reasonable assessment of the tale is that Chaucer appreciated some elements in it and wanted it where it is...all twenty pages of it.

28 This position is developed at some length by Lumiansky, *Of Sondry Folk*, pp. 97-104, and by Trevor Whittock, *A Reading of the Canterbury Tales*, pp. 218-20. It is, I believe, the most satisfactory explanation of a minor Chaucerian puzzle, how the worldly Monk comes to tell the tale he does.

29 See Claude Jones, "The Monk's Tale, a Mediaeval Sermon," *Modern Language Notes*, 52 (1937), 570-72.

30 R. K. Root, in *The Poetry of Chaucer* (New York: Peter Smith, 1957), calls the tales "unspeakably monotonous"; Whittock speaks of "mindless repetition of (almost) meaningless incident" (*A Reading of the Canterbury Tales*, p. 220).

31 Lumiansky (*Of Sondry Folk*, p. 102). A similar position is taken by Joella Owens Brown in "Chaucer's Daun Piers: One Monk or Two?" *Criticism*, 6 (1964), 44-52.

32 William C. Strange, "*The Monk's Tale:* A Generous View," *Chaucer Review* 1 (1967), 167-80.

33 See R. E. Kaske's excellent study, "The Knight's Interruption of the *Monk's Tale*," *English Literary History*, 24 (1957), 249-68.

34 "The Nun's Priest in the *Canterbury Tales, PMLA*, 68 (1953), 896-906.

35 Marie Padgett Hamilton, "The Convent of Chaucer's Prioress and Her Priests," *Philologica; The Malone Anniversary Studies* (Baltimore, 1949), pp. 179-90; and Arthur Sherbo, "Chaucer's Nun's Priest Again," *PMLA*, 64 (1949), 236-46.

36 *The Art of the Canterbury Tales*, p. 184.

37 *Chaucer: Poet of Mirth and Morality*, p. 212.

38 *A Reading of the Canterbury Tales*, p. 228.

39 See especially G. R. Owst, *Literature and Pulpit in Medieval England* (Cambridge, Eng.: Cambridge U. Press, 1933) and Owst, *Preaching in Medieval England* (Cambridge, Eng.: Cambridge U. Press, 1926).

40 It scarcely bears mentioning that an entire school of Chaucerians, led by D. W. Robertson, Jr., views virtually all of Chaucer's work (and all of medieval literature) as conscious exemplum, either of *caritas* or its antithesis, *cupiditas*.

41 See Kate O. Peterson, *On the Sources of the Nunne Priestes Tale*, (Boston, 1898), Radcliffe College Monograph, No. 10; reprinted New york: Haskell House, 1966).

42 Fables had also achieved considerable popularity with teachers, who used them as subjects for assigned compositions, R. T. Lenaghan has shown. It seems more likely that the Nun's Priest, being a clergyman, would produce a parody of a sermon than that the tale parodies such

compositions, as Mr. Lenaghan argues in "The Nun's Priest's Fable," *PMLA*, 78 (1963), 300-7.

43 See Nicole Bozon, *Les contes moralises de Nicole Bozon*, ed. Paul Meyer and P. Toulmin Smith (Paris, 1889); Odo of Cheriton, *Fabulae*, ed. Leopold Hervieux (*Les Fabulistes Latins*, vol 4), Paris, 1897, reprinted New York: Burt Franklin, n.d.; and Jacques de Vitry, *The Exempla and Illustrated stories from the Sermones Vulgares of Jacques de Vitry*, ed. Thomas Frederick Crane (London, 1890), Folklore Society, vol. 26.

44 "The Morall Fabillis of Esope the Phrygian" in Robert Henryson, *Poems and Fables of Robert Henryson*, ed. H. Harvey Woods (Edinburgh: Oliver and Boyd, 1958). Note that all Henryson's fables are not out of the aesopic tradition.

45 See Kenneth Varty, *Reynard the Fox*, (New York: Humanities Press, 1967).

46 Chaucer was familiar with the work of Odo of Cheriton and used his exempla in the *Pardoner's Tale*. See Albert C. Friend, "Analogues in Cheriton to the Pardoner and His Sermon," *Journal of English and Germanic Philology*, 53 (1954), 383-88. And see Robert A. Pratt, "Three Old French Sources of The Nownes Preestes Tale," *Speculum* 47 (1972), 422-44 and 646-68.

47 "Chaucer's Anti-Fable: *Reductio ad Absurdum* in the *Nun's Priest's Tale*," *Leeds Studies in English*, 4 (1970), 1-10.

48 *Chaucer the Maker* (London: Faber, 1951), pp. 185-93.

49 "Colfax vs. Chauntecleer," *PMLA*, 39 (1924), 762-81.

50 "The Nun's Priest's Fable," *PMLA*, 78 (1963), 300-7.

51 See Speirs (above); Huppé (*A Reading of the Canterbury Tales*, pp. 174-84); Mortimer J. Donovan, "The 'Moralite' of the Nun's Priest's Sermon," *Journal of English and Germanic Philology*, 52 (1953), 498-508; Bernard S. Levy and George R. Adams, "Chauntecleer's Paradise Lost and Regained," *Medieval Studies*, 29 (1967), 178-92; and Judson Boyce Allen, "The Ironic Fruyt: Chauntecleer as Figura," *Studies In Philology*, 66 (1969), 25-35.

52 See Stephen Manning, "The Nun's Priest's Morality and the Medieval Attitude Toward Fables," *Journal of English and Germanic Philology*, 59 (1960), 403-16.

53 "Colfax vs. Chauntecleer," above.

54 p. 778.

55 Donovan, p. 507.

56 Kenneth Varty (*Reynard the Fox* plate II) has photographed one depiction of the cock and fox story which juxtaposes this fable to the story of St. George and the dragon. The moral here

is obvious: as St. George is a type of Christ, the New Adam, slaying the demon-dragon and winning salvation, Chauntecleer is a type of the old Adam, carried to his damnation by a demon-fox.

57 Chaucer, *The Nun's Priest's Tale* (London: Harrap, 1959), p. 27.

59 The Christian allegory is all but destroyed by E. Talbot Donaldson, who concludes his discussion with the observation, "Even if one were to accept the allegorical interpretation of this tale, I cannot see that much has, critically speaking, been gained." See "Patristic Exegesis in the Criticism of Medieval Literature: the Opposition," *Speaking of Chaucer* (New York: Norton, 1970), p. 148. To this I can only add that any interpretation of this tale which involves cloaking high theology in the burlesque of mock epic raises serious questions about Chaucer's taste; I must reject flatly Spiers' notion of "a targi-comic allegory of the Fall" and "Universal chaos of the Fall as burlesque" (*Chaucer the Maker*, p. 192).

52 This reading is close to the conclusions reached by Donaldson (*Chaucer's Poetry*, p. 942) and Muscatine in *Chaucer and the Trench Tradition*. Muscatine finds in the fable the epitome of Chaucer's *Canterbury Tales:* a blurring of distinctions, an erasure of boundaries, an undercutting of fine distinctions of theme and art. "Unlike fable, the *Nun's Priest's Tale* does not so much make true and solemn asertions about life," Muscatine writes, "as it tests truths and tries out solemnities...The only absolute virtue that its reading educes is an enlightened recognition of the problem of perception itself. (p. 242.) The difference between Muscatine's view and my own is, of course, that I read Chaucer as searching for and, in a tale not too distant from this, finding perception, truth, and solemn assertions about life.

CHAPTER V

FRAGMENTS VIII-X: THE PILGRIMAGE COMPLETED

During the final four tales of the Canterbury pilgrimage, social, metaphysical, even physical transmutations come thick and fast. The route of the pilgrims moves through the road from London to Canterbury to an allegorized road to the New Jerusalem; Host Harry Bailey exhibits a transformation of character which turns him first into a servant of the other pilgrims and finally into a member of the Parson's flock; Chaucer's metaphysics and aesthetics come together with a force which, after a moment's backsliding, propels him headlong into his retraction. These final *Canterbury Tales*, long relegated to a position of critical inattention and, implicitly, artistic and thematic unimportance, prove to be among the most crucial of the collection, as they measure and record the culmination of the various movements we have been tracing in the *Canterbury Tales*. They draw together in a final statement all the thematic and imagistic strands of the pilgrimage and transform them (quite literally in the case of the Canon's Yeoman) into new forms and visions, aesthetic, metaphysical, and social.

THE SECOND NUN'S TALE

The *Second Nun's Tale* is the first step in this consolidation and transmutation, an aesthetic and metaphysical vision embodying the religious order and degree, and the attitude toward art toward which Chaucer's pilgrims have been moving ever since they left the Tabard Inn. No matter that the tale is generally conceded to be a remnant of Chaucer's youth, integrated like the *Knight's Tale* into the Canterbury scheme long after it was written;1 the issue is, as Trevor Whittock has noted, not when the tale was written, but its function in the *Canterbury Tales*.2 And what we discover is a classic example of an element in Chaucer's dialectic fitted to a position arrived at by the poet long after he had written the piece—after, in fact, he had written pieces adopting differing perspectives. The early date of the *Second Nun's Tale* illustrates not its irrelevance to the Canterbury scheme—far from it—but the contrivance of Chaucer's dialectic.

The tale's chief concerns are familiar to us by now: the profitless squandering of time in game and idleness, work as an antidote to sloth, and the centrality of will and intent to all fruitful human endeavor. Intent, busyness, and time are all brought together in the Nun's initial stanzas, set moving in a thoroughly Christian cosmos and incorporated into a thoroughly Christian metaphysics. Echoing the *Friar's Tale* and its implicit warning about the devil's subtle entrapment, but giving her admonition new and deeper significance by relating her admonition directly to the pilgrims' experience, the Second Nun warns that man is caught too easily in the trap of idleness before he himself is aware the devil has taken him. And the devil waits ever anon with his thousand subtle cords (he is, in fact, riding to overtake the pilgrims at this very moment, as we discover in the next tale). "Men dradden nevere for to dye," she warns (15), looking forward to the end of life's pilgrimage with the eyes of the Parson, and men are not careful to do good.

The antidote to such sloth, we are told, is work in all its various forms:

> And for to putte us fro swich ydelnesse,
> That cause is of so greet confusioun,
> I have heer doon my feithful bisynesse
> After the legende, in translacioun
> Right of thy glorious lif and passioun
> Thou with thy gerland wroght with rose and lilie,—
> Thee meene I, mayde and martyr, Seint Cecile.
> (22-28)

For herself the Nun chooses the labor of writing, a translation of the life of St. Cecilia. For the medievals, as Russell Peck has observed, translation was not necessarily a literary matter,3 and St. Cecilia (whose very name is glossed in one case as a combination of piety with bisyness) is herself an example of translation in the non-literary sense: she removes men from their mortal blindness and transplants them to the realms of light, she transforms everyone she meets from this world to the next. The busyness of translation, then, may have been meaningful to pilgrims mindful of concerns other than their story-telling, to readers other than Chaucer's friend Gower. On the other hand, work is, for the purposes of the Second Nun, cast in specifically literary terms: work is writing, and in this sense the story touches closely on Chaucer's own pilgrimage as Christian and artist. The good Christian writes, the Second Nun suggests, not so much to teach either explicitly or implicitly, not even to wrestle with aesthetic or metaphysical problems, but simply to avoid idleness and increase good works.

Here is a possible answer to the negations of the *Nun's Priest's Tale* and the *Tale of Thopas:* narrative art may fail to convey morals, given a certain type of art and a certain kind of audience; satirical art is potentially monotonous and dangerously indirect. Yet the creation of worthy art, inspired by good intent, may win for the artist a place in heaven by keeping his mind and hands from idleness and sin. In fact, this Nun tells us echoing the Physician, the prototype of the artist is God himself, "Creatour of every creature" (49). Cration is a work of faith which proceeds without didactic intentions: "And, for that feith is deed withouten werkis,/So for to werken yif me wit and space,/That I be quit fro thennes that most derk is!" the Nun prays (64-66). In fact, it may well be that the very act of working justifies the work, regardless of man's very human and unavoidable inadequacies which ultimately mar the poem:

> Yet preye I yow that reden that I write,
> Foryeve me that I do no diligence
> This ilke storie subtilly to endite,
> For bothe have I the wordes and sentence
> Of hym that at the seintes reverence
> The storie wroot, and folwen hire legende,
> And pray yow that ye wole my werk amende.
>
>   (78-84)

Socially, it behooves the community of pilgrims to work, for the night is coming; artistically it behooves the artist to work, for his art is the manifestation of his faith in the Christian order of things. It does not matter that the artist's mortal inadequacy flaws his product and that much may deserve retraction; reward follows sincere effort and hard work.

Significantly, Chaucer's own personality begins to intrude in the *Canterbury Tales* at this crucial juncture of translation and salvation. In a passage which has not ceased to perplex critics, the Second Nun refers to herself as an "unworthy sone of Eve" late in her prologue. Later she addresses those who *read* what she has *written*. This is clear evidence, we are told, that Chaucer wrote the translation before the Canterbury scheme was conceived and well before it was assigned to the Nun.4 Is it not possible, however, that Chaucer here intentionally drops the mask a trifle, as he will drop it at the close of the *Tales*? The position of the Second Nun closely anticipates his own in the retraction: "And if ther be any thyng that displese hem, I preye hem also that they arrette it to the defaute of myn unknonnynge, and nat to my wyl, that wolde fayn

have seyd bettre if I hadde had knonnynge" (X 1081). And in that
retraction, Chaucer will not only restate the plea of human
fallibility, but drop the fiction articulated in the *General Prologue*
that other persons, not himself, are responsible for the *Canterbury
Tales.* Strange, nearly allegorial action marks these final tales, and
I for one would not be surprised if the reference to an unworthy son
of Eve and the address to *readers* were intentional self-revelations
on the part of an artist whose fictional pilgrimage happened at this
particular juncture to be impinging especially close upon his
personal, non-fictional life.

The Nun's tale itself brings together work and teaching, as well
as the minor themes of intent, salvation, fruition, and appearance
vs. reality. Clearly Cecilia's work, manifestation of a faith which
seems initially naive and superstitious, is fruitful: her converts
quite literally people paradise. The conversion of the Romans is an
on-going process throughout the tale, and an emblem for the
transmutation of pilgrims and Host in these late stages of the
pilgrimage prior to their entry into a New Jerusalem. The tale is a
miracle, a saint's life in the mold of the Man of Law's and
Prioress's tales, and yet it is a saint's life with a difference.5 What
seemed unrealistic in the Clerk's and Man of Law's tales is here
made more palatable: these people die when confronted by the
forces of this world in the personage of Almachius. We may not
appreciate their eagerness for death, the miracle of the fiery
furnace, the angels who keep popping up all over the place, but we
appreciate the fact that the children of this world prove wiser in
their generation that the children of light. And those angels are
explained as Griselda's patience and the constant divine
intervention which rescued Constance were not:

> Tiburce answerede, "Seistow this to me
> In soothnesse, or in dreem I herkne this?"
> "In dremes," quod Valerian, "han we be
> Unto this tyme, brother myn, ywis.
> But now at erst in trouthe oure dwellyng is."
>
> (260-64)

The Parson will repeat the motif:

> And Jhesu, for his grace, wit me sende
> To shewe yow the wey, in this viage,
> Of thilke parfit glorious pilgrymage
> That highte Jerusalem celestial.
>
> (X 48-51)

Those angels represent a new reality, a new way of seeing things contraposed to more mundane shadows by Chaucer and his Nun. As Almachius' power is illusory, so the mundane world is illusion. We may not agree, but somehow the explanation makes this tale seem more sophisticated than earlier saints' lives.

And the tale is far and away more sophisticated than the Prioress's pietistic legend. This is, in fact, a heavily intellectual, almost larded tale6 which buttresses itself at every juncture with generous servings of church doctrine., explanation, and authority, from the Nun's explications of the name Cecilia to Cecilia's own lecture to Almachius (and pilgrims, and readers) on true and illusory might. "That shal I telle," Cecilia promises Tiberius, and she does. And in explaining clearly but learnedly, she lifts the tale beyond pietism and superstition, beyond the level of the *Prioress's Tale*. We accept the tale and its point: earthly governance is circumscribed by a higher governance (a point not lost on the Host, as the *Canon's Yeoman's Prologue* and subsequent action makes clear), and good work inspired by honest intention cannot fail to populate heaven. As the Romans of the tale are converted from a false governor to a true, the pilgrims on the pilgrimage will turn from Harry Bailey to the Parson, and those of us reading this remarkable journey become decidedly less skeptical about the Christianity Chaucer will so orthodoxly expouse in the *Parson's Tale*. Like the pilgrimage, then, the tale involves conversion, a regaining of sight, and—from Chaucer's point of view—honest effort that staves off idleness and wins eternal life. Like the pilgrimage and very appropriately, the tale ends at the shrine of a saint.

THE CANON'S YOEMAN'S TALE

The Canon's Yeoman's prologue and tale are linked closely to the *Second Nun's Tale*, far more so than the first line of his prologue might indicate ("When ended was the lyf of Seinte Cecile"), and far more so than Professor Robinson would have us believe.7 In fact, the transmutations of the Yeoman's confession are anti-types of those we have just heard in the Nun's life of Saint Cecilia. There God's saint won souls for the heavenly kingdom; here the devil's agent (or is it Old Scratch himself?) wins souls for the lower kingdom. Ceceilia was an "ensample" by her good teaching (93); the Yeoman pleads with the pilgrims, "Lat every man be war by me" (737). Both tales are learned, the Nun's filled with church doctrine, the Yeoman's confession filled with alchemical lore. Both tales provide us with glimpses of a new reality, divine in the one case, demonic in the other. Far from being totally unrelated, the pair form a carefully matched set, counterposing the sacred and the demonic, the elect and the damned. Saint Cecilia burns unharmed in the fiery furnace this Yeoman puffed his health away to stoke.

The transmutations of the *Canon's Yeoman's Tale* begin with the very fact of the yeoman himself: his presence, as has been noted elsewhere before this,8 brings the total number of pilgrims from twenty-nine to thirty, with all the numerological significance of such a change. The yeoman's association with alchemy and Chaucer's insistence on the number twenty-nine in the *General Prologue* and the *Parson's Prologue*, even though the figure is at variance with the actual number of pilgrims listed by Chaucer, assure us that this numerological point is neither accidental or without significance. Twenty-nine is, simply, a bad number, suggestive of spiritual deficiency, transgression, moral decrepitude.9 Thirty, by contrast, is an extention of three and a multiple of ten, thereby reflecting the Trinity, completion, perfection. In addition, thirty is a marriage number and a sign of fruitfulness.10 Simply by joining the pilgrimage, then, at this significant juncture, the Yeoman represents an emblematic numerological transformation of the company of pilgrims from spiritual deficiency to spiritual fulfillment.

Transmutation continues with the *Prologue* proper, in which both landscape and action become suprarealistic and vaguely apocalyptic:

> Er ew hadde riden fully fyve mile,
> At Boghtoun uner Blee us gan atake
> A man that clothed was in clothes blake,
> And under-nethe he hadde a whyt surplys.
> His hakeney, that was al pomely grys,
> So swatte that it wonder was to see;
> It seemed as he had priked miles three.
> The hors eek that his yeman rood upon
> So swatte that unnethe myghte it gon.
> About the peytral stood the foom ful hye;
> He was of foom al flekked as a pye...
> I demed hym som chanoun for to be.
> His hat heeng at his bak doun by a laas,
> For he hadde riden moore than trot or pass;
> He hadde ay priked lik as he were wood.
>   (555-65, 73-76)

Here comes the pair, the one dressed in a black cape which billows around him, riding on a storm of lathered horses. Obviously something is up. ''Faste have I priked,'' the Canon informs this company, ''for youre sake'' (584). It is an explanation which won't wash, as even the Host realizes. He has ridden for his own sake, we decide, to con the pilgrims out of their gold and silver. But even this explanation will not do: why should the Canon and his Yeoman ride "as though they were insane" to catch a company of pilgrims five miles out of town when pilgrims passed by almost every day and victims were to be had in town, close at hand, ripe for the plucking? The more one turns matters over in his mind, the more one is drawn to the conclusion that there is something more to these pilgrims, and something to this canon than meets the eye. We recall the Nun's admonition about Satan ever ready to catch mortals, and we note the persistent identification of this canon, of alchemy, of gold itself with the devil ("Though that the feend noght in oure sighte hym shewe," the Yeoman states in lines 916 and 17, "I trowe he with us be, that ilke shrewe!") and we conclude that here is the devil himself, riding hard upon these pilgrims in a desperate attempt to catch them unawares before they enter Canterbury.

But, significantly, this devil does not catch the pilgrims or the host sleeping; in fact, Harry's actions during this prologue reveal a ruler who is wise, vigilant, careful of his people, a governor tutored by the events of the pilgrimage and, more immediately, by the *Second Nun's Tale*. The initial exchange between Canon and Host is interesting and significant:

"God save," quod he, "this joly compaignye!
Feste have I priked," quod he, "for youre sake,
By cause that I wolde yow atake,
To riden in this myrie compaignye."

(583-86)

"God save" suggests, and not particularly obliquely either, the destination of the pilgrims from which this Canon would like to divert them, as he has diverted others; "joly" and "myrie" suggest the game which marked the early and middle stages of the journey, stages now past, when the pilgrims' minds were not intent on their destination; "wolde" indicates an assertion of will not in keeping with the spiritual purpose of pilgrimage, although certainly appropriate to this demon-alchemist, an assertion which, we have already learned, can produce nothing but discord, ignorance, and disaster; "for youre sake" suggests the Canon's false motives and the role he would like to play: pied piper down the crooked path of the *Pardoner's Tale*, with gold at the top of the hill and death just over the crest. But Harry, still spokesman for the company, is cautious, verbalizing what one senses to be a collective reaction. "He would *seem* wise..." Whether the

reservations arise from Harry's perception of a threat to his
position or a newly acquired concern for his and everyone elses'
souls is not clear. In either case, Harry is suspicious of the
Yeoman's proud boast that his lord and sovereign could turn to
gold "al this ground on which we been ridyng,/Til that we come to
Caunterbury toun" (623-24). The claim may be preposterous, but
the intelligence required to see through it is no greater than that
required to measure accurately the pilgrims described in the
General Prologue, understand many of the tales Harry has missed,
or realize that May is not struggling with Aurelius up in that pear
tree just to regain January his sight. We have seen blindness
before on this pilgrimage, but here the Host is not blind:

> And whan this Yeman hadde this tale ytold
> Unto oure Hoost, he seyde, "*Benedicitee!*
> This thyng is wonder merveillous to me,
> Syn that thy lord is of so heigh prudence,
> By cause of which men sholde hym reverence,
> That of his worshippe rekketh he so lite.
> His overslope nys nat worth a myte,
> As in effect, to hym, so moot I go!
> It is al baudy and totore also.
> Why is thy lord so sluttissh, I the preye,
> And is of power bettre clooth to beye,
> If that his dede accorde with thy speche?
>
> (627-38)

Regenerate, Harry sees through illusion and is suspicious of the
gold which has so impressed him in other pilgrims (the Prioress,
the Monk, to name only a couple). He knows a tree by its fruit, and
a bad tree by its bad fruit.

The Yeoman's response to Harry's questioning deals with the
misuse of power, the concealment of one's true nature, and the
common confidence line "I kan sey yow namoore" (651). None of
this can be expected to ennoble the Canon in anyone's opinion;
most damaging of all the Yeoman's revelations is the news that
this Canon abuses his high powers, that his wisdom is so extensive
as to be a vice, that he and his man disguise themselves like
robbers and thieves who "Holden hir pryvee fereful residence"
(660). Harry is even more incredulous and inquires about the
yeoman's facial disfigurement, a deformity which, like those of
other pilgrims, emblemizes a spiritual deformity. This last pricks
the Yeoman to confession: the Canon's work, proceeding from evil
intention, cannot reach fruition. He does not achieve the
Philosopher's Stone, and he does not overtake this pilgrimage.
With this confession of his Yeoman his projection collapses, and he
knows it. Interrupting the Yeoman, the Canon reveals his own

intent in lines reminiscent of the Pardoner:

> Hoold thou thy pees, and spek no wordes mo,
> For if thou do, thou shalt it deere abye.
> Thou sclaunderest me heere in this compaignye,
> And eek discoverest that thou sholdest hyde.
> (693-96)

Here, two centuries before Marlowe, the tactics of Mephistophilis in that last scene with Faust:

> Thou traitor, Faustus, I arrest thy soul
> For disobedience to my soverign lord;
> Revolt, or I'll in piecemeal tear thy flesh.

Faust revolts; the Yeoman does not. At the urging of Host Harry Bailey the Yeoman is about to tell all, risking discomfort of his flesh for the salvation of his soul. Seeing this, the Canon, unable to endure truth or confession and fixed like Satan in his sin, rides off from the pilgrims and from the road to salvation.11 "My lord is goon," the Yeoman observes (718); he will now take another. For a moment our minds flash back to the opening of the prologue: the Canon's horse had ridden fast and furious three or five miles, but it was his Yeoman's horse that "So swatte that unnethe myghte it gon."

The tale proper is a confession in the general tradition of the later *Mirror for Magistrates*: "Lat every man be war by me for evere!" the Yeoman warns us. "What manner man that casteth hym thereto,/If he continue, I hold his thrift ydo./For so help me God, therby shal he nat wynne" (737-40). Alchemy, quite literally the setting of one's self in the position of God, the Lord of creation, does not prosper.12 One does not attain grace thereby. It is "madness" and "folly," clearly the devil's own work.

The remainder of part one of the *Canon's Yeoman's Tale*13 is given over to a recounting of the particulars of "this cursed craft" as they pop quite randomly into the Yeoman's mind. The long lists of vessels and materials, terms and methodology may seem disconnected and a trifle dull to the modern reader, especially when introduced by lines the likes of "Yet forgat I to maken rehersaille/Of. . ." But complete recital is important to complete confession. This is surely the devil's own business, the Yeoman concludes, revealing the fruits of their incessant labor to be confusion ("The pot tobreketh, and farwel, al is go!"), dissention ("But wel I woot greet strife is us among"), accusation ("Every man chit, and halt hym yvel apayd.") and the foul odor by which Harry recognized the Canon's fraud ("Men may hem knowe by smel of brymstoon.''). All that gitters, the Yeoman warns us, verbalizing a truth which has become increasingly apparent over the course of the *Canterbury Tales*, is not gold. He who seems wisest, by Jesus, is the greatest fool (967-68). The children of darkness are wiser only in their generation.

Part two of the tale turns from alchemy as a fraud and a waste of time to alchemy as a metaphor for spiritual and metaphysical contagion.14 The canon (and, despite the protestations of the Yeoman, elicited most probably by lingering dread of his old master's parting threat, that the canon of this tale is not *his* Canon, we suspect the two are of a piece)—the canon is a religious person, and will infect an entire town (Canterbury?) if not exorcised immediately:

> If any Judas in youre covent be,
> Remoeveth hym bitymes, I yow rede,
> If shame or los may causen any drede.
>
> (1007-9)

The advice anticipates the position Chaucer takes in his retraction, and echoes remotely the Physician's advice: forsake sin, er that sin forsake you. It might appear to be directed at other churchmen on the pilgrimage, but it is in effect directed at all of us: ''false governaunce'' (989) is as fatal as it is attractive. ''What shall I pay?'' asks the priest of this tale; the answer is, of course, not forty pounds or four hundred pounds, but his soul. The unfortunate man is brought to spiritual as well as physical and financial destruction, the former for having placed his faith in the false gold of the world instead of the true gold of spiritual salvation.

The concluding lines of the *Canon's Yeoman's Tale* tie alchemy again to sin and assert once more that the end is inevitably ruin and damnation. ''Flee the fires heete'' (1408) has a double meaning, especially in light of the Second Nun's life of St. Cecelia: avoid alchemy, eschew sin. The Yeoman has done just that: he has separated himself from his Canon, and through confession he has left the heat of sin. As a result he is able to reach a conclusion at long last:

> Thanne conclude I thus, sith that God of hevene
> Ne wil nat that the philosophres nevene
> How that a man shal come unto this stoon,
> I rede, as for the beste, lete it goon.
> For whoso maketh God his adversarie,
> As for to werken any thyng in contrarie
> Of his wil, certes, never shal he thryve,
> Though that he multiplie terms of his lyve.
>
> (1472-79)

Leave off wordly pursuits, subject your will to the Lord, and you will thrive; otherwise "ye shul nothyng wynneon." And "bet than nevere is late" (1410).

The confession of the Canon's Yeoman—and this tale is, despite the denial of 1087-90, the quintessence of tale-as-confession, since it is intentionally so—is more than the reflections of an alchemist's assistant, a clerk gone bad, and the disastrous results of his seven-year commitment to the dark science; it is a confession of Everyman who has turned away from the path of sin, from the "false governaunce" of a bad lord, to join—late but not too late—this pilgrimage to spirituality. As such it reprsents the confession described by the Parson as a prerequisite to grace and entry into the New Jerusalem. It is the second to last state of pilgrim and artist.

THE MANCIPLE'S TALE

Taken out of its context in the Canterbury pilgrimage, the *Manciple's Tale* is probably the most puzzling of all the *Tales*: it is artistically thin, didactically inept, and in a sense confused—we are admonished to remember the crow and his experience and remain silent when prudent, even though what we might say happens to be the truth. The injustice of such a position has lead one critic to read the tale as "betraying the essentially cold-bloodedness of the man [the Manciple], the cruelty of the true cynic."15 It has lead another critic to find in the tale "the deft play of the parodist's craft" and view it as "a parodic mockery of the immoral 'moral tale'."16 It has lead the vast majority Chaucerians to ignore pologue and tale entirely, thereby playing things safe.

Taken in the context of the other *Canterbury Tales*, however, and viewed as a part of the various movements I have been tracing through the pilgrimage, the tale and the prologue make more sense. The time of judgment is at hand; it is a moment for meditation on sins of physical action and of verbal commission, especially in light of the verbal nature of the pilgrimage. And it is a time for some back-sliding as well, for a final moment of hopelessness and despair, a final bobbing down before the triumphant arrival in the New Jerusalem. We can understand the Manciple's concern for verbal sin, then, as we can appreciate—especially after the action of his prologue—his erroneous depiction of a god of wrath and vengeance before whom silence becomes the better part of wisdom. Furthermore, the Parson will correct matters, reassuring us of a God of mercy and forgiveness, before whom the speech of confession brings not instant death but eteranal life.

If the action of the *Canon's Yeoman's Prologue* moved us well out of the ordinary and into the surrealism of allegory, the action of the *Manciple's Prologue*, for all the apparent reflections of "the burgeois tradition of low realistic comedy,"17 is not an exercise in realism but symbolism, not in cruelty but in charity. It reads like a passage from *Piers Plowman:*

> Woot ye nat where ther stant a litel toun
> Which that yeleped is Bobbe-up-and-doun,
> Under the Blee, in Caunterbury Weye?
> Ther gan oure Hooste for to jape and pleye,
> And seyde, "Sires, what! Dun is in the myre!
> Is ther no man, for preyere ne for hyre,
> That wole awake oure felawe al bihynde?
> A theef myghte hym ful lightly robbe and bynde.
> See how he nappeth! se how, for cokkes bones,
> That he wol falle fro his hors atones!
> Is that a cook of Londoun, with meschaunce?
> Do hym come forth, he knoweth his penaunce:
> For he shal telle a tale, by my fey,
> Although it be nat worth a botel hey.
> Awake, thou Cook," quod he, "God yeve thee
>   sorwe!
> What eyleth thee to slepe by the morwe?
> Hastow had fleen al nyght, or artow dronke?
> Or hastow with som quene al nyght yswonke,
> So that thow mayst nat holden up thyn heed?"
> This Cook, that was ful pale and no thyng reed,
> Seyde to oure Hoost, "So God my soule blesse,
> As ther is falle on me swich hevynesse,
> Noot I nat why, that me were levere slepe
> Than the beste galon wyn in Chepe."
>
>   (1-24)

Now there is coarseness in these lines, no denying it, and there is a rough reassertion of the agreement between pilgrims and Host which places Roger the Cook under Harry's rule, to tell a tale where and when he demands. But there is charity here, and allegory as well. The Cook, we know only too well, has begun to tell a tale earlier; there is no reason why he should tell another here.

Moreover, there is simply no town the likes of "Bobbe-up-and-doun/Under the Blee" about which we are queried. "Do you know where it is?" Chaucer asks. No, we don't.18 Something is up. On the physical road from London to Canterbury there may be no Bob-up-and-down, but in the metaphysical sense there has been a lot of bobbing up and down on this pilgrimage, and there will be a good deal more in the prologue and tale we are about to hear; could it be that the town is nothing more than a spiritual condition through which the pilgrims are passing, a village of the mind? I think so—it certainly sounds allegorial (even in England one does not find towns called Bob-up-and-down, or towers called Truth)—and in asking us if we don't know the place Chaucer gives us a broad hint as to his purposes here. Furthermore, the allegorical quality of the town is developed in the allegory of succeeding lines. The Cook is drunk, a most inexplicable drunkenness to hear him tell it. Harry jokes coarsely, but then makes the point that a thief might easily take Roger, or he might fall into the mire, and is there no man "for preyere ne for hyre" who will help him out? We need no explanation of the theological significance of sleep, not here after the *Nun's Priest's Tale*, and we need no gloss on a thief robbing or binding the Cook. We have seen that thief just a tale ago, and know that he watches and waits to see just what straggling pilgrims he might devour. There is mockery in Harry's voice, to be sure, but there is also charity, for the Host awakens and warns the Cook, and will not let him fall. One might even argue that the tale Harry urges reflects the philosophy of the Second Nun: let us busy old Roger telling a tale, thereby keeping him awake and saving his soul.

Into this exchange intrudes the Manciple. He has his own strong sense of justice, and while it is severe in an a-Christian manner, he is right in realizing that speech may damn as well as redeem, and given the Cook's present condition, his speech would much more likely condemn than save. In fact, the Manciple makes Roger an example to the others:

> Se how he ganeth, lo! this dronken wight,
> As though he wolde swolwe us anonright.
> Hold cloos thy mouth, man, by thy fader kyn!
> The devel of heele sette his foot therin!
> Thy cursed breeth infecte wole us alle.
> Fy, stynkyng swyn! fy, foule moote thee falle!
> A! taketh heede, sires, of this lusty man.
>   (35-41)

The Manciple is self-righteous, a bit severe in his religion and strict in his judgment, but the point he makes harkens back to the Canon's Yeoman's admonition: better the Judas be cast out of a company than that he infect an entire population. It is for the pilgrims to restore the Cook to his senses, not for the Cook to pollute the pilgrimage. The Cook takes offense at the Manciple's self-righteousness (as well he might, we object), turns angry and falls off his horse into the mire, a symbolic action in keeping with his drunkenness and sleep.

What is significant is the ministry of the Manciple and the other pilgrims (for the entire company is involved in this work of charity), who help the fallen Cook back on his horse, treating his spiritual wounds, offering him drink. The consort of effort here, the communal shoving to and fro, is in itself an emblem of the harmony and charity now to be found among the group, coarse jokes and self-righteous sermoning aside. The Host observes that because the man is drunk—in a state of sin—he would obviously tell a lewd—sinful—tale; he notes that it is all Roger can do to keep himself on his horse; and, with the characteristically practical observation that if he falls again, Roger will be difficult to raise up to his horse, he passes over person and tale. He also reproves the Manciple for his sermon, suggesting that we all have our days and one day soon the Cook might take the Manciple to task. The Manciple's response is to deny serious malice in his lecture to the Cook, and to offer him a drink of wine. Why, one asks himself, would the Manciple offer wine to a drunken Cook? Why should the Cook, who formerly desired sleep more than the best gallon of wine in Cheapside, be so "wonder fayn" of such a drink and thank the Manciple "in swich wise as he koude" (93)? Even Chaucer the pilgrim wonders. And why should drink "turne rancour and disease/T'acord and love, and many a wrong apese" (97-98)? Certainly drink had none of these effects on the Miller, or on the Cook either. We can only conclude that the wine, like the initial drunkenness and that fall from the horse, has allegorical significance, that this is the wine of the mass offered to a man trapped in the mire of sin, the wine which restores individual, community, and creation to a state of grace, accord, and love. Significantly, after much bobbing up and down, after mixed coarseness and charity, the *Prologue* concludes in peace and harmony after an emblematic communion.

The tale proper, to which the Host is pointedly directed to lend an ear, develops three major points: the severity of divine judgment, man's insistence on sin, and the need to take keep of what one says. The three are not fully integrated, and that is one of the tale's artistic defects, but they are not entirely unrelated either. The severity, indeed the injustice of Phoebus' justice, for example may be explained by reading his wrath and myopia as but another manifestation of irresistible human impulses, although in anthropomorphizing God in this manner the Manciple understandably but inaccurately depicts divine justice in terms reminiscent of the *Knight's Tale*.19 It is a verbal sin committed by this, the pilgrim most conscious of verbal sins, an indication that he, like his fellow pilgrims, is not immune from the human tendency to err. The pilgrimage has, in fact, exemplified nothing so much as the attraction of sin to mortal man. Although we have seen a general movement through (and away from) sin, tales like those of the Knight, the Wife, the Reeve, the Friar have demonstrated beyond a shadow of a doubt how prone man is to wrath, lechery, idleness, and despair. These seem to be natural appetites, like the desire of a caged bird for freedom, like the cat's attraction to mice, the desire of wolves to couple. "Flesh is so newefangel, with meschaunce,/That we ne konne in nothyng han plesaunce/That sowneth into vertu any while," the Manciple concludes in 193-95. This, it would seem, is as much the sin of despair as the *Knight's Tale*, but the persistence of vice through the *Canterbury Tales*, the Cook's fall from his horse just as the company was approaching its destination, all the many conscious and unconscious confessions of the pilgrims make it appear a just assessment of the human condition. Surely the pilgrims are damned by their own confessions, condemned by the tales they have told.

> Lordynges, by this ensample I yow preye,
> Beth war, and taketh kep what that ye seye.
> (309-10)

and again,

> But he that hath mysseyd, I dar wel sayn,
> He may by no wey clepe his word agayn.
> Thyng that is seyd is seyd, and forth it gooth,
> Though hym repente, or be hym nevere so looth.
> He is his thral to whom that he hath sayd
> A tale of which he is now yvel apayd.
> (353-58)

And yet even as the Manciple tells his tale of absolute and terrible retribution for false speech, he is aware of the need to watch his speech, for he is looking ahead with the eyes of Chaucer toward the judgment now in sight. The excuses which allowed the Miller's and Reeve's tales, and many a lecherous lay besides, which suggested that a reader simply turn the page and select another tale if such broad comedy were not to his taste—these excuses will simply not do here. "Certes, this is a knavyssh speche!/Forveveth it me, and that I yow biseche," the Manciple begs (205, 6). One becomes the slave of what he says, Chaucer realizes, and articulates the position through his pilgrim. And, in terror of the judgment which here appears overly severe, the pilgrim, if not the poet, despairs. The god of this tale is a jealous god, justice without mercy, and a blind justice at that, enough to terrify even the most self-righteous Christian. But he is not the Christian god, as the Parson will make abundantly clear. This unfounded fear of wrathful and terrible judgment is itself a fall into the sin of despair, a final bobbing down before the good news and affirmation of faith which will end the pilgrimage. The *Manciple's Tale* is Chaucer's farewell to this world.

THE PARSON'S TALE

The Parson's sermon, as I have suggested earlier and others before me have noted,[20] brings the *Canterbury Tales* to its spiritual fulfillment and thus to its conclusion. The end of pilgrimage is grace, not confession or game, and when grace is attained, pilgrimage ends, confession ceases, game is over. Such is indeed the case with the *Parson's Prologue* and *Tale*, in which we see the physical transformed entirely into the metaphysical, game resolved unequivocally in earnest, art absorbed into theology, and doubt and uncertainty purged by faith.

These shifts of metaphysics and aesthetics are, characteristically, signalled by shifts in social relationships and narrative developments in the fiction of the pilgrimage. A minor but significant change, for example, is from secular to canonical time: most manuscripts read "ten of the clock" instead of "foure of the clock" in line 5, a reading which makes no sense at all when taken to be secular time (ten o'clock will simply not accord with the declination of the sun recorded in lines 2-4) but makes plenty of sense when understood as canonical time.[21] A second important change has occurred in the number of pilgrims: the imperfect twenty-nine has been transmuted by an alchemist's helper turned repentant to the perfect thirty, a transmutation of which we are reminded in the opening lines:

> By that the Maunciple hadde his tale al ended,
> The sonne fro the south lyne was descended
> So lowe that he nas nat, to my sighte,
> Degrees nyne and twenty as in highte.

(1-4)

Twenty-nine degrees, for twenty-nine pilgrims—now become thirty.

A third transformation is found in the character of the Host. Earlier he has denigrated the Parson, speaking contemptuously of him as a Lollard and a Jenkin; now, quite inexplicably except from al allegorical interpretation of the *Tales*, he seems submissive, humble, subservient:

> Oure Hoost hadde the wordes for us alle:
> "Sire Preest," quod he, "now faire yow bifalle!
> Telleth," quod he, "youre meditacioun.
> But hasteth yow, the sone wole adoun;
> Beth fructuous, and that in litel space,
> And to do wel God sende yow his grace!
> Sey what yow list, and we wol gladly heere."
>
> (67-73)

What a dramatic turnabout from the Shipman's previous "Nay, by my fader soule,...heer schal he nat preche!" In a scene which can only remind us of Harry Bailey's election in the *General Prologue*, the Parson has by unanimous consent assumed governance of the pilgrimage—with Harry Bailey acting as spokesman to announce the pilgrims' will and urge the Parson to be fruitful! For his part, Harry seems to realize that his hour is past and the Parson's come: "Almoost fulfild is al myn ordinaunce," he says in line 19, knowing good and well that he has not heard two tales from each pilgrim, knowing good and well that he planned a trip back to the Tabard for dinner. Regenerate and tutored by the discussion of the pilgrimage thus far, the Host realizes that his is not the final word (as Chaucer, in his retraction, recognizes that his is not the final aesthetic judgment) and stands ready to yield control to the representative of a higher order. Besides, Harry has committed his own verbal sins, although he has told no tale, and he has those to meditate upon. Little wonder he entreats the Parson, "Be fruitful, and that in little time."

The *Parson's Tale* is, clearly, Chaucer's own tale told in Chaucer's own voice, whether we moderns like the fact or not.[23] It was stitched together carefully from a number of sources,[24] grows directly out of earlier tales of the pilgrimage, and leads directly to the artist's own retraction of some of his more sinful works. Rigidly orthodox in its theology, comprehensive to the point of boring anyone except a medieval Christian, unequivocably affirmative and theologically comic, the tale stands as the capstone of Chaucer's metaphysical and aesthetic pilgrimage. While we may not reject it as an aberration, as a satire, as death-bed piety, we might be tempted to view it but one element in Chaucer's multi-faceted *Tales* and thus of only qualified authority.[25] This, I believe, is also to misread Chaucer: the *Parson's Tale* is the final statement of Chaucer's dialectic, the point to which his long pilgrimage finally brings him. It has the authority of finality and the poet's personal acceptance in the stance taken in his retractions. The tale is undeniable.

It is a sermon on sin, confession, penance, and–finally–absolution and grace. It assumes a Christian cosmology with the certainty and absolutism inherent in such a cosmos: "Stondeth upon the weyes, and seeth and axeth of olde pathes (that is to seyn, of olde sentences) which is the goode wey,/and walketh in that wey, and ye shal fynde refresshynge for youre soules" (77, 78). There are two ways and two ways only, the straight and the crooked. In one is refreshment and salvation, in the other damnation. We have seen the crooked way earlier, in the *Pardoner's Tale* of course, but in all those many tales which left us uncertain, confused, unrefreshed—the Knight's romance no less than the Merchant's morose commentary. The dualism recalls the two voices of the *General Prologue*, but here is a difference: there we found ambiguity, a *both...and*; here there is no equivocation and no ambiguity, an *either...or*. Unlike the folk of Jeremiah's prophecy, who would not walk therin, this company has— sometimes with considerable difficulty, as in the case of the Cook—managed to persevere in the road to Canterbury and the new Jerusalem. "Every tyme that man falleth," the Parson notes, "Be it never so ofte, that he may arise thurgh Penitence, if he have grace" (91). But there is great doubt, he goes on to say, and it is only "repentant folk, that stynte for to synne, hooly chirche holdeth hem siker of hire savacioun" (92). It is important to cease sinning, a fact relevant to the *Parson's Tale*, to the pilgrims' behavior, and to Chaucer as artist and pilgrim. He himself must not only confess his sins, but leave off sinning. The requirements of perfect penitence are contrition of heart, confession of mouth, and satisfaction, we discover. All are required of pilgrims and artists before the completion "Of thilke parfit glorious pilgrymage/That highte Jerusalem celestial" (50, 51). In return for proper penitence, the pilgrims are promised much:

> Thanne shal men understonde what is the fruyt of penaunce; and, after the word of Jhesu Crist, it is the endelees blisse of hevene,/ther joye hath no contrarioustee of wo ne grevaunce; ther alle harmes been passed of this present lyf; ther as is the sikernesse fro the peyne of helle; ther as is the blisful compaignye that rejoysen hem evermo, everich of otheres joye;/ther as the body of man, that whilom was foul and derk, is moore cleer than the sonne; ther as the body, that whilom was syk, freele, and fieble, and mortal is immortal, and so strong and so hool that ther may no thyng apeyren it;/ther as ne is neither hunger, thurst, ne coold,

> but every soule replenyssed with the sighte of the
> parfit knowynge of God./This blisful regne may
> man purchace by poverte espiritueel, and the
> glorie by lowenesse, the plentee of joye by hunger
> and thurst, and the reste by travaille, and the lyf
> by deeth and mortificacion of synne.
>
> (1076-80)

In one sense the sermon is directed to the pilgrims. We need not
schematise Chaucer, making each pilgrim reflect one or two sins or
subsins to recognize this fact.26 The centrality of the Parson's
sermon to the *Canterbury Tales* and its applicability to his pilgrims
is apparent in the many verbal echoes one discovers here of earlier
tales: "stynte for to synne, and forlete synne er that synne forlete
hem" (the *Physician's Tale*), "that syngen evere *Placebo*" (the
Merchant's Tale), "the root of alle harmes is Coveitise" (the
Pardoner's Tale), "a man may sleen hymself with his owene knyf"
(the *Merchant's Tale*), "for mariage is figured bitwixe Crist and
holy chirche" (the *Clerk's Tale*), "Seint Jerome seith" (the *Wife
of Bath's Prologue*), "Al that is writen is writen for oure doctrine"
(the *Nun's Priest's Tale*). And on and on. The pilgrims must read
themselves in the *Parson's Tale*, as must every one of us.

But Chaucer also reads himself in the tale and its prologue, for
he must also leave off sinning and the Parson's directives come to
him as well as to the others. Moreover, the Parson makes an
aesthetic statement applicable only to the poet:

> This Persoun answerde, al atones,
> "Thou getest fable noon ytoold for me;
> For Paul that writeth unto Thymothee,
> Repreveth hem that weyven soothfastnesse,
> And tellen fables and swich wrecchednesse.
> Why sholde I sowen draf out of my fest,
> Whan I may sowen whete, if that me lest?"
>
> (30-36)

The denial here, as is generally recongized, is not of fable in the
sense of animal story, but fable in the broader sense: all fictional
narrative. A broad condemnation, this, but one which grows out of
the *Nun's Priest's Tale* and Chaucer's discussion of aesthetics in
fragment VII. This is important directive, and one to be taken
seriously. "And for he shal be verray penitent, he shal...nevere
to doon thyng for which hym oghte moore to biwayle or to
compleyne, and to continue in goode wekes, or elles his
repentance may nat availle" (87).

And so, with considerable reluctance I imagine, Chaucer
repents and promises to sin no more:

> Wherfore I biseke yow mekely, for the mercy of
> God, that ye preye for me that Crist have mercy on
> me and foryeve me my giltes;/and namely of my
> transclacions and enditynges of worldly vanitees,
> the whiche I revoke in my retracciouns.
>
> (1083-84)

This is a harsh statement for moderns to accept, and many have refused to bite the bullet, circumscribing the retractions with all manner of qualification to prove that Chaucer really didn't retract much of anything, turning the piece into a death-bed repentance, attributing the retraction to someone, anyone other than the poet. More sophisticated commentators wish to balance beginning and ending, this world with the other, Miller with Parson, allowing multiple realities and committing Chaucer to none. I confess there was at time when I too believed this—after all, read correctly any tale *might* induce morality, and Chaucer did lavish so much attention on so many poems apparently rejected here. But such argument is self-delusion, for Chaucer was not deceived. The retraction was implicit, we realize in retrospect, in the very beginning of the *General Prologue* where sensuality and worldly procreation gave place to the asceticism and spirituality of the saint's shrine. Certainly it has been a foregone conclusion ever since the failure of the *Nun's Priest's Tale* to convey moral sentence. There comes a time when art seems not enough, Trevor Whittock observes, when the wisdom it can offer seems inadequate to the urgent demands of life.27 The artist is, finally, a man, and what is art compared with a man's soul? What is this world when compared with another? Would not we too opt, were we able, for the "grace of verry penitence, confessioun and satisfaccioun" that would bring us to salvation, that would make us "oon of hem at the day of doom that shulle be saved"?

The matter of Chaucer's religion has attracted its fair share of critical attention recently, partially because of the *Retraction* to the *Tales*, partially because of remarks elsewhere in the Chaucer canon. There is the doubt implicit in that remark which closes Arcite's life, "His spirit chaunged hous and wente ther,/As I cam nevere, I kan nat tellen wher" (I 2809, 10). There is the satire of ecclesiastics and ecclesiastical institutions of the *General Prologue*. And there are those troublesome opening liens to the *Legend of Good Women:*

> A thousand tymes have I herd men telle
> That ther ys joy in hevene and peyne in helle,
> And I acorde wel that it ys so;

> But, natheless, yet wot I wel also
> That ther nis noon dwellyng in this contree,
> That eyther hath in hevene or helle ybe,
> Ne may of hit noon other weyes witen,
> But as he hath herd sayd, or founde it writen;
> For by assay ther may no man it preve.
> But God forbede but men shulde leve
> Wel more thing then men han seen with ye!
>
> (F 1-11)

All of these imply a certain skepticism on the poet's part. On the other hand there are the apparently unequivocable affirmations of Parson's and Second Nun's tales, the closing scenes of *Troilus and Criseyde*, and the troublesome *Retraction* itself. The evidence has let to a variety of conclusions: Chaucer took no real stand on religious issues (Loomis), Chaucer was a Wycliffite (Simon), Chaucer was an orthodox Christian (Root, Coulton), Chaucer was a good Christian in his youth but turned agnostic in later life (Lounsbury).28 Most recently Sheila Delany has argued Chaucer's attitude to be one of "literary fideism":

> Fideism differs from faith; it is a last resort, the only kind of faith available to those who can find no reason to believe. Chaucer is no ideological poet like Jean de Meun or Dante. Religion is not his first idea but his last, so that it enters the structure of his work not as a credible solution to dialectic, but in fact as another term is dialectic...Chaucer fails, then, as a Christian poet: his success is with his art rather than with his ideology. That Chaucer is aware of some such distinction in his work, and that it makes him uneasy, is clear from the retraction appended to the *Canterbury Tales*.29

But such is not the case, as we have seen. What fails Chaucer in that series culminating in the *Nun's Priest's Tale* is in fact his art. Where art is affirmed it is as a means of driving away sinful idleness. It is the art of wheat without chaff. And it is an art out of which *Retraction* grows, not an art to which *Retraction* is appended. Ms. Delany makes the same mistake made by those who would weigh equally the Knight's and Parson's statements, the *terminus a quo* and the *terminus ad quem* of Chaucer's aesthetic and metaphysical pilgrimage, or by those who would view the tales as a series of randomly ordered points suspended between Tabard Inn and Canterbury Cathedral. The direction taken by Chaucer in his Canterbury pilgrimage should make clear nothing so much as the poet's religious orthodoxy, an orthodoxy tested by intelligent and sincere probing of alternatives and legitimate philosophical doubts, but in the end a very honest and affirmative orthodoxy. It makes as little sense to argue Chaucer a skeptic on the basis of positions taken in those early tales as it does to argue Chaucer's struggle insincere because its conclusion is prefigured in its beginning eighteen lines. The Canterbury pilgrimage is no more or less rigged than any morality play is rigged, no more or less than the life of any Christian is rigged. Always grace extends to the end; always salvation is assured if only a man persists. But the doubts and the dangers are real too, be they personified into Venus or Youth or Mamon or presented as artistic and metaphysical statements from Miller or Wife or Manciple. Chaucer was no theologian; neither was he an agnostic. He was, as we have seen, a thoughtful, orthodox Christian wrestling with matters of faith and art in a Christian poem in a Christian age. To view him as less is to impose modern doubt, modern aesthetics, modern faith in the artifice of poetry on his quintessentially medieval position.

FOOTNOTES TO CHAPTER V

1 The opinions of authorities cited in Tatlock's *The Development and Chronology of Chaucer's Works* (1907; rpt. Gloucester, Mass.: Peter Smith, 1963) on date of composition are as follow: Furnivall, 1373; ten Brink, about 1373; Kock, 1373-4; Mather, shortly after 1373; Skeat, 1369-73; Pollard, 1370-4; Root, 1373-4. An extant "Lyf of Seynt Cecyle" is mentioned in the *Legend of Good Women*, so the poem in some version antedated the *Canterbury Tales'* inception. I, for one, am not entirely convinced by arguments for a date as early as 1373; the poetry seems far more subtle and well wrought than his other early work. The tale does, however, share some of the artistic self-consciousness of such early works as the *Book of the Duchess* and the *House of Fame*.

2 *A Reading of the Canterbury Tales*, p. 251.

3 "The Ideas of 'Entente' and Translation in Chaucer's *Second Nun's Tale*," *Annuale Mediaevale*, 8 (1967), 17-37.

4 However, W. B. Gardner has argued, "When Chaucer had the Second Nun refer to herself as a 'sone of Eve,' he was merely using a word-pattern from the *Salve Regina* which he knew every Religious actually used every day of her life in reciting the Divine Office whether in Latin or English." See "Chaucer's 'Unworthy Sone of Eve'," *Studies in English*, (Austin: University of Texas, 1947), pp. 77-83.

5 Trevor Whittock has drawn this same distinction; see *A Reading of the Canterbury Tales*, pp. 255-56.

6 Chaucer's immediate source for this tale was the *Legenda Aurea* of Jacobus de Voragine, but both prologue and tale have been discovered to contain elements from Alanus ab Insulis, various Latin hymns, Dante's *Paradisio*, Jehan de Vignay, Jacobus Januensis, and Mombritius' version of the legend. See Robinson's notes, p. 756, and Paul M. Clogan's brilliant study, "*The Figural Style and Meaning of the* Second Nun's Prologue *and* Tale," *Medievalia et Humanistica*, 3 (1972), 213-40.

7 "The first line of the *Canon's Yeoman's Prologue* indicates that it was to follow the *Second Nun's Tale*. Otherwise there is no connection between either *Prologue* or *Tale* and what precedes" (p. 759).

8 Russell A. Peck, "Number Symbolism in the Prologue to Chaucer's *Parson's Tale*," *English Studies*, 48 (1967), 205-215.

9 See Peck, p. 207, and behind him Vincent F. Hopper, *Medieval Number Symbolism* (New York: Columbia University Press, 1938), p. 152.

10 See Peck, p. 208 and John Steadman, "Chaucer's Thirty Pilgrims and the *Activa Vita*," *Neophilologus*, 45 (1960), 224-30.

11 "The failure of the Canon to remain in pilgrimage, for whatever reason, implies a truly terrible judgment," observes Paul Ruggiers in *The Art of the Canterbury Tales*, p. 133.

12 See especially Edgar H. Duncan, "The Literature of Alchemy and Chaucer's Canon's Yeoman's Tale: Framework, Theme, and Characters," *Speculum*, 43 (1968), 633-56.

13 Samuel McCracken wishes to read the Yeoman's prologue as introduction; his tale, part one as "confessional prologue"; and his tale, part two as the tale proper. It seems to me such a reordering is as unnecessary as it is uncalled for. See "Confessional Prologue and Topography of the Canon's Yeoman," *Modern Philology*, 68 (1970), 289-91.

14 Joseph E. Grennen writes, "There seems to me little doubt that the Yeoman's story, Pars Secunda, is an ironic image of the sacri-religious aspect of alchemy, just as Prima Pars deals ironically with the pretensions of ordinary alchemical theory and the folly of the 'puffers'." See "The Canon's Yeoman's Alchemical 'Mass'," *Critisicm*, 3 (1962), 546-60.

15 Corsa, *Chaucer: Poet of Mirth and Morality*, p 229.

16 Richard Hazelton, "The Manciple's Tale: Parody and Critique," *Journal of English and Germanic Philology*, 62 (1963), 1-31. I find this interpretation unlikely, in that it would involve an almost precise repetition of the position of the *Nun's Priest's Tale* (and in the *Canterbury Tales*, whether viewed as dialectic or anthology, we find that Chaucer never repeats himself precisely) and unsupported by the tone of the poem. When Chaucer parodies, we find either raucous humor (*Sir Thopas*) or obvious burlesque (the *Nun's Priest's Tale*); in the *Manciple's Tale* we find neither.

17 Ruggiers, *The Art of the Canterbury Tales*, p. 248n.

18 Leading candidates for this role are Harbledown, mentioned in several early accounts of Canterbury pilgrimages, and Up-and-Down Field in Thannington. See especially Henry Littlehales, ed., *Some Notes on the Road from London to Canterbury in the Middle Ages*, Chaucer Society II. No. 30 (London: Trubner, 1898), pp. 36ff.

19 Such is, in fact, the reading of this tale given by William Cadbury in "Manipulation of Sources and the Meaning of the

Manciple's Tale," Philological Quarterly, 43 (1964), 538-48.

20 See especially Baldwin, *The Unity of the Canterbury Tales,* pp. 95-105; Ruggiers, *The Art of the Canterbury Tales,* pp. 247-57; and Trevor Whittock, *A Reading of the Canterbury Tales*, pp. 285-99.

21 See Peck, "Number Symbolism in the Prologue to Chaucer's *Parson's Tale,"* p. 209.

22 E. Talbot Donaldson, *Chaucer's Poetry* (New York: Ronald Press, 1958), pp. 948-49.

23 John Findlayson reads this tale as satire, relying in part for support on a tone established in the *General Prologue.* Nothing, to use a tired but appropriate expression, could be further from the truth. See "The Satiric Mode and the *Parson's Tale," Chaucer Review,* 6 (1972), 94-116.

24 See Kate O. Peterson, *The Sources of the Parson's Tale* (Boston: Ginn, 1901), and Alfred Kellogg, "St. Augustine and the Parson's Tale," *Traditio,* 8 (1952, 424-30.

25 Such is the conclusion of Whittock.

26 I refer, of course, to Frederick Tupper, "Chaucer and the Seven Deadly Sins," *PMLA,* 29 (1914), 93-128.

27 *A Reading of the Canterbury Tales,* p. 297.

28 For a thorough and useful review of criticism on this point, see Mary Edith Thomas, *Medieval Skepticism and Chaucer* (New York: William-Frederick Press, 1950), pp. 95-108.

29 *Chaucer's House of Fame* (Chicago: University of Chicago Press, 1972), pp. 118, 19.

INDEX

Aquinas, 58.

Adams, George, 161.

Adams, John, 113.

Alanus ab Insulis, 185.

Allegory, 3, 54, 55, 59, 78, 80-81, 84, 114, 150-154, 162, 163, 179-84.

Allen, J. B., 161.

Augustine, 5, 36.

Bailey, Harry (Host), 3, 4, 5, 8-9, 13, 14, 21, 23, 24-27, 29, 36, 39, 42, 43, 46, 48-50, 55-56, 70, 72, 75, 79-80, 85, 93, 95, 98, 101-2, 115, 124, 125-26, 129, 131-32, 137-38, 142-45, 147, 148, 163, 166-67, 169-71, 174-76, 178-79.

Baker, Donald C., 13, 73, 113, 119.

Baldwin, Ralph, 1-2, 8, 10, 57, 187.

Baugh, A. C., 115, 116.

Baum, Paul, 156.

Beichner, Paul, 113.

Benjamin, Edward, 119.

Birney, Earle, 113.

Block, Wm., 53, 63.

Bob-Up-and-Down, 15, 18, 173.

Boccaccio, 30.

Boethius, 29, 31, 35, 39, 45, 50, 52, 68, 89, 149.

Bolton, W. F., 40.

Bonjour, Adrian, 113.

Book of the Duchess, 152, 185.

Bowden, Muriel, 27, 59.

Bradshaw Shift, 12, 13.

Brewer, D. S., 118.

Bronson, Bertrand, 20, 57, 116.

Brooks, Douglas, 28, 58.

Brown, J. O., 160.

Brown, Wm., 40, 61.

Burrow, J. A., 88.

Cadbury, Wm., 186.

Calderwood, James, 157.

Canon's Yoeman, 163, 167-69.

Canon's Yeoman's Tale, 15, 120, 167-73.

Canterbury Tales, unity of, vi, 1-5, 163, 183-84.

Cawley, A. C., 76, 113.

Chapman, Robert, 157.

Chaucer, as narrator/ pilgrim, 8, 9, 20-23, 25, 50, 94, 128, 141-46, 173.

Chaucer, as poet, 3, 4, 5, 8, 10, 29, 40, 50, 62, 70, 84, 94, 98-99, 121-23, 125, 140, 141-46, 148, 151-52, 163, 165-66, 173, 177-78, 180-84, 186-87.

Chaucer Society, 13, 18, 120, 186.

Clarke, C. C., 158.

Clerk, 59, 79-80, 114.

Clerk's Tale, 11, 78-86, 89, 92, 108, 116, 181.

Clogan, Paul, 185.

Coghill, Neville, 116, 154.

Colfax, Nicholas, 153.

Cook, 46-47, 173-76.

Cook's Tale, 4, 22, 41, 46-47.

Copland, M., 45, 61.

Corsa, H. S., 18, 58, 116, 117, 149, 156, 186.

Craik, Henry, 159.

Dante, 6, 7, 119, 185.

David, Alfred, 62.

Delany, Shiela, 10, 61, 183.

De Legibus et Consuetudinibus Regni Angliae, 58.

Dempster, Germaine, 116.

Destiny, 31-35, 38-39, 52, 58, 147-49.

Donaldson, E. T., 14-15, 18, 20, 21, 57, 157, 162.

Donovan, Mortimer, 161.

Duffey, Bernard, 61-63.

Duncan, Edgar, 57, 186.

Ellesmere Order, vi, 12-15, 64, 120, 156.

Elliott, John, 116.

Exemplum, 73, 121, 148, 150, 160.

Falstaff, 65.

Farrell, Robert T., 63.

Fifield, Merle, 58, 59.

Finlayson, John, 16, 60, 187.

Fortune, 31, 32, 39, 52, 53, 83, 106, 107, 145, 147-48, 149, 152.

Fowler, Alastair, 28, 58.

Franklin, 95, 101-2.

Franklin's Tale, 64, 79, 95, 100-10, 120-121.

Friar, 20, 68, 70-78, 177.

Friar's Tale, 1, 9, 22, 26, 70-76, 149, 164.

Frost, Wm., 58, 60.

Garbaty, Thomas, 20, 57.

Gardner, W. B., 185.

Gawain, 15, 20, 132.

Gaylord, Alan, 16, 107, 140, 157.

General Prologue, 10, 11, 18-27, 28, 41, 48, 56, 64, 74, 78, 128, 135, 139, 147, 157, 166, 168, 180.

Gerhard, Joseph, 106, 119.

Gower, 50, 62, 164.

Green, Wigfall, 158.

Grennan, Joseph, 186.

Hadow, G. E., 116.

Hamilton, Marie Padgett, 160.

Harrington, David, 157.

Hatton, Thomas, 27.

Hauser, Arnold, 16.

Hazelton, Richard, 186.

Heidtmann, Peter, vii.

Henderson, Arnold, 11.

Heninger, S. K., 114.

Henry Bolingbroke, 153.

Henry de Bracton, 58.

Henryson, Robert, 161.

Hinckley, H. B., 118.

Hoffman, Arthur, 57.

Holland, Norman, 111.

Holman, Hugh, 115.

Hopper, Vincent, 186.

Host—see Harry Bailey.

Hotson, J. Leslie, 153.

House of Fame, 4, 8, 10, 185.

Howard, Donald, 3.

Huppe, Bernard, 2, 16, 17, 18, 20, 30, 57, 58, 60, 64,

86, 89, 112, 113, 115, 156, 161.

Intent, 9, 53, 70-78, 91, 121, 130-32, 164.

Jacobus de Voragine, 185.

Jacobus Januensis, 185.

Jacques de Vitry, 151, 161.

Jehan de Vignay, 185.

Job, 123.

John Bromyard, 151, 161.

John of Gaunt, 27.

John of Salisbury, 58, 68.

Jones, Claude, 160.

Jonson, Ben, 142.

Josipovici, G. D., 17.

Judgment, 25, 49, 61, 81, 176-77, 180.

Kane, George, 7-8.

Kaske, Robert, 61, 160.

Kellogg, Alfred, 157.

Kenyon, John, 118.

Ker, W. P., 159.

Kittredge, G. L., 16, 64, 95, 100, 101, 115, 117, 118, 156, 158.

Knight, 26, 27-30, 38, 39, 45, 46, 59, 80, 132, 148, 177.

Knight's Tale, 1, 5, 9, 10, 19, 27-36, 39, 40, 44, 52, 53, 78, 83, 93, 95, 111, 163, 176.

Ladner, Gerhart, 16.

Lawlor, John, 3.

Lawrence, W. W., 118, 157, 159.

Legend of Good Women, 4, 8, 50, 120, 182.

Leneghan, R. T., 160.

Levy, Bernard, 161.

Lewis, Robert, 61, 62.

Lounsbury, Thomas, 113, 183.

Lumiansky, R. M., 20, 57, 118, 149, 156, 157, 160.

Lyons, C. P., 118.

Madeleva, Sister Mary, 158.

Major, John, 20, 57.

Malone, Kemp, 57.

Manciple, 173, 184.

Manciple's Tale, 4, 15, 98, 120, 152, 173-77.

Manning, Stephen, 161.

Manly, John, 59, 62, 116, 158, 159.

Mann, Lindsay, 104, 118.

Man of Law, 48-55, 59, 62, 64, 65, 80.

Man of Law's Tale, 11, 12, 13, 14, 20, 47-56, 64, 68, 70, 78, 80, 83, 84, 111, 133, 134, 149, 166.

Markman, Alan, 9.

Marriage of Sir Gawain & Dame Ragnel, 67.

McCracken, Samuel, 186.

Melibee, 133, 142-46, 159.

Merchant, 129.

Merchant's Tale, 79, 86-94, 133, 181.

Miller, 9, 23, 36-37, 39, 46, 111, 128, 182, 184.

Miller's Tale, vi, vii, 9, 19, 22, 36-41, 42, 44, 52, 61, 77, 78, 79, 87, 111, 133, 177.

Miller, Robert, 66, 67, 156.

Mitchell, J., 114.

Moore, Arthur, 157, 159.

Mroczkowski, Premyslaw, 10.

Meech, Sanford, 17.

Mitchell, Charles, 28.

Monk, 21, 23, 39, 89, 146, 170.

Monk's Tale, 146-49.
Morrow, Patrick, 85, 90, 114.
Muscatine, Charles, 38, 58, 60, 114, 115, 156, 162.
Nature, 5, 122, 124.
Neville, Marie, 117.
Nevo, Ruth, 57.
Nicole Bozon, 151, 161.
Nine-and-twenty, 18, 168, 178-79.
Nominalism, 45, 47, 83.
Nun's Priest, 149.
Nun's Priest's Tale, 11, 14, 98, 100, 103, 120, 143, 165, 181, 182, 186.
Ockham, Wm., 58.
Odo of Cheriton, 67, 151, 161.
Ovid, 50.
Owen, Charles, 39, 60, 106, 118, 158.
Owst, G. R., 160.
Pardoner, 9, 20, 68, 71, 126-32.
Pardoner's Tale, 70, 120, 125-32, 169, 181.
Parliament of Fowles, 5, 8, 98, 118.
Parson, 3, 8, 11, 24, 27, 28, 35, 55-56, 70, 125-26, 164, 178-79, 182.
Parson's Tale, 5, 15, 19, 35, 36, 76, 100, 104, 120, 123, 146, 150, 155, 168, 178-81.
Parzival, 23.
Payne, Robert, 16.
Pearsall, D. A., 116, 117.
Peck, Russell, 185, 186, 187.
Pelerinage de la Vie Humaine, 6-7.

Peterson, Joyce, 116, 117.
Peterson, Kate, 160, 187.
Petrarch, 85.
Physician, 127, 165.
Physician's Tale, 120-25, 126, 133, 134, 136, 181.
Piers Plowman, 5, 6, 174.
Pilgrimage, 5-7, 9, 10, 11, 17, 46, 49, 50, 51, 56, 59, 65, 68-69, 84-86, 97, 121, 124-25, 132, 135, 144, 155, 163, 164, 167, 178-81.
Pilgrim's Progress, 5.
Plato, 24.
Plowman, 24.
Polycraticus, 58.
Power, Eileen, 158.
Pratt, Robert, 13, 14, 17, 112, 119, 161.
Preston, Raymond, 139.
Prioress, 18, 21, 22, 28, 138-39, 141, 149, 170.
Prioress's Tale, 70, 137-40, 144, 149, 152, 167.
Providence, 9, 33, 47, 52, 106-10, 119, 126, 140, 147-48.
Pygmalion, 123.
Ramsey, Roy Vance, 72, 112.
Realism, 11, 37, 41, 45, 46, 54-55, 61, 85, 114, 167.
Reeve, 9, 128, 129, 177.
Reeve's Tale, 22, 40, 41-45, 46-47, 52, 78, 111, 177.
Reiman, Donald, 114.
Reiss, Edmund, 16.
Renoir, Alain, 17.
Retraction, 22, 51, 123, 124, 146, 150, 163, 170, 181-84.
Richard II, 153.

Richardson, Janette, 158.

Robertson, D. W., Jr., 35, 58, 59, 65, 112, 116, 118, 156, 160.

Robinson, F. N., 13, 17, 28, 59, 116, 117, 167, 185.

Roman de Renart, 151.

Romulus, 151.

Roosevelt, Theodore, 113.

Root, R. K., 160, 183.

Ruggiers, Paul, 2, 8, 18, 29, 35, 37, 54, 60, 61, 111, 114, 115, 116, 149, 156, 157, 158, 185, 186, 187.

St. Jerome, 65, 66, 68, 112.

St. Paul, 65, 89, 91.

Saint's Life, 55, 63-64.

Salter, F. N., 112.

Satire, 44, 58, 60.

Scale of Perfection, 5.

Second Nun's Tale, 133, 163-67, 169, 172.

Sedgwick, 128, 156.

Sheps, Walter, 151.

Shipman, 21, 23, 71.

Shipman's Tale, 4, 11, 12, 13, 55, 68, 120, 133-37, 140.

Sidney, 1.

Silverman, Albert, 118.

Silverstein, Theodore, 111.

Silvia, Daniel, 112.

Sittingbourne, 13, 71.

Sledd, James, 104, 114, 119.

Solomon, 67, 79.

Song of Songs, 88, 92.

Southwark, 70.

Spiers, John, 152.

Squire, 94-99, 101, 127.

Squire's Tale, 11, 94-100, 101, 117.

Steadman, John, 186.

Steinberg, Aaron, 111.

Stokoe, Wm., 60.

Strange, Wm., 160.

Strohm, Paul, 159.

Sullivan, Wm., 61.

Summoner, 9, 70-78, 129.

Summoner's Tale, 22, 70, 76-78, 95.

Swart, John, 21, 28.

Tabard Inn, 20, 23, 24, 26.

Tale of Florent, 67.

Tatlock, J. S. P., 17, 62, 113, 115, 157, 185.

Theofrastus, 68, 112.

Thomas, Mary E., 187.

Thopas, 11, 94, 141-43, 144, 147, 159, 165, 186.

Thurston, Paul, 30, 58.

Time, 27, 42, 47-49, 78-80, 132, 178.

Tolkien, J. R. R., 154.

Trivet, Nicholas, 51, 63.

Troilus & Criseyde, 8, 29, 50, 119, 183.

Tupper, Frederick, 157, 187.

Varty, Kenneth, 161.

Wenzel, Siegfried, 16.

Westlund, Joseph, 59.

Whittock, Trevor, 3, 18, 111, 114, 116, 117, 118, 122, 149, 156, 157, 159, 163, 187.

Wife of Bath, 20, 23, 64-70, 80, 85, 95, 102, 105, 111, 125, 129, 133-35, 177, 184.

Wife of Bath's Tale, 12, 26, 64-70, 79, 128, 149, 181.

Will, 9, 53, 68, 70-78, 90, 97-99, 103-4, 109, 123, 164, 172-73, 177, 178-84.

Winstanley, Lilian, 159.

Wycliff, 183.

Yunck, John, 62, 63.